Andràs Török's

BUDAPEST
A CRITICAL GUIDE

András Török's

BUDAPEST
A CRITICAL GUIDE

Illustrated by
ANDRÁS FELVIDÉKI

The Chapter on Drinking Wine
Fully Rewritten by
ANDRÁS EGYEDI

PALLAS ATHENE
Publishers

For MÁRTA and GYÖRGY, my parents, who have never had enough time to enjoy their home town, and now that they do have time, are reluctant to do so

Special thanks to

DR ZOLTÁN SZENTKIRÁLYI and DR BALÁZS VARGHA[†], who were kind enough to go through the manuscript as consultants of the very first edition

ANDRÁS BARABÁS who improved on the text and who could possibly write a much better book on Budapest

PETER DOHERTY who comes from Dublin and who knows better than anyone what to enjoy and laugh at in Budapest

The author and the illustrator are also indebted to

Márta Aczél, Judit Béres, Ákos Birkás, Éva Blaschtik, Ferenc Bodor[†], Alexander Brody, Endre Bojtár, Mária Borbás, László Darvas, Anne Dauvergne, Katalin Délceg, Klára D. Major, Győző Duró, Ágnes Eperjesi, Edit Erki, Zoltán Erő, Péter Esterházy, Katalin Farkas[†], András Ferkai, József Finta, Ádám Fischer, Doris Fischer, András Fűrész, George and Julie Gábor, Zsuzsa Gáspár, Éva Gedeon, János Gerle, Tibor Frank, József Hegedüs, Robert Hetzron, Iván Horváth, Éva Jeles, György Kassai, Mária Kemény, János Kenedi, Károly Kincses, Gábor Klaniczay, János Mátyás Kovács, László Kúnos, László Kis Papp, Pál Kövi, Endre Lábass, George Lang, Tony Lang, Alain Lombard, László Lugosi Lugo, István Margócsy, Miklós Molnár, Ákos Nagy, Ádám Nádasdy, Vilma Nádasdy, András Nyerges[†], Ágnes Padányi, Walter Peruzzi, Vera Pécsi, Klára Péter, Attila Pogány, Péter Polgár, Gábor Preisich, Mihály Ráday, István Rév, András Rochlitz, András Román, Róbert Sarlós, Jean-Luc Soulé, Erzsébet Szabados, György Tibor Szántó, Anna Szemere, Ákos Szilágyi, István Teplán, Lionel Tiger, Ágnes Tompa, Iván Tosics, Mihály Vargha, Benedek Várkonyi, Anna Veress, Tibor Vidos, Miklós Vincze, Júlia Váradi, Péter Virágvölgyi, Richard Saul Wurman, Zsófia Zachár.

Design by András Felvidéki
DTP by graphoman
Ground Plans by Andrea Réti
Cover design by László Lugosi Lugo

Original English version translated by Peter Doherty and Ágnes Enyedi, edited by Zsuzsa Gáspár
Third edition revised with the assistance of Flóra Török and Alexander Fyjis-Walker
This revised edition went to press on 15 March 1998
Edited by István Bart
Published in the UK and US by Pallas Athene,
    59 Linden Gardens, London W2 4HJ
ISBN 1 873429 62 2

CONTENTS

WHAT IS THIS BOOK FOR?

Introduction to the First Edition

BUDAPEST, my birthplace, used to be compared to Vienna by visitors. 'The Danube, the ring boulevards, the many eclectic and revival buildings — the city is a second Vienna, in a more modest edition,' they would say. Others might remark, 'True, Mother Nature has been more generous, but as regards historic buildings, it cannot even hold a candle to Vienna. On top of that, the Hungarian language does not resemble any other European language.'

Budapest has now earned a higher reputation than this among the young who come from Paris, Amsterdam, Warsaw or St. Petersburg. There are many back-packing tourists in Budapest but the number of 'non-package', independence-loving visitors, who arrive in their own car, has also much increased recently. Those friends of mine, mostly my age, whom I have shown around in the last fifteen years have usually sung the city's praises beyond the point of politeness.

They said they found Budapest to be truly cultured, truly European. They said that from certain points of view it had preserved the old, humane qualities of days gone by better than many other cities, where development has swept the past away. They remembered staircases badly needing renovation, locksmith's workshops with wooden floors and the smell of oil, and small suburban family-run restaurants. They were fascinated by the grand riverbank architecture, and the beauty of the three bridges in the middle. They also said that the historic buildings seemed to be familiar to them (perhaps because quite a few of them are copies?) and were very accessible.

It was not so much the grandeur as the prettiness of the buildings that captivated them. They even said that the city was like a Sleeping Beauty still hidden from the eyes of Europe. My friends who have returned after two, three or more years have said that Budapest has changed a lot. New shops and restaurants have opened, and now you can even get a taxi. They noticed some nice modern buildings. They found their money still went a long way, though not as far as it had done.

'We would not have got too far without you,' my friends said. And that was more than a simple compliment. The spirit of the city had revealed itself to them, a spirit which can get close to you only with the help of a native. This book was written in order to provide an invisible host for you.

THIS BOOK tries to combine three types of guides with the advantages of all three: the Baedeker type, the critical guidebook and the alternative guidebook. Obviously it will not be exhaustive in all three modes.

THERE IS a Hungarian saying for things that seem impossible: 'an iron ring made out of wood'. Even if this book cannot overcome the language difficulties, it is designed to put the visitor at ease when making his own plans to discover the city. After all, it is easier to get help with the language from friends, business-partners, interpreters or hotel receptionists, than to get ideas for spending one's time.

THE COW AND THE SOCIAL SAFARI

Introduction to the Third, Revised Edition

Budapest, my native city, has changed a lot in the eyes of serious travellers, since this book was first published eight years ago. I don't mean the growing number of luxury restaurants, the ever nicer shops, the Viennese prices in some places.

It has changed so much even for me — almost beyond recognition. The society of scarcity has changed to a society of affluence and squalor. Respect for the traditional cityscape has returned; and there is also unbelievable visual pollution: billboards by the thousand in the city, and with the brand names of the two biggest, ever-warring soft drinks manufacturers on thousands of shop signs. And little, lit-up cigarette packets on façades.

Even I don't really remember that meek and mellow dictatorship, which melted away in front of our very eyes, around 1989. Just for your education, Gentle, Serious Reader, since the good old days are still here, in every cupboard, all over town, under every carpet — let me give you a short lecture.

You should know that this ancien régime was different from all the others in Eastern Europe. Most Hungarians did not cry out against it every day after getting up; on the contrary, they had to remind themselves of what kind of a régime they were living in, at the weekend. They laughed at the ignorant 'politicians', and — at least my class, the egghead dissident folks — detested money.

We wore ragged blue jeans from twenty to thirty and our hair was reluctant to follow the Zeitgeist into a shorter and shorter style. We read a lot of books, but very few newspapers, and then always between the lines. We didn't expect this world to disappear in our lifetimes. We were conditioned to irreverence and to having absolutely no responsibility outside the family.

Until one day some of us found ourselves in the government, responsible for billions of forints of budgets.

Being born in 1954, I didn't have any memories of the revolution in 1956. My best friend, a poet and scholar, did. He kept telling me the story of the Cow.

He explained that in the dark fifties his family didn't think the régime would last. They felt as if a big dark cow that was grazing over a beautiful meadow (Hungary) had suddenly sat down. But that darkness, they thought, cannot last forever: it is the very nature of cows that one day they get up. And the Cow did get up. For only twelve days — a glorious but short time. After that nobody thought that she would ever leave. Some people — including me — thought it was not a cow, just a cow-shaped piece of solid rock. And it is possible to live under a rock — if you are some species of fungus.

Around 1982 the government decided to introduce some 'reforms': after inventing lukewarm water they opted for inventing hot water. Letting small businesses start and flourish was about to erode the remaining ideological features of the system. Earlier, a district hall official could refuse permission for a shoemaker's shop just by saying that there were enough shoemakers in a given neighbourhood.

That made a slow but dramatic impact on Budapest. There were better and better shops. The gentrification of the Inner City started again, first making the tourist reservation just a bit bigger, later spreading throughout the area within the Grand Boulevard. That slowly changed my generation as well. Some of us felt that it was worth earning money so as to spend it in an intelligent way. Some of us were not interested in money at all — we published the half dozen underground papers, for a couple of thousand people. Some were interested in both. Some in nothing. But everyone thought that the régime could not become more liberal than it had already become. Yet common sense was infiltrating everyday life more and more – if not enough to abolish one of the stupidest laws, my own favourite. Until the autumn of 1989 (!) if you had a car less than three years old, you could only sell it to the state, at a depressed price. Thus, a three-year-and-one-day-old car was much more expensive than a three-year-old car...

But who remembers these days? Suddenly, to our astonishment, the Cow began to fidget, and slowly, very slowly to get up. It was a slower and less dramatic event than in the countries around Hungary; nobody was killed and there were hardly any demonstrations, so the world press showed much less interest.

Now there is a free Parliament, free business, even a free press. In a couple of years' time Hungary might become one of those smaller, prosperous, boring countries. Not yet though.

When the Cow left, we hoped the grass would recover overnight. Alas, no. There came new Cows from our very own barns. Some swore they spotted some new Cows coming in from the West. Some patches of grass have recovered wonderfully by now. Some others are in worse shape than ever before.

You should come and check it out from time to time. It can easily amount to a Social Safari for the Discerning Traveller.

(October 1997 — February 1998)

A CITY

A CRASH COURSE IN BUDAPEST

An Exercise in Civic Boosterism
(The Absolute Minimum You Should Know if You Aim to Be Called
Well-Informed by Locals on Your First Day)

Budapest is the overgrown capital of the Republic of Hungary, inhabited by about two million restless inhabitants — most of them readers, and not only of the telephone numbers in the television commercials. It was officially established in 1873 by joining Buda, Pest and northern Old Buda (Óbuda). It consists of 23 municipal districts.

Roughly two-thirds of the city is in Pest, on the eastern bank of the Danube and almost completely flat; the rest is in the hilly part called Buda, on the western bank and a much older settlement.

The following tries hard to list places where Budapest eggheads go to, meet at, or point out to foreign egghead friends they desperately try to impress.

WEATHER is far from boring in Budapest. It is pretty predictable: it can be very hot in the summer, and can theoretically be very cold in the winter; the latter happens every five or six years. In Hungary we celebrate name-days which are usually the feast days of a saint of that name. The name-days of Sándor, József and Benedek fall between March 18th and 21st and, according to the saying, they 'bring the warm weather in their bags'. Indeed this is usually the time when spring allows us to shed our winter topcoats — a good time for a visit too. A really heavy fall of snow is somewhat rare, but it is followed by slush and filthy piles of frozen snow pushed to the edges of the pavement. Dusk falls early in winter, between 3.30 and 4.30 in the afternoon and the sun is rarely seen. However, the other three seasons make up for this. Stormy days total about 30. Summer is warm and temperatures of 30° C (86° Fahrenheit) are by no means unusual. Nevertheless raincoats or umbrellas should not be left behind, especially if it rains on Medárd Day (June 8th). Tradition has it that the next forty days will also bring rain. $X°$ Celsius $= ((9X/5) + 32)°$ Fahrenheit

NOT AN EXOTIC COUNTRY ANY MORE As an associate country of the European Union, there are no special, unusual visa, customs or registration regulations in Budapest. Visas are not required for citizens of European countries. The exception, at the time of going to press, is the countries of the former Soviet Union (if you are not a package tourist). They (and citizens of non-European countries, with the exception of the USA and Canada) should obtain a visa from a Hungarian consulate abroad. A visa is valid for six months and entitles the holder to a stay of up to thirty days. For a longer stay, you must extend the visa at the local police station. Visas can also be obtained at road frontier crossing points or at Budapest Ferihegy Airport. There visas cost somewhat more.

Passengers arriving by train or boat must buy their visas in advance.
If you are in doubt, you can always call Tourinform Budapest: (36 1) 1179-800.

TRANSPORT
Budapest has proverbially good public transport which has become increasingly foreigner-friendly to use. Maps are to be found at more and more tram stops, ticket vending machines now tend to speak in several languages. If I were you, I would walk and walk and walk, before using the underground and tram lines. But at least they are never blocked by cars, which have multiplied insanely. Bus routes are more difficult to find out about.

If you remember — apart from the three underground lines — Tram 2 (on the Pest riverfront) and Trams 4 and 6 on Grand Boulevard, you will be able to get to pretty much everywhere you are unwilling to walk to.

You are likely to find *The Budapest Citymap for Tourists* very useful; it is published by Budapest Transport Ltd, and available from ticket vendors in the larger underground passages. (There is a yellow tram and a pink tram ticket on the cover, and 'Budapest 1997' in large lettering.)

The average Budapest citizen tends to have a car, usually over seven years old, but they often walk and rarely resort to the ever more expensive taxis. If they do, yes, then they order it from home, and do not hail one in the street. They try to call a CityTaxi (211-1111), a Főtaxi (122-2222) or a Yellow Pages Taxi (155-5000).

The real Budapest patriots often use the underground and admire the lamps in the carriages on line 2 (the Red Line). These lamps reflect the thirties in Russia. Budapest citizens are not surprised if caught in a hurricane on one of the endlessly long escalators. (That's how the metro is ventilated.) And they are wary of pickpockets.

PHONES & FAXES
Budapest people love the recent changes for the better. They are about to forget that once upon a time there was a scarcity of phone lines. Waiting for installation literally lasted years, sometimes a dozen or more. In the early eighties an MP in the all-Communist Parliament made an ironic suggestion that telephone applications should be made inheritable...

Budapesters fancy the big blue coin-operated telephones imported from South Africa, but almost everyone prefers to use telephone cards.

The card-operated phones are imported from France, and they 'speak' in Hungarian and English, alternately. Phone cards are sold at newsagents all over the town. The proper way to ask for one is 'Kérek egy telefonkártyát' (Keeh-rek edy telefon-kaahr-tyaaht). Then comes the inevitable question about the kind. There are two kinds, one of fewer units and the more substantial one. Find your way out of this by writing the number on a piece of paper.

Faxes are to be found everywhere in businesses, but you have to queue up for them in post offices. And if you want to receive a fax, you have to browse among dozens of other faxes for strangers with the same initials as you. Or you can go to the elegant business centre of Kempinski Hotel, downtown.

The first floor of the Inner City Telephone Centre (Belvárosi Telefonköz-pont) is a place where you can personally browse in all the printed direc-tories of the world, and can sit down in reasonably comfortable booths. (V. Petőfi Sándor utca 17-19.)

Various services are provided by the telephone company called MATÁV: they include alarm calls, jokes and bedtime stories — in Hungarian, of course. The only service for which you don't need the local dialect is an 'A' for tuning: 117-1822.

MONEY
The Forint (Ft) became the Hungarian currency in August 1946, after a period of extremely high inflation was brought to an end.

The denominations of notes are: the white 10,000 Ft with St Stephen, King of Hungary, the first in a controversial new series; the brown 5,000 Ft with Count Széchenyi, the early 19th-century aristocrat and reformer; the green 1,000 Ft with Bartók, the composer; the purple 500 Ft with Endre Ady, the poet; and the red 100 Ft with Kossuth. (For more details, look them all up in the chapter 'Who Was Who'.) You can occasionally spot brown 50 Ft notes with Ferenc Rákóczi II, who led an unsuccessful struggle for inde-pendence against the Habsburgs in the early 18th century. The blue 20 Ft note has the picture of György Dózsa, the leader of a 15th century peasant revolt and the green 10-Ft note, with Sándor Petőfi, the poet, are collectors' items now. They have been replaced by oversize coins.

Coins come in denominations of 200, 100, 50, 20, 10, 5, 2 and 1 Ft. You may find some fillér coins in your change (100 fillér = 1 forint), but there is now nothing you can buy for less than 1 Ft. The coins look a ridiculous mess, thanks to the autocratic President of the National Bank in the early nineties who exercised his right to the final say in the design process and decided to go with the different results of both a competition and an opinion poll; that's why the reverse and the obverse of the coins are so different. The 1 forint coins are said to be too small (Budapest people call them 'shirt but-tons'). The 100 Ft coin is too large, and was recently replaced by a two-metal smaller coin. This one is said to be withdrawn soon, since the inner part falls out, if you put it in a freezer, as a recent TV programme found out. (Why should coins survive in a freezer? Don't ask me...)

On the back of the 5,000 forint bill there is the building of the Academy of Sciences and Letters, established by Count Széchenyi, who is on the front of the banknote. As a comic biweekly found out after the note was issued, the etching was made after a contemporary photo: the designer has parked a selection of East-European-made cars at the building. Certainly not in production when the Count was around.

CHANGING MONEY
January 1997 was a historic date in the modernization of Hungary: changing forints into foreign currencies was totally liberalized. There came a veritable revolution in changing money for tourists. There are hundreds of services that change your money, and you can get forints from ATM's too. Despite this you will no doubt be solicited to change money in the street at a slightly better rate; there are a large number of con-men walking the streets: some pass on forged notes but most simply work a switch whereby the tourist finds himself with a heap of toilet paper bundled up in genuine notes at either end of the roll.

THE SINGLE MOST IMPORTANT BOOKSHOP

is certainly Írók Könyvesboltja ('Writers' Bookshop', VI. Andrássy út 45, at Liszt Ferenc tér) in a former, famous, café called 'Japan', for its once fine Oriental décor, which is still to be spotted behind the awful, nondescript mid-sixties panelling-cum-fluorescent tube interior. You can sit and have tea, watch the crowd leafing through the incredibly high number of new publications and literary reviews from all over Hungary and from the Hungarian speaking regions of the nearby countries. Hungarian literature is the shop's forte, and there is a book launch almost every afternoon at 4 p.m. Also look for the innovative window displays of new titles. After a great deal of toing and froing, the shop was sold to its enthusiastic staff, who had to borrow a huge amount of money for the purchase, of course.

THE SINGLE MOST IMPORTANT ANTIQUARIAN BOOKSELLERS

are obviously Mr and Mrs Borda, in their home. They used to work for a state-owned chain, then opened a small, elegant shop in a remarkably civilized part of New Leopold Town. But they found the rent too high, and had to deal with too many customers just looking for some detective novel 'they just had to have', so they retreated to their home. They have published about a dozen carefully compiled lists. (One of the first items in the most recent one was the bus card of Endre Ady, the great poetic genius of the 1910's.) It's a very serious operation, open only on Tuesday and Thursday afternoon, 4 to 8, and other times by special appointment. (VII. Madách Imre tér 5. IInd floor No 1. T: 267-3723.)

THE LISZT MUSIC ACADEMY

is the most important venue of the prodigiously lively classical music scene. (VI. Liszt Ferenc tér 8, at Király utca.) It's in a landmark art nouveau block with a big concert hall, worth visiting even on the occasion of a minor musical event. The smaller room opens from the first floor, where there is a huge painting: *The Spring of Arts*. Musical graffiti in the Gents' downstairs: 'Viva Brüggen!'. Béla Bartók and Zoltán Kodály used to teach upstairs. The State Opera House (VI. Andrássy út 22) is a jewel, completed in 1884, lovingly restored for its centenary. It seats 1200 people. There is another, much bigger, much less fancy opera venue, called the Erkel Színház (VIII. Köztársaság tér), where the productions that attract really large crowds are performed.

STAMPS & LETTERS

Everyone thinks that bigger post offices are quicker because they have more staff — they do, but they are also busier and queues are long. Try the smaller post offices. Since our walks begin at Vörösmarty tér, note the side-street at the northern end of the square, with Post Office No. 51 at Dorottya utca 9. (T: 118-6441.)

The only post office open round the clock is Post Office No. 62 at Western Railway Station (VI. Teréz körút 51 - 53.)

You will notice that some addresses are given with the district number in Roman numerals first, and some with a four-digit postcode in Arabic numerals. For speedier delivery of letters, the postcode should be used. The correct way to address an envelope in Hungary is:

KOVÁCS JÁNOS

BUDAPEST
King Kong utca 6.
1052

The logic of the postcode is that 1 indicates Budapest, the next two digits the Budapest district, and the final digit the sorting-office's division of the district. The same address would be found under. 'V. King Kong utca 6.' in a directory.

ART MOVIES AND THE RECENT MULTIPLEX CRAZE
General conversion pains (i.e. to the free market) somewhat delayed the Hungarian movie scene's attempt to follow international trends. While a remarkable art movie network was retained in Budapest, mainstream movie theatres looked more and more neglected. Reluctantly, capital gathered momentum in the mid-nineties: by the end of 1997, the number of movie seats rose from about 11,000 to over 15,000. Almost at the same time three new multiplex cinemas opened. One of them, Corvin Film Palace, is the investment of a company owned by the city of Budapest (see Walk Five, p. 154)

The kinds of Hungarian films so popular with serious movie-goers back in the seventies and eighties have hardly been produced for a long time. The mild totalitarian dictatorship poured money like water into the film industry, and it had its special expectations. Now little over two per cent of moviegoers are interested in the local crop. Signs of change can now occasionally be spotted. A younger generation of directors and producers has learnt to find its way to European film funds. A great example is *Witman Boys* by János Szász, which is a must.

Meanwhile, the unbelievably rich art movie supply is still here. On a level with Paris and New York. No kidding.

THE SINGLE MOST IMPORTANT FOREIGN LANGUAGE BOOKSHOP
is the one with the deceptive name 'Bestsellers', operated by an immigrant from Britain, Tony Lang, who had some Hungarian blood, but no prior command of the Hungarian language. He moved to Hungary to buy a shop — it happened to be a food shop, with permission to sell 'other goods'. For a year there were some bottles and some Heinz sauces to demonstrate that it was a food shop after all. It sells all kinds of fiction, non-fiction and reference books. Also newspapers and magazines and fine stationery. A centre for the expatriate community. Open until 6 p.m. — on Saturday, too.

KATONA JÓZSEF THEATRE
is one of Europe's best theatre companies, a member of the eight-theatre European Theatre Union, (the British members are the National Theatre and the Royal Shakespeare Company) and veterans of over a hundred performances

abroad. They have a large repertory, including *Platonov* by Chekhov, *The Taming of the Shrew* and *A Midsummer Night's Dream*. Their latest hit is *The Broken Jug* by Kleist. They play in a small house, and in an even smaller studio nearby, called *Kamra* or Larder, established in 1982, by innovative (though mainstream) actors and directors forced out of the National Theatre. There are only about 250 seats, so it's not easy to get in. Budapest eggheads tend to know someone in the company. Worth the effort! (V. Petőfi Sándor utca 6.)

EXPAT PAPERS *Budapest Week*, the first weekly for expats, by expats, established in the early nineties is a professional, easy to use publication now, with reliable listings & insiders' information on every conceivable topic. (I especially like Bob Dent's "What's in a Name" column.)

They have recently launched a monthly side publication, meant to be a glossy paper for beside reading, called "Budapest Style". Seems promising.

The *Budapest Sun* was established by an American professional couple a couple of years back. They provide excellent TV and movie listings for English speakers. But they don't have access to real inside information about politics and life, so don't always realize when opinions are biased. Also, the staff turnover is far too high. They don't have long enough memories, if you know what I mean.

There is also the *Budapest Business Journal*, which is serious stuff and even has an excellent Parliamentary Diary, written by a proper political analyst, who heads the local branch of a British firm.

PAPERS BUDAPEST EGGHEAD EXPATS READ

They tended to read the now defunct *Budapest Week*, out of tradition, and they hesitated to change over to the *Budapest Sun*. They are all said to subscribe to *The Hungarian Quarterly*, a prestige review, notable for its translations of modern short stories and poetry and with a lively review section, and articles on the country and its history. A most readable publication written in impeccable English by senior Hungarian opinion-makers.

Also, expatriate eggheads are beginning to appreciate the *Budapest Review of Books*, another quarterly, with a very funny column at the end called the BRB Guide to Budapest, about life in Budapest intellectual salons and with comments on the cultural scene. Some of the occasional readers are on the brink of subscribing – and perhaps to the *Quarterly* too. But most of them go through them in libraries. (See under 'Reading', p. 220.)

THE SINGLE MOST IMPORTANT ESOTERIC CLASSICAL RECORD SHOP is Concerto. The attention of

some Budapest eggheads was drawn to the shop by the British magazine *Gramophone*. The owner (now living in Toronto) made a small fortune by importing a carefully selected list of LP's from the then Soviet Union, then selling them as rarities to Western eggheads, those who still think analogue is better than digital, and consider LP's far superior to CD's. The shop is in a curious block called 'Block 15' — where the Budapest City Hall launched its abortive rehabilitation campaign. They never managed to lure similarly chic businesses here. The street name means 'Drum street'. No tourist ever sets foot here, though it's not far from the city centre (VII. Dob utca 33. T: 121-6432).

STAIRS

STAIRS The most famous, the best known stairs in Budapest, the most appropriate to meet a wife, girlfriend or girl friend are of course those of the National Museum, in Museum Gardens (off Kálvin tér). That is where people think Sándor Petőfi, the youthful leader of the 1848 Revolution, recited his freshly written poem, the *National Song* on the afternoon of March 15. (Research proved he did not. Not here, not him.)

Another one, ideal for first or second date, first kiss in daylight, is on the Pest riverbank, off the embankment, halfway between the Chain Bridge and the Elizabeth Bridge, somewhat nearer the latter. The more passionate the relationship is, the nearer the water you have to sit, in order not to be disturbed by others.

The trendiest stairs these days are indoors: not in a staircase, but in the foyer of the French Institute. If you have a look at it on the occasion of a opening, you will see how well it serves its purpose: to see better and be seen better. The two reasons for which one goes to an opening.

The naffest and by far the most ridiculous stairs are to be seen at the corner of XIII. Váci út and Dózsa György út, at the base of the 'skyscraper' of the Municipal Waterworks. A stretch of staircase about twenty meters wide that never got to be used. There are dozens of pre-cast concrete flowerbeds placed across the stairs, very near the bottom. The world's ugliest and least used stairs.

TWELVE PLACES TO MEET A BUDAPEST FRIEND

7 a.m. Burger King (!), the second floor, by the rail, with a view of the Grand Boulevard. Recent, post-modern glitz. (VI. Oktogon tér 3.)

9 a.m. Café Gerbeaud, in the middle, flat-ceilinged room, under the oil painting *The Altar Boy and the Apprentice Confectioner*. It opens at 9, so try to be there before the other tourists whom Budapest eggheads avoid. (V. Vörösmarty tér 7.)

11 a.m. The big oak table in the main hall of the Museum of Ethnography, the former Supreme Court. (V. Kossuth Lajos tér 12. Closed on Monday.)

1 p.m. The top of the stairs of the National Museum — the left side. A landmark building from 1847, the setting for the start of the 1848 Revolution. (VIII. Múzeum körút 14-16.)

3 p.m. CD Bar, a small shop where you can listen to some Purcell sarabandes through headphones, sit sipping coffee, and not admit you are just waiting. (VIII. Krúdy Gyula utca 6.)

5 p.m. The gallery of Café New York — but don't expect to be served there. The birthplace of modern Hungarian literature. (VII. Erzsébet körút 9-11.)

7 p.m. In front of the fancy modern clock, in the courtyard of the Hotel Taverna (V. Váci utca 20.)

9 p.m. The Korona Passage in the Korona Hotel, at the very back, under the mural depicting the siege of Buda in 1686. (V. Kecskeméti utca 14. The left wing.)

11 p.m Café Művész, the inner room. Traditional splendour, elderly clientèle — but not at that hour. (VI. Andrássy út 29.)

1 a.m. Paris, Texas, trendy new café (IX. Ráday utca 36.)

3 a.m. Epicentrum Salad Bar, between the upper and lower embankment, south of the Buda end of Margit Bridge. Without the crowd at that time, when the slow service is not unnerving.

5 a.m. Copy General. Since the owners of Talk Talk Café were forced to discontinue their round the clock operation, there is no public indoor place other this very smoothly run shop, where you are likely to bump into architecture students desperately trying to meet their last deadline, and some eccentric composers with fresh music to be given to the string quartet the coming morning. If your friend happens to be late (which is highly uncivilized at that time of the day), and you want to pretend you are busy, please don't photocopy this book, choose something else... (And buy another copy for your friend.)

STARING AT OTHERS
AND GETTING AWAY WITH IT
Coming up and down on the escalator of any of the underground stations. Especially at Kossuth Lajos tér (lower middle class), at Lehel tér (working class, no escalator, though) and at Blaha Lujza tér (perfect mix). Or riding Bus 15 from terminus to terminus at sunset. People switch on their lights, but do not draw their curtains right away; to take advantage is not nice, not even in Hungary. You could be scholarly and call it 'applied people-watching'.

HUNGARIAN PAPERS
HUNGARIAN EGGHEADS READ
They tend to read *Magyar Hírlap* (a Swiss-owned, formerly liberal daily; they switched to it from *Magyar Nemzet*, the one they had read for thirty years), *Heti Világgazdaság* (the fifteen-year-old Economist-like weekly, no longer printed on green paper), *Élet és Irodalom*, a literary weekly (this one they may just have cancelled), *Hócipő* (a hilariously funny biweekly — ask a Budapest friend about the meaning of the name), but they also keep an eye on the formerly Communist, now (German-owned) independent *Népszabadság*, the daily with by far the biggest circulation. (Some years ago Péter Esterházy, the influential writer wrote about this paper: 'Now it is only the name of it that I hate'. (The *Népszabadság* used this quotation the next week to advertise itself.)

THE HOMEPAGE OF THE AUTHOR
Before you leave for Budapest, have a look at www.internetto.hu/budapest. Every week I am writing something about the city. A continuation of the book. I call them "vignettas". There you can find the earlier ones, too.

THE PRESIDENT OF THE REPUBLIC Bare-headed,
grey-haired, rotund, with an eternally knowing smile, his face is to be seen everywhere in the media. Árpád Göncz speaks fantastic English with an unmistakable Hungarian accent (in prison, after 1956, where he learned his English, there were books, but no tapes). Unlike eggheads, he is never hot-headed, and can talk to kings, peasants and billionaires alike. Will pay attention even to you if bumped into at a reception. His book of short stories, *Homecoming,* was published by Corvina, my publisher.

BUDAPEST BESTS : : BUDAPEST BESTS : : BUDAPEST BESTS

Ferenc Bodor, gallery director, columnist, a fine judge of pubs

My favourite outings in the city. The strangest and most engaging panorama of the town is to be had by taking the Cogwheel Railway up to the Széchenyi Hill stop and walking from there along Melinda út to the former Majestic Hotel. From behind the building the vista of an unknown metropolis lies before us. And we can marvel at those buildings constructed between the wars, in the functionalist vein, now a little run-down and used for housing.

The discreet pleasures of the proletariat. From the Pest abutment of Margit bridge we cross by ferry to the Kék Duna landing stage on Római part, watching the city shrink to the size of a picture postcard. Going across the bulky iron bridge — which is now a monument — keeping an eye on the city to the right, we reach Népsziget ('the people's island') which, in the people's language is also known as Mosquito Island. From one of the few restaurants with gardens comes the sound of dancing. In another garden it's time to indulge in eating fish from the bottle. At the city end of the island a concrete bridge leads to the metro station. An outing only recommended for those who enjoy the simple, proletarian pleasures of summer.

A stroll through Socialist Realist Past. 'Socreal' architecture is, in our days, ripe for appreciation.

The finest example of a housing estate in the style is that in the XIVth district, between Nagy Lajos király útja and Kerepesi út. The reliefs over the entry doors and the whispering trees give it the appearance of a film set. The strange, enclosed spaces, the passages and deserted playgrounds are lit by ancient striplight advertisements. Coming out towards Fehér út metró station brings us to the 'Mimóza Eszpresszó', where the lonely piano player caters for those who want to dance. Recommended for lovers of *couleur locale* at weekends.

(Ferenc Bodor died in 1994 — he did not live to see signs of positive changes in his beloved city, most of which — no doubt — he would praise.)

CHOOSING A PLACE TO STAY

Budapest is no hotel paradise, though the situation has improved a lot. Staying at a hotel in Budapest is obviously a situation I have never been in — I have only a limited pool of independent information to rely on. What comes next is not a comprehensive list. That is available at every tour operator all over the world.

As unfortunately most serious travellers come only for a few days to Budapest, location is crucial. So my tips tend to have a bias towards reasonably good locations.

For a Conference-hopper who Wants to Avoid Fellow Conference-hoppers

ALBA *I. Apor Péter utca 3. T: 175-9244. F: 175-9899.* On the corner of Hunyadi János út. A 95-room hotel in Buda, at the foot of the Castle Hill. No panorama, as it overlooks a side street off Main Street (Fő utca), which is parallel to the river. Very near Castle District. Very good access to main sites. There is a fine Greek restaurant in the same, tiny street.

LIGET *VI. Dózsa György út 106. T: 269-5300. F: 269-5329.* 139 rooms. A singularly pleasant, though not very quiet location, opposite the side of the Museum of Fine Arts and the Zoo, that is to say, the City Park (Városliget). Nice post-modern building with a sauna and gym. The somewhat too obtrusive copper statue at the corner is often ridiculed; some locals, however, call it 'Ophelia Mad Scene'.

VICTORIA *I. Bem rakpart 11. T: 201-8644. F: 201-5816.* 27 rooms. Right on the Buda riverbank, overlooking the old Chain Bridge. For years the owner was in a fierce legal battle with the City Hall: he had added an extra floor, hoping that in those turbulent times (when democracy knocked on our doors) it would go unnoticed. It didn't. The extra floor is still there. Try to book a room on the top floor, that particular one.

For Affluent Newly-weds Who Want to Rejuvenate themselves After Eventful Nights

RAMADA GRAND HOTEL *XIII. Margitsziget. T: 311-1000. F: 153-2753.* 246 rooms. A hundred-year-old establishment on a large island, ideal for jogging and long walks. You need a car to get to town comfortably in five minutes. Say hi to me if you pass me and my pal, as we jog contentedly on the path on the Pest side. Around 9 a.m., on Sundays. The Mayor of Budapest, Gábor Demszky, always overtakes us. (No bodyguards.)

For a Tennis-freak Junior Manager of a Multinational Company

FLAMENCO *XI. Tas vezér utca 7. T: 161-2250. F: 165-8007.* 348 rooms. A less well-known hotel, close to the centre of South Buda, with quiet grounds and an artificial lake. Large indoors tennis facility 200 metres from the hotel.

Am Express here

Hotel for a Man to Impress Highschool Sweetheart, After 50 Years

HILTON *I. Hess András tér 1-3.* T: 214-3000. F: 156-0285. 323 rooms. Superb location on Castle Hill, overlooking the Danube. Remains of a 13th-century convent are built into this fine building. (See 'First Walk' for details.)

KEMPINSKI HOTEL CORVINUS BUDAPEST *V. Erzsébet tér 7-8.* T: 266-1000. F: 266-2000. 367 rooms. This post-modern tour de force by the contemporary Hungarian architect József Finta and associates occupies a whole block. Three of the façades are elegant and the fourth plain — the last is said by insiders to be a kind of revenge. It faces the headquarters of the city police, who allegedly demanded that no windows should face in their direction. You should check the result. By the way, the police building was traded for a new police building, also designed by Mr Finta. It is called 'Cops' Palace' (corner of XIII. Róbert Károly körút and Teve utca, near the Pest end of Árpád bridge.)

did not take time
To en— west
right

Ideal Hotel for the Affluent Expatriate, Who Loves Downtown, and Is On the Verge of Buying a Flat of His/Her Own

MILLENNIUM COURT *V. Pesti Barnabás u. 4.* T: 235-1800. F: 235-1900. A brand new Marriott Executive Residence building for those who stay more than three weeks, but less than half a year. The nearby Marriott offers all the services for this brand new institution in a relatively small street between the textbook shopping street and the river.

Prices are much lower than you would expect anywhere near the name Marriott.

'I Hate Big Hotels'

ART INN-SIDE *V. Királyi Pál utca 12.* T: 266-2166. F: 266-2170. 32 rooms. Few Budapest people have heard of this place — a block of flats that was, briefly, an important student movement stronghold and student hostel after World War II. Very conveniently located in a quieter part of the inner city, 100 metres from the underground, 200 from the busy centre. A nice memorial tablet inside.

'I love the Opera and Classical Music'

K + K HOTEL OPERA *VI. Révay utca 24.* T: 269-0222. F: 269-0230. 115 rooms. An obvious, purpose built hotel for music lovers, with immaculate service. With function rooms. It is parallel to splendid Andrássy út. Literally 50 metres from the Opera House, with phenomenal public transport connections. Ask for the room where Peter Greenaway and his wife stayed.

'I Want Fin-de-siècle Splendour and Want to Have a Pool Indoors'

GELLÉRT *XI. Szent Gellért tér 1.* T:185-2200. F: 166-6631. 233 rooms. Traditional grand hotel with windows looking over the most beautiful of the bridges, Gellérthegy, and its own large swimming pool. (See more of it during 'Walk Three'.)

'I don't Want to See the Marriott from the Outside'

BUDAPEST MARRIOTT *V. Apáczai Csere János utca 4. T: 266-7000. F: 266-5000.* With 362 rooms and suites. All rooms overlook the Danube. As the building is really prominent, the only solution to the problem is to stay there, and enjoy the panorama. President Carter stayed here during his two Budapest visits. He insisted that I follow him to the Presidential Suite, and gave me an autographed edition of his book — in return for me showing him around. I thought I would never see him again. Since then I have seen him again, twice. Once, the next morning, while jogging on the riverfront (he was doing the same), and once again when he came to Hungary on one of his campaigns building wooden houses for the poor. Never say never (more)!

'I like Traditional Splendour, but I Don't Mind Minor Glitches in Decoration and Service if I Can Pay Accordingly'

ASTORIA *V. Kossuth Lajos utca 19-21. T:117-3411. F: 118-6798.* 130 rooms. Landmark in centre — the crossroads here is named after it — and recently redecorated, but so as to retain its old-fashioned style. The first democratic government was formed here — the one that declared independence from Austria, in October 1918. You can visit the room, but can't stay in it.

NEMZETI *VIII. József körút 4. T: 269-9310. F: 114-0019.* Traditional splendour of the Grand Boulevard days before cars had spoiled this crossroads or the National Theatre was pulled down, poured its fashionable crowd into the restaurant of this hotel. 76 rooms, a suite and a conference room. Built over an underground station: Blaha Lujza tér (Line 2).

'I Love the Urban Jungle'

SAS BÉKE RADISSON *VI. Teréz körút 43. T: 132-3300. F: 153-3380.* 246 rooms. Recently modernized hotel on the city's main thoroughfare. Well served by public transport. Right on Grand Boulevard. Some 15 years ago they quite justifiably razed 90 per cent of the hotel, keeping only the façade and some interior embellishments, including the oversize wall paintings in the 'Shakespeare Restaurant'. The 'Café' on the first floor is posh but has nice confectionery and good espresso; don't expect quick service.

'I Want to Stay in a Historical Area, but Don't Want to Pay for it'

KULTURINNOV *I. Szentháromság tér 6. T: 155-0122. F: 175-1886.* 16 rooms. One of the most improbable small hotels in the world. In the grand building of the pre-war Ministry of Finances, now owned by the Foundation for Hungarian Culture, which was established to facilitate connections with ethnic Hungarians in neighbouring countries. Modest, dormitory-type rooms, for a reasonable price, 200 metres from Matthias Church (150 of which are taken up by the endless corridors of the building, some grand, some shabby). The fancy name used to belong to a state-owned company for training executives for cultural institutions and businesses.

'I Want a Small, Old-fashioned, Family-run, Five Star Hotel'

I'm afraid this is the wrong place to come to. The genre does not exist in Budapest or anywhere else in Hungary, unfortunately.

Swapping Flats with My Hungarian Peers

WHAT AD TO PUBLISH AND WHERE Any of the two English-speaking weeklies, either the *Budapest Week* or the *Budapest Sun*. You can rely on one of the agencies advertising themselves there — competition is fierce and it makes them do a fairly good job. You can also try to write a letter to the Internet paper called 'Internetto': a Letter to the Editor, *http://www.internetto.hu*.

Twelve Acceptable Second Choices if You Desperately Want to Come

ATRIUM HYATT *V. Roosevelt tér 2.* T: *138-3000.* F: *266-9101.* With 355 rooms, 28 suites. Town centre, on the river, the usual quality, if you can afford it. Replicas of classic Hungarian paintings hang along the first floor — you can order an official replica of any of the paintings in the National Gallery. They have it painted for you, and issue a certificate as well. Oh yes, and there is the aeroplane, too. (See 'Walk One'.)

DUNAPART *I. Szilágyi Dezső tér.* T: *155-9244.* F:*155-3770.* 32 rooms. Anchored at the Buda embankment, the converted steamer is an interesting addition to the Budapest hotel scene. Obviously, it has different prices depending on what your room faces: the Houses of Parliament or the noisy embankment full of traffic. Also a restaurant, with reasonably good food, run by efficient, very pleasant Chinese waiters.

GRAND HOTEL HUNGÁRIA *VII. Rákóczi út 90.* T: *322-9050.* F: *268-1999.* 511 rooms. Ten minutes walk from inner city. Some rooms overlook Keleti (Eastern) Railway Station. Entirely rebuilt in 1985. Largest hotel in the country. Excellent food in the 'Fiaker Söröző', or beer hall, which in fact is quite a good restaurant, serving oversize, tasty portions. (There is a 'fiaker', a two-horse coach, at the entrance.) Real Budapest patriots know the difference between the 'fiah-ker' and the 'khonf-lish'. The difference between the Trabant and the Volkswagen Golf, in fin-de-siècle terms.

By the way, kids love the ceramic relief in the foyer – in the shape of a giant paper aeroplane.

HELIA THERMAL *XIII. Kárpát utca 62-64.* T: *270-3277.* F: *270-2262.* 262 rooms. Just opposite the middle of Margaret Island, in the immediate vicinity of a pre-fab housing estate. Thus, half the rooms have superb, the other half less than perfect views. Don't forget to inquire when reserving a room. Water from the springs of the island. Swimming pool. Not very far from a station on the Metro 3 line.

MERCURE BUDA *I. Krisztina körút 41-43. T: 156-6333. F: 155- 6964.* 396 rooms. Just between the Southern Railway Station and beautiful Blood Field, or Vérmező, the name of which commemorates the execution of the Hungarian Jacobins in 1795. Also, from this side, a nice panorama of Castle Hill. Again, not very pleasant to look at, but very nice to look out of.

MERCURE KORONA *V. Kecskeméti utca 14. T: 117-4111. F: 118-3867.* An unmistakable, much discussed building on a key dowtown site, on busy, noisy Kálvin tér (special treble-glazing). (See 'Walk Three'.) 433 rooms, plus small conference facilities on either side of a street, with a 'Bridge of Sighs' between the two parts. Excellent access to all the sights, three minute walk to the river. The reception is in a pleasant atrium, hung with some history paintings bought by the hotel, by maverick, visionary painter Győző Somogyi, who lives north of Lake Balaton, in a village called Salföld, a frequent destination of egghead pilgrimage.

NOVOTEL BUDAPEST CENTRUM *XII. Alkotás utca 63-67. T: 186-9588. F: 166-5636.* 324 rooms. On the road leading to Elizabeth bridge, surrounded by hills, completed at the beginning of the eighties. Beside it stands the Budapest Convention Centre, also a concert venue. Not a very good location, unless your conference is here.

ORION *I. Döbrentei utca 13. T: 156-8583. F: 175-5418.* 30 rooms. A small place near the Buda end of Elizabeth bridge. This was the very first private hotel after the small business boom of the early eighties. It was built according to the rules. When it was ready, the authorities realized that it was bigger than they had anticipated – and lowered the acceptable maximum number of rooms – and the proprietor had to sell the place to some state business... A good location if you want to go for long walks on the hills nearby.

PANORAMA *XII. Rege utca 21. T: 175-0522, F: 175-9727.* On top of Szabadság hegy, with a large park, and newly built bungalows. Try to book into the main building, for the sake of a better panorama. And try to use the old cog-wheel railway ('fogaskerekű vasút'). The hotel is just by the terminus. By the way, it was called the Red Star Hotel for forty years. Would you believe it?

TAVERNA *V. Váci utca 20. T: 138-4999. F: 118-7188.* 224 rooms. Impossible to be more central and in Pest's main shopping street to boot. Discussed in the 'First Walk' in connection with its post-modern style. As a minority opinion I admit that I like the concrete connecting element at the top. It was so refreshing after so many decades ruled by the rectangle. Especially in Budapest. (I still like it, together with the statues on the pillars.)

THERMAL HOTEL AQUINCUM *III. Árpád fejedelem útja 94. T: 250-3360. F: 250-4672.* On the Buda riverfront, near the Buda end of the northernmost bridge over the river. Aquincum was a Roman settlement. To the left of the main entrance there is a large tablet from a Roman find. Some interesting pieces of architecture nearby, including the nearby neo-Classical synagogue; (the style is a rarity in Hungary) which is now used as a television studio, a 900-year-old Catholic Church, and a branch of the Municipal Gallery, in a pretty 18th-century house. One of the best, non-naff Hungarian restaurants is in walking distance. (See 'Kéhli' in the Chapter 'Eating Well'.)

THERMAL MARGITSZIGET *XIII. Margitsziget. T: 311-1000. F: 269-4589.* 206 rooms. On the island in the Danube, the hotel offers a wide range of services. Much less elegant than the Grand Hotel. But the air is the same. If you have kids, you can rent two kinds of four-wheeled carts made up of doubled-up bicycles: the 'bringóhintó' or the 'sétacikli'.

THREE OFFICES

American Express *V. Deák Ferenc utca 10. T: 268-8680. F: 267-2028. Open October to May: 9 a.m. to 5.30 p.m. Monday to Friday, from June to September 9 a.m. to 6.30 p.m., Saturdays all year 9 a.m. to 2 p.m. Proverbially quick and efficient service: it is said that management use computers to moni- tor the average number of rings it takes an employee to answer a call, and reward accordingly. Hotel reservation for a 10 dollar fee.*

IBUSZ *V. Apáczai Csere János utca 1. Open 24 hours a day. The oldest trav- el company in Hungary still books rooms for about 80 per cent of the hotels, rents out rooms of all kinds, sells plane tickets, and changes money.*

Tourinform *V. Sütő utca 2. T: 117-9800. They don't book hotels, but give suggestions. Plenty of hotel brochures. Open every single day of the year, from 8 a.m. to 8 p.m.*

BUDAPEST BESTS : : BUDAPEST BESTS : : BUDAPEST BESTS
Péter Molnár Gál (MGP), wit, theatre critic; the wickedest pen

There is a small restaurant in the old Józsefváros, the **Gólya** (in Bókay János utca). Its regulars include the local shopkeepers and tradesmen, folk musicians and the occasional off-duty whore. Outside in the court- yard in summer a curtain of trained vines almost reaches your soup plate. Inside it's all wood-panelling; the old white of the hall cup- board has been given a fashionable brown coat. The menu card has four or five simple dishes, always a delight. Your conversation scin- tillates at the Gólya's tables. (Provided I cut the band's amplifier lead with a pair of pliers.)

Wherever you eat well, eat plenty. For the next time you get there you won't find again what it was you so enjoyed first time round.

There is still a **tobacconist's** at No. 2. Nádor utca. A white-haired, smiling, elderly lady stands behind the counter. I'm always in a good mood for a few hours after dropping in there.

In Budapest you can't dunk your bread in the same sauce twice. The city is going through a time of transition. As it has been doing for five hundred years.

Don't eat! Smoke! It makes you slim.

Help is always at hand for visitors to Budapest at a friendly office just half a minute's walk from the junction of the three underground lines, the

Tourinform office: 117-9800

Right in the heart of the city, at Sütő utca 2, the office is open from 8 a.m. to 8 p.m. seven days a week. (There is a second one now, off Vörösmarty tér, in 2. Dorottya utca.)

You can get virtually all information here in German, English, Russian and French, sometimes even in Italian. The office has the most up-to-date information on transport, accommodation, activities, sights, on everything a tourist might be interested in, and it's all on their computer. They will help you to get accommodation only in certain special cases but they will always help you with the necessary addresses and telephone numbers. They keep a range of travel brochures here as well. There are about twenty people on its changing, but remarkably experienced staff, who are always happy to pass on their own knowledge of the city. They will also do some detective work to find out where some special goods can be bought. I spent a whole morning in this office checking various data and was struck by their enthusiasm. In need you can always rely on them. In the heroic times — before the changes — they were rumoured to have sewn a button back on a student traveller — which they can't do as a rule.

TOUCHSCREEN INFORMATION You'll find eight touchscreen information sets over town — two at Ferihegy Airport, one each in the Southern Railway Station, the Astoria underground station, the Central Market Hall, the Royal Castle and the Hungarian Culture Foundation, and two at the Tourinform offices. The number of machines is soon to treble, and the awesome variety of information available in Hungarian will soon be available in English and German as well. (Currently only some of it is.)

Apart from the usual kind of information, the system provides sophisticated orientation advice — it helps with routes by mass transit, or by car. The owner and the initiator of the project is a new organization, Tourism Office, Budapest; they are eager to hear what visitors think about the system, so be so kind as to send them your comments, flattering or devastating: H-1364 Postafiók 215. Or *info@budtour.hu*.

THE BUDAPEST CARD is another new institution, introduced in 1997, a sort of three-day, general, non-transferable pass offering free travel on public transport, free entry to 55 museums, and substantial discounts on sightseeing, baths, restaurants and a plethora of other things. Everything that makes Budapest special. The date of purchase is stamped when the card is issued, and you have to sign it the way you do a credit

card, which it altogether resembles. It makes life more comfortable, and puts many things at your fingertips. The 1998 price is 2400 forints for adults and there is a reduction for kids. You can buy it everywhere, from travel agencies to Budapest Transit Authority ticket offices, museums and other places.

MAPS
In hotels and travel agencies you are given a miniature one-page map — a highly unsatisfactory one. The ideal solution depends on your aims and status.

The Best Map for the One-weekend Conference Tourist
Who Wants to Get Away for a Short While

BUDAPEST: THE INNER PART *(Budapest belső területe)* Inside the not very attractive, green and red cover there is a very practical, easy-to-use map. The back shows the inner city areas in such detail that even the numbers of the buildings are indicated at corners of the streets. (Scale: 1:7500!) There is a comprehensive street index for both sides of the map.

The Best Map for a Couple Staying Downtown
But Who Want to Discover the City for Themselves on Foot

BUDAPEST "FALK" A regular but beautifully printed map which you can unfold at home and leaf through in the street. It shows the structure of the city very clearly. The inset map shows such a small area that it is almost useless. Full street index. Attracts muggers.

Map for a Young Couple from Ukraine on Honeymoon,
Who are Staying with Relatives in the Outskirts

THE MAP OF BUDAPEST A map showing the whole city with the districts in different colours — which is sometimes helpful even to a foreign visitor. All tram and bus routes are indicated. Full index. Includes a very well designed inset map of the centre.

Map for a Serious, Lonely Traveller Who Swapped
His Turin Flat for an Elegant Home Near City Park

EURO CITY BUDAPEST A red, spiral-bound booklet, very clearly and cleverly designed, somewhat expensive, though. It must have been designed far from Budapest — it covers a very large area of Pest, but very little of Buda. Full, easy-to-read index.

Map for the Business Traveller Who Wants to Find New
Premises for His/Her Central European Headquarters

THE ATLAS OF BUDAPEST A large-format, spiral-bound book, covering 28 districts around the city. The scale is 1:20000, (Sections 8-81, and 1:10000 in the inner city parts). With street numbers and one-way indication. There is a haystack of soulless information, not really of much use, at the back of the book. Also easy to use, quite large print, full index.

Map for an Architecture Freak Who Wants to Visit
Every Single Address in the 'For Serious Addicts' Part of This Book

CARTOGRAPHIA'S BUDAPEST *(in a transparent plastic folder)* Basically a brand new, locally edited version of the Falk map, simply printed as a traditional flat map (i.e. you cannot leaf through it). A separate section details the metro system. Full index on the back. Landmark buildings in primitive but useful 3-D drawings.

MAP SHOPS

TÉRKÉPBOLT VI. Bajcsy-Zsilinszky út 37. T: 112-6001. Off Arany János utca Underground, Blue Line 3. A small shop — don't expect a vast, London or New York style shop (the sort where you can buy the surface of the globe in small sections, even if they are totally sea-covered). But have a look at the awkwardly coloured wall maps for schools.

TÉRKÉPKIRÁLY XIV. Bosnyák tér 5. Shares a building with its parent company, the map-makers Cartographia. At the end of the No. 7 bus line. T: 221-9707. F: 163-3402. Full range of maps of Budapest. If you are there, have a quick look at the double map: the replica of an 1896 map of Budapest, paired with a remake of the same area, same colouring, same size. You will be sorry that you don't read Hungarian: the otherworldly, great-grandma flavour of the words is as appealing as the charming typography and design. The two come in a plastic folder. A good present for a Hungarian who has made your Budapest stay nicer than you expected.

THE BASIC SETUP OF THE CITY
Now let's lay out a map in front of us and try to keep the structure of the city in mind. It is very rare that a city has two parts that are so different from one another. The hilly part in the west is Buda; across the river, twice the size and totally flat, is Pest.

In the Middle Ages the two were independent; in fact it was only just over 125 years ago that they joined with Óbuda to form the modern city. In the 15th century, when Buda was in its heyday, it was considerably larger and more important than Pest. The number of its inhabitants is estimated to have been about 24,000, whereas Pest had only 4,000. (After the Turks were driven out, towards the end of the 17th century, Buda had about 600 and Pest about 300 inhabitants.)

THE DANUBE,
which is strictly speaking the main thoroughfare, divides the capital in two as it flows southwards. At the northern limit of the city the river is almost a kilometre wide, a little further down it encircles two islands. Downriver from Margit (Margaret) Island the Danube narrows considerably. It is at its narrowest at the foot of Gellért Hill, only 230 metres across. Its average water-level here is 96 metres above sea level. The hills of Buda are between 150 and 500 metres in height and, with the exception of Gellért Hill, rise gently. The higher peaks form a semicircle some eight or so kilometres from the city centre. Even Pest is not as flat as it seems to be, since it rises steadily and the X. (Tenth) District, Kőbánya, is at the same height as Castle Hill. All this explains why we get such a magnificent view of Pest from the vantage points in Buda. Since the rise on the Pest side also forms a semicircle, Budapest could with some poetic exaggeration be said to compete with Naples or Rio de Janeiro. It is also rare that a large city reflects the characteristic landscapes of the whole coun-

try. To the west, beyond Buda, there are the hills and valleys typical of Transdanubia, whereas to the East, not so far from Pest, behind some small hills, the Great Hungarian Plain stretches out perfectly flat. True, to the north there are mountains, though with the highest peak at 1,015 metres they are not very high.

A lot more will be said about the history of the seven bridges over the Danube, and we will also have a close look at them during our walks. Just now, let's find them on the map. In this book they will always be referred to by their Hungarian names. (Remember that 'híd' is the Hungarian for 'bridge'.) There is an island between two of the bridges. The bridge south of the island forms an obtuse angle in the middle. This is Margit híd. Let's take this as our starting point.

BRIDGES AND BOULEVARDS

The historic centre of Buda can still be seen today on Castle Hill; almost nothing has survived of that of Pest. Historic Pest was situated between Lánchíd and Szabadság híd; that is, between the first and the third bridges south of Margit híd. This is what even today we call the city centre or downtown; officially it is the southern part of the V. district. The edge of this district is flanked by

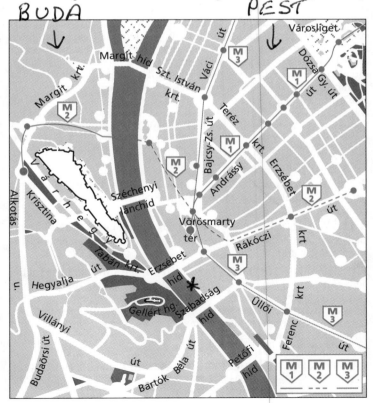

the Kiskörút (literally the 'small boulevard'), which consists of József Attila utca, Károly körút, Múzeum körút and Vámház körút.

The main street in the city is Váci utca. Halfway along this street there is the Pest end of Erzsébet híd, the first of the two modern bridges in the city. On the Buda side, the road from the bridge turns sharply to the right and starts climbing steeply. It leads straight onto the motorway to Vienna and to Lake Balaton.

From the Pest end of Margit híd runs a semicircular avenue, built after the Parisian pattern. This is called the Nagykörút (literally the 'great boulevard') and reaches the Danube at both ends, joining Margit híd in the north and Petőfi híd in the south. 'Grand Boulevard' is actually a nickname — no part of it is actually called that. It is the overall name of Szent István körút, Teréz körút, Erzsébet körút, József körút and Ferenc körút.

The semicircle continues on the Buda side, although not quite as regularly as in Pest. Thus the circle is completed by Irinyi József utca, Karinthy Frigyes út, Villányi út, Alkotás utca and Margit körút, and there we are again at Margit híd (most of this can be travelled by Trams 4 and 6).

It is more or less true to say that Budapest was built within this circle by the turn of the century, with some additional building along main roads running out of town such as Andrássy út, which ends in Városliget in the east. The bridge north of Margit híd, Árpád híd, is the beginning of an outer semicircular ring. Its sections are called Róbert Károly körút, Hungária körút and Könyves Kálmán körút. The latter has just reached the Danube again in the south, when Lágymányosi híd, with its special, over-size mirrors (to light the road evenly) was built, right beside the present rail bridge, Déli Vasúti híd. Pest had spread more or less this far by the beginning of World War II. The outer ring roads join five major roads that carry traffic from the city towards the suburbs: Váci út, Andrássy út, Rákóczi út which continues in Kerepesi út, Üllői út and Soroksári út. Metro lines run along all of these except the last.

Budapest, with an area of 525 square kilometres, is the home of something less than 2 million people, one in every five citizens of this country.

VIEWPOINTS
The most famous viewpoints, Castle Hill and Gellért Hill, are included in our first and third walks. Some more places worth visiting are:

THE LOOK-OUT TOWER ON JÁNOS-HEGY The tower is situated at the highest point over the city, on top of the 529 metre high János-hegy or John Hill. Four platforms, one above the other, encircle the wall of the tower. On an average day visitors can see places 75 kilometres away in all directions, but on especially clear days some have even seen the High Tatra Mountains, 215 kilometres away. The best way to get there is by Bus 190 or the Chairlift.

THE TERRACE OF THE RESTAURANT *BELLEVUE*, **MARRIOTT HOTEL** *(on the bank of the Danube)* The restaurant is on the 10th floor of the hotel. Only for patrons of the restaurant.

THE LOOK-OUT TOWER ON JÓZSEF-HEGY *(II. Józsefhegyi út)* This small look-out tower, built in brown stone, is neither very well known nor in very good shape. There is a full view of the city with all the bridges, the Danube Bend and all the Buda hills. The easiest way to get there is by Buses 91 or 191. I hope the neo-Nazi graffiti will have gone by the time you get there.

MARGIT HÍD — THE 'ELBOW' At the 'elbow' of the bridge, opposite the island, as close to the river as possible. This is a breathtaking, unusual view, a kind of third panorama of the river. A famous playwright and theatre director proposed building the new National Theatre here. The idea wasn't taken seriously, mainly because of the cost. (And other problems.)

MARTINOVICS-HEGY *(at the top of XII. Gaál József út)* From this 259-metre high hill there is an unusual view of the city, especially of Castle Hill. In fact the top of the hill is a nature reserve almost directly above the busy Moszkva tér. It is also a favourite rendezvous for dog owners and their dogs. Dusk, when streetlamps are being lit, is an especially pleasant time to walk up here. Fifteen minutes from Moszkva tér on foot.

ÁRPÁD TOWER Best to get there by Bus 11 and then walk up Látó hegyi út from the terminus. A charming spot, unknown to tourists or travellers. The tower itself has echoes of the rural folk architecture of Transdanubia.

THE DOME OF BUDAPEST CATHEDRAL (THE 'BASILICA') *(V. Szent István tér)* Opened relatively recently, the lower observation deck around the dome is still not known to Budapest people. There are 302 steps (a lift will open soon). Some steps after 200 the scene changes: you climb out of a specially built tube into the inside of the dome, in a wrought iron construction. Then you get to the space between the inside and the outside of the dome — quite a thrilling experience. The panorama outside will keep you amazed for at least fifteen minutes. Take your time, and try to discover the hidden sights that are always kept secret from ordinary mortals. Don't forget about the Drop on top of the Nationale Nederlanden building, and other delicacies. (For more about the church see 'Walk Two'.)

TAXI

As with everything in Budapest, there are far-reaching changes on the taxi-front as well. As opposed to the grim situation of some years back, nowadays you can get a taxi at any time and in almost every part of the city within minutes and there are also a number of taxi companies waiting for your telephone call.

But chaos on the taxi-front still prevails. Obviously, it doesn't matter how serious an offence they commit, nobody can really be stripped of their permit.

You can be charged anything, but the driver should tell you the price. There are about five kinds of rates, according to the time of the day and the zone — even I don't understand it. City Hall wanted to regulate this jungle by maximizing the prices, but the Constitutional Court overruled the decision. Every six months new ideas emerge, and nothing happens.

Taxis can be hailed in the street; they are for hire only if the 'TAXI' sign is lit up. If you are ordering one by phone, give the address, then your full name and telephone number. English is almost always understood.

Try to avoid the 'hyenas' queueing at hotels and at the railway stations.

The worst are those working at the airport. Insist on the meter being turned on — and on paying in forints. At the airport the situation is so bad, you are better off taking the Airport Shuttle or the universally praised Airport Minibus Service. When you land, a leaflet is given to you about this service operated by the airport authorities, and you can pay for it while you are waiting for your luggage. When leaving Budapest you can get it to pick you up from where you are staying. This is a fair, reliable and affordable sevice. At hotels insist on the receptionist ordering a taxi for you. Otherwise, you can be sure of going on a zigzag route and of being over-charged.

I may be biased, and I don't very often resort to taxis, but there are four companies who do seem straightforward, so I can pass this information on to you. Ring them up yourself, or insist that the receptionist in your hotel use one of them when ordering your taxi. You can usually ask for a non-smoking car, I mean a car whose owner doesn't smoke and who doesn't let passengers smoke.

Budataxi: 120-0200
Citytaxi: 211-1111
Főtaxi: 222-2222
Yellow Pages Taxi: 155-5000

Taxi drivers in Budapest are generally outgoing and talkative people who actually do circulate the latest news and know about everything. It is worth asking them if they can speak any foreign languages. And remember to check whether the meter is on. You are not obliged to pay if it isn't. However, an English-speaking driver is still a rarity in Budapest, and will probably be working for a VIP service.

Most locals remember the telephone number of the first and at one time the only (state) taxi company; however most of their best drivers, who used to know the city inside out, have gone private. (Look for the taxi driver's badge of honour on the dashboard: a plaque given for $1/4$, $1/2$ and 1 million accident-free kilometres.) One of the oldest of taxi driver jokes: A driver drives straight through all the red lights without hesitation. When he arrives at a crossing where the traffic lights are green, he stops immediately. 'Can't we go now?' asks the customer, who is shaken up from the ride. 'No way,' the driver says. 'This is when the taxis are coming from the right.'

METRO (Underground)
As most Budapest residents travel with a monthly card, they do not really understand the recent changes in the fare structure, which attempted to cater more efficiently for the needs of internal travellers and tourists, and old people over 70 (the latter travel free of charge). As you will probably buy a Budapest Card, and not bother about tickets, you may not be interested either. If for some reason the Budapest Card does not appeal, you can buy a 'metro szakaszjegy' that entitles you to ride 3 stops away on the same line, a 'metró szakasz-átszál-lójegy', that entitles you to ride 5 stops with one change, and a 'metró-átszállójegy', that lets you go wherever you want, on any of the lines, though again with one change and no more. Of course, the day ticket can be used on the underground as well.

The first underground line, the yellow line, runs between Vörösmarty tér in the city centre (all our walks start from this square) and the terminus at Mexikói út. The journey takes just over 10 minutes. The entrances to most stations and the notices on the walls are copies of the originals; it was only in the 1970s that the old trains were unfortunately replaced by more modern carriages.

The second, red, line, takes passengers from a large housing estate in the east of Pest to the centre of Buda to Moszkva tér and to the Déli (Southern) Railway Station. The line crosses under the river, between the Parliament and Lánchíd. The journey takes about 20 minutes. In the rush hour, trains run at 2 minute 7 second intervals. In all stations, there is a rubber strip on the edge of the platform. You may not step on this until the train has stopped in the station. If you do stray onto it, a voice will, with increasing hysteria, start coming over the loudspeakers: 'A biztonsági sávot kérem elhagyni'. (*'Leave the Security Strip, Will You?!'*) Naturally, most foreign visitors do not understand the warning, which will be repeated until a Hungarian passenger taps the visitor on the shoulder, and gestures to him to step back.

The third, blue, line is the newest. It takes passengers from an industrial district in the south-east through the downtown area to the northern part of the city in 28 minutes. In the rush hour the trains on this line run every 2 minutes and 20 seconds.

The three lines have a busy junction at Deák tér. Tickets are available at every station at the regular 'pénztár' until about 8 p.m. After that time you can get one in the section called 'forgalmi ügyelet'. There you can look at the black and white monitors that keep an eye on the network.

Underground trains run between 4.30 a.m. and 11.10 p.m.

Night Bus 78 serves most of the route of the second underground line, while Night Bus 182 follows the route of the third line.

BUSES
Most people in Budapest, some 40% of all mass transit passengers, travel by bus. There are more than 200 bus routes, all of them travelled by Hungarian-made buses with automatic gearboxes. They are manufactured at Ikarus, once the fifth largest bus factory in the world, a stumbling industrial giant whose reorganization is now gathering momentum. Perhaps half of them are articulated buses — as characteristic of Budapest as double-deckers are of London. On busy routes, buses with the number in red are fast buses; the route is the same as that of the buses with the same number in black but there are far fewer stops. Boarding these buses requires careful consideration. Bus numbers in red which are also followed by a red letter E (e.g. 73E) are express non-stop service, and stop only at the two termini. Most bus stops indicate the routes and stops on a board.

After boarding the bus, passengers must look for a punch-machine to validate their tickets. You put your ticket into the slot of the machine upside down and pull the rim of the slot firmly towards you. The machine punches the ticket or, at least, indents it and such tickets are accepted by the inspectors, who either wear a uniform when getting on the bus or disguise themselves as housewives carrying large shopping bags. In either case an inspector states: 'Kérem a jegyeket ellenőrzésre' (*Keh-rrem ah yedj-e-ket e-len-owr-zesh-re*), i. e. 'Show me your tickets for checking'. Inspectors are not often tolerant of confused foreigners. City buses are traditionally blue; but now they are coloured all over with advertisements. You can board the bus through any door. The bus stops only if there is someone waiting to get on or to get off. If you wish to get off, you signal to the driver by pushing the button above any of the doors. People do not queue at bus stops: you board the door nearest you when you can.

TRAMS
There have been trams in Budapest for more than a century, the tracks laid by competing companies, all of which kept their trams in their own livery. Until only twenty years ago there were still various types of trams and people had various sentiments towards certain types. Some trams had an open platform and more adventurous passengers, or those who could not find any room inside the tram, stayed outside. Most Budapest children naturally preferred the platform, which gave you the sense of being master of a ship as the tram swayed along.

Nowadays all the trams are yellow and all have doors that close automatically. A few years ago many tram routes were replaced by buses but this trend has now stopped and there has even been a new tram line laid (Tram 1 on the Outer Boulevard). If the tram is packed, pass your ticket over to someone beside the punch and they will punch it for you.

Trams start running early in the morning, some as early as 3 a.m. Information on the first and the last trams on a route can be read at every stop. (*Utolsó kocsi indul* = The last one leaves.)

TROLLEY-BUSES
There have been trolley-buses in Budapest since 1949 and there are 13 routes at present. Their numbers allegedly start from 70 only because it was on Stalin's 70th birthday that the first line started operating. You can travel on trolley-buses with tram tickets. The current-collectors of trolley-buses frequently come loose, providing a favourite piece of street-theatre when the driver jumps out of her seat, assembles a long pole, catches the loose current-collector with it and puts it back onto the overhead wire. (Trolley-buses and trams are usually driven by women.)

Every bus, tram and trolley stop has a sign which shows when the last vehicle starts from the terminus on that route, usually between 11 and 12 p.m. You can find information on all-night trams and buses that run even after midnight. For the visitor the best value is, no doubt, the Budapest Card, or a day ticket. **A Word of Warning:** You cannot buy tickets on trams or buses. You have to buy them in underground stations or at newsagents, or slot machines. Another rule is that after 8 p.m. you can only use the front door, and there you should produce your pass or ticket to the driver.

OTHER TRANSPORT
THE COG-WHEEL RAILWAY (Fogaskerekű) began running in 1874 and has since been electrified. It climbs up into the Buda hills, starting from Városmajor near Moszkva tér and reaching Széchenyi-hegy station in 16 minutes. The distance between the two termini is 3,7 kilometres and the difference in height is 327 metres. The trains run from 4.25 a.m. to midnight.

CHILDREN'S RAILWAY starts from where the cog-wheel train line ends up on the hill. The trains run on an 11 kilometre narrow-gauge track and provide an enchanting trip through the woods. What is special about it is that the line is run by children, naturally with adult helpers for some of the tasks.

THE CHAIRLIFT runs 8 metres above the hillside from a valley called Zugliget up to the highest peak in the city, the look-out tower on János-hegy. There is a 262 metre difference in height between the two termini and it takes 12 minutes to make the journey. It is in operation between 9.30 a.m. and 4 p.m., in summer between 9 a.m. and 5 p.m., except every other Monday (the odd ones).

THE CABLE CAR (Sikló) train was reopened in 1986, having been entirely reconstructed after damage suffered during the war. It takes visitors from the Buda end of Lánchíd up to Castle Hill in one minute. It carries prams and wheelchairs as well. Tickets on the spot.

DRIVING

I wouldn't recommend it to anyone who doesn't know the town very well. Not even the occasional emigré who comes back for a visit. A couple of factors make it hell to drive in Budapest.

Cars are more than seven years old on average. Pollution is somewhat less than before, since more and more cars run with a catalytic converter, but still the air can be heavy. Cars double-, even treble-park.

There has been a small revolution in Budapest recently: a parking enforcement revolution. Hundreds of meters were installed, with notices in three languages.

There are new entrance gates to the Castle District, which will keep you entirely out of certain areas. So you should park before you reach the plateau, and use one of the dozen stairs.

The former régime was strong in politics, but — perhaps it's not common knowledge — was weak in everyday life, unable to enforce its petty rules (traffic, parking, housing, building, etc. regulations).

Vans still load in daylight, at high noon, causing bottlenecks at every corner. Also cars go wrong, even my one-year-old wonderful company car, a very dark blue Opel Astra, with 16 valves (registration plate: FFH 619. If you dent it, just leave your cheque under the wipers).

Traffic manners are non-existent. The bigger the car you have, the more aggressive you are.

Women drivers are considered easy game. If you want to see Budapest driving at its best (worst), try the Pest side of the Lánchíd (Chain Bridge). There is only one lane of the three around the square (the middle one) that entitles cars to get onto the bridge. Stand at the corner with a gas mask and watch the Ayrton Senna manoeuvres to get into that lane; within five minutes you are guaranteed a fine display of mutual recrimination when fender meets offender.

So take a taxi. Or take a tram. Best of all: walk.

AT THE WEEKEND

Budapest empties every Friday evening between spring and autumn for the weekend. Families rush off to 'Balcsi'

— Lake Balaton — or to their 'plots'. Their summer places are somewhere along the 180 kilometres of the shore of the lake. The more desirable places are on the hills of the northern shore of the lake, which shelves more steeply than the other side. Family 'plots' are usually somewhere around Budapest and are, quite simply, a small piece of land with a small house built of stone or wood, usually with a lovingly cared-for lawn and vegetable garden. For many years, the very high number of 'summer houses' has been due to the restrictions of the housing market; people simply have not been able to afford to buy their own home in the green belt or on the fringe of Budapest but have wanted to have a sense of space, a garden of their own. Significantly, the first motorway built in Hungary linked Budapest not with Austria or Yugoslavia, but with Lake Balaton. During the Sunday evening jam the number of lanes could be doubled without having any noticeable effect. At the weekends then, the tempo of Budapest becomes more relaxing. Buses and trams run less often, and far fewer cars take to the streets. Shops are open between 9 a.m. and 1 p.m. on Saturdays, food shops generally until 2 and the larger stores until 3.

A FOOD MARKET ON SUNDAY XIII. Lehel út, corner of Váci út, at the Lehel tér stop on the Blue (No. 3.) Metro. Not packed. A spectacle in itself. From 7 to 11 a.m.

NIGHT PHARMACIES
Pharmacies close at 8 p.m. at the latest, but those listed below provide a night service. When you ring the bell, the duty pharmacist gets up, opens a small window and dispenses the required medicine. All pharmacies display the address of the nearest night pharmacies in the window. (*A legközelebbi éjszakai ügyeletet tartó gyógyszertár.*) The list here, therefore, is not complete. You have to pay a 100 forints surcharge if it is not an emergency.

II. Frankel Leó út 22. T: 115-8290
VI. Teréz körút 41. (*On the corner of Szondi utca*) T: 111-4439
VII. Rákóczi út 86. (*At Baross tér*) T: 122-9613
XI. Kosztolányi Dezső tér 11. T: 166-6494
XII. Alkotás utca 1/B. (*At Déli Railway Station*) T: 155-4691
XIV. Bosnyák utca 1/A T: 183-0391

As in so many other places in this book, your attention is drawn to the number 117-9800, the **Tourinform** number, which is in operation between 8 a.m. and 8 p.m. They will be able to understand the problem you are trying to communicate and will be able to give you accurate advice on where you can turn to for help.

AMBULANCE: 104 If for any reason you cannot get through to this number, ring 111-1666. They can usually handle calls made in English or German. However they recommend that you get someone on the spot to report the incident and its location in Hungarian and only as a last resort try to make the call yourself. To use this and any other emergency number, you still have to insert a coin into a call-box. This will be returned to you after the call.

FIRE BRIGADE: 105 The alternative number if 105 is unobtainable is 121-6216. Calls can be dealt with in Russian, speakers of other languages should contact the police. (See below.) Under Hungarian law, even fires that have been extinguished have to be reported. Otherwise you can't claim on your insurance. Call-boxes return your coin after an 105 call.

POLICE: 107 If you cannot get through, call 118-0800 or 111-8668. These numbers are for emergencies only, not for enquiries or for routine police business. Calls can be handled in English, French, German, Polish, Russian and Spanish. For calls in other languages an interpreter can be obtained. For other police affairs, see General Information for a list of the Budapest District Police Stations.

'I DON'T FEEL WELL!' Many of the embassies hold a list of

doctors and dentists speaking the language of their nationals. And there are some ads for English-speaking doctors in the English-speaking weeklies. If you are in real trouble, you can try the following Medical School clinics:

I. SZÁMÚ BELGYÓGYÁSZATI KLINIKA (Internist Unit)
VIII. Korányi Sándor utca 2/a. T: 133-0360.
II. SZÁMÚ BELGYÓGYÁSZATI KLINIKA (Internist Unit)
VIII. Szentkirályi utca 46. T: 113-8688.
III. SZÁMÚ BELGYÓGYÁSZATI KLINIKA (Internist Unit)
XII. Eötvös út 12. T: 175-4533.
I. SZÁMÚ SEBÉSZETI KLINIKA (Surgical Unit)
VIII. Üllői út 78. T: 113-5216.
**I. SZÁMÚ GYERMEKGYÓGYÁSZATI KLINIKA
(Paediatrics Unit)**
VIII.Bókay János u. 53. T: 134-3186.
**II. SZÁMÚ GYERMEKGYÓGYÁSZATI KLINIKA
(Paediatrics Unit)**
IX.Tűzoltó utca 7-9. T: 133-1380.
FOGPÓTLÁSTANI KLINIKA (Dental Unit)
VIII. Mikszáth Kálmán tér 5. T: 113-1639.
NŐGYÓGYÁSZATI KLINIKA (Gynaecology Unit)
VIII. Baross utca 27. T: 133-1130.

PHARMACIES The Hungarian word for a pharmacy, *gyógyszer-*

tár, bears little resemblance to its name in other European languages. The alternative is a loan-word from Latin, *patika*. They are listed in the telephone directory under this latter heading. In town there are some fine old pharmacies which are highly regarded; simply looking into them seems to have a curative effect. Most of the pharmacists speak English and German. An old custom is to have a jug of water and glasses laid out on a table in the pharmacy so that medicines can be taken on the spot.

Some Pretty Pharmacies

PÁZMÁNY PÉTER PATIKA V. Egyetem tér 5. T: 117-5306.
Open 8 a.m. to 5 p.m., closed Saturday and Sunday.
KÍGYÓ PATIKA V. Kossuth Lajos utca 2/a. T: 118-5679.
Under the arcade. Open 8 a.m. to 5 p.m., Saturday 8 a.m. to 2 p.m., closed Sunday. Advice given in English and German.
OPERA PATIKA VI. Andrássy út 26. T: 153-1753.
Open 8 a.m. to 8 p.m., closed Saturdays and Sundays.

THAT AWFUL HUNGARIAN LANGUAGE

Enzensberger, the globetrotting German poet, once complained that Hungary was the only country with Latin script he had ever visited where he couldn't make out even a pharmacy sign. He was right: pharmacy is *gyógyszertár* in Hungarian. This monster of a word was coined, together with hundreds of others, to save the country from becoming a German-speaking one for good, as it almost did during the first two decades of the 19th century. And miraculously, Hungary did manage not to become another Ireland, that is, a small country with very old, lively arts and literature, but without its own language. By the way, the official language of Hungary until 1844 was not German, but Latin. (Literacy in Latin was widespread in the educated classes and lingered on for another hundred years, until the otherwise beautiful Russian language was forced on Hungarian schools.)

One can learn how to read Hungarian in half an hour (its spelling is logical), but a lifetime is too short to understand it, let alone speak it. It is not even an Indo–European tongue: it belongs to the Finno–Ugric family of languages. Finnish is a distant relative: totally incomprehensible to us.

If you have a look at a Hungarian book, you will see a lot of diacritical marks: two of which, 'ő' and 'ű' are missing even from the IBM standard character set, which makes life hell for Hungarian computer buffs. On average every sixth Hungarian letter is accented in some way or other — though only the vowels. There are long and short vowels: consequently, it is still possible to write 'metric poetry' (e.g. hexameters) in Hungarian, while in English, or Modern Greek, for instance, it is not.

The only good news is for the very obstinate: there is no gender for nouns, and word order is quite free — or, as experts say, 'fluid' – though a word will carry slight difference in meaning in different positions. This freedom, needless to say, is due to the unusually rich morphology of the language. If you take a closer look at any Hungarian book you will see very long words, most of them divided at the end of lines.

Though there are only three tenses, present, past and future, Hungarian conjugation is incredibly tricky: there are two separate sets in each of the three tenses: the 'transitive set' and the 'intransitive set'. So when I want to say 'I read a lot' or 'I am reading', I use one set, and the other when I read something in particular. And what is really weird for students with an English background: the imperative is the most complicated business to put together... For most foreigners Hungarian is intriguing, if not barbaric in sound. Eva Hoffmann, an American author talks about the 'utterly perplexing sounds of Hungarian language, with its Bartókian syncopations and sensuousness. Even when they speak English, Hungarians manage to transport some of the off-rhythms and softness of their own language into that flatter tongue, English, and give it strange, lunar resonances.' Do we?

Believe me, Hungarian is not an ugly language. Here is the list a Hungarian poet made of what he thought are the most beautiful words in our language: *láng* (flame), *gyöngy* (pearl), *anya* (mother), *ősz* (autumn), *szűz* (maiden), *kard* (sword), *csók* (kiss), *vér* (blood), *szív* (heart), *sír* (grave). In a language where words tend to be three syllables long…

TWELVE MOST IMPORTANT HUNGARIAN WORDS AND PHRASES

Yes – **Igen**; *No* – **Nem**; *Thanks* – **Köszönöm**; *Hungarian* – **Magyar**; *Nice (in most sentences):* – **Szép**; *Can I Have a Glass of Water?* — **Kérek egy pohár vizet**; *Red Wine* – **Vörösbor**; *White Wine* – **Fehérbor**; *Naff* – **Ciki**.

TWELVE COMMONPLACE SENTENCES YOU CAN MAKE US HAPPY WITH

Maga sokkal jobban tud angolul, mint én magyarul.
Your English is far better than my Hungarian.

Nagyon szép ország Magyarország.
Hungary is a very pretty country.

Budapest rengeteget fejlődött, mióta itt jártam.
Budapest has developed a lot since I was here.

A magyar boroknak alig van párja a világon.
Hungarian wines have hardly any rivals anywhere in the world.

A magyar nők nagyon csinosak.
Hungarian women are very pretty.

Mindenki tudja, hogy a magyar diákok szokták megnyerni a matematikai olimpiát.
I've heard that Hungarian students tend to win the Mathematical Olympics.

A mai napig jól emlékszem arra, amikor az Önök aranycsapata 6:3-ra legyőzte az angolokat a Wembley stadionban…
I clearly remember when your Golden Team beat England 6–3 at Wembley. — Only for people over 50, since it happened in 1953.

Szépek a magyar bankjegyek!
How nice Hungarian banknotes are! — A downright lie.

Szeretnék Szentendrére elmenni, megnézni a világhírű Kovács Margit Múzeumot.
I want to get to Szentendre, to visit the 'world famous' museum devoted to the art of the late Margit Kovács, the ceramist. — Practically unknown abroad.

Szerintem Önöket már az isten sem mentheti meg attól, hogy 2000 körül bekerüljenek a NATO-ba és az Európai Unióba.
I think you can take it for granted that you're going into NATO and the uropean Union around 2000. — An idiomatic phrase, literally 'now not even God can save you from going into.'

Tényleg nagyon igazságtalan volt az 1920-as Trianoni Békeszerződés, de ha bent lesznek az Unióban, egész Európa az Önöké lesz, az összes tengerekkel.
The Versailles Peace Treaty was really very unjust, but when you are in the Union, you'll have all Europe, with all its seas.

THE SHORTLIST

The Good, The Ugly and The Naff

THE GOOD

The Most Important Accessory to Tour Budapest with: A pair of binoculars. (Cheap and reasonably good Russian ones in the fleamarkets.) You should examine the façades and spires.

Best Place to Sip a Coffee and Feel the Tremor of the Underground Under Ground: Café Gerbeaud, at the tables to the far left.

Best Place to Feel You Are Just a Piece of Dust, Doomed to Failure: The Hungarian History Paintings Galleries on the second floor of the National Gallery, Royal Castle.

Probably the Nicest Small Museum, if You Want to Meet Your Girlfriend in Secret: *Ráth György Museum* in a beautiful, art nouveau villa in VI. Gorkij fasor 12. More guards than visitors.

Waitress with the Nicest, but not Sexy Smile: *In Kanári Salad Bar,* XIII. Pannónia utca 3.

Best Traditional Glove Shop: *Ékes,* V. Régiposta utca 16.

Nicest Pharmacy: *Pázmány Péter Patika,* V. Egyetem tér 5.

Most Artistic Burger King In All The World, and Best Obvious View of Budapest: VI. Oktogon tér. Fancy interior, looks like a 'grand café' in Amsterdam. With a big mural by László Lakner.

Best Antique Shop for Art Nouveau: V. Kammermayer Károly tér 3.

Best Place to View St Stephen's Church ('The Basilica') from: The terrace of a small, shabby café that changes owners and names all the time: VI. Bajcsy-Zsilinszky Endre út 19.

Nicest Art Nouveau Bank Hall: *Post Office Savings Bank,* V. Hold utca and Perczel Mór utca.

Biggest Pancake: *Korona Passage,* a New York style public space on the left side of Hotel Korona. Self-service.

Grandest Public Bath: *Gellért Bath,* XI. Kelenhegyi út 4.

Cosiest Map Shop: In the Arcade called *Párisi Udvar,* V. Ferenciek tere 5.

Fanciest Thirties Cinema: *Atrium,* Margit körút 55.

Biggest Public Building: Obviously the *Houses of Parliament,* built 1887-1904. It's 268 metres long, built on a 2 meter thick concrete foundation. Far too big for the square, for the purpose, for the country.

Narrowest Block: *I. No. 26. Döbrentei utca,* corner of Döbrentei tér. There seems to be no gate at all. (It's on the other side.)

Longest and Most Mysterious Chain of Arcades: In *VI. Terézváros,* between No. 16 Dob utca and No. 11 Király utca.

Biggest Architectural Hoax: *Vajdahunyad Castle* in Városliget, originally built out of cheap materials, for the Millenary Exhibition (1896), to represent the various styles in Hungarian Architecture. Later rebuilt to last for good.

Ice Rink in the Most Romantic Setting: *The lake* in front of the above castle, in winter.

Loveliest Great Flood Memorial Tablet from 1838: *corner of V. Királyi Pál and V. Szerb utca.* The area flooded in 1838 is shown in red marble in a map. The water level is also shown, as it is on many buildings.

Most Moving Monument: The *Raoul Wallenberg Monument*, II. Szilágyi Erzsébet fasor and Küküllő utca.

Fanciest Gilded, Old Style Cinema: Probably the *Uránia*, VII. Rákóczi út 21.

'Green Tram' Rebuilt: *VII. Rózsák tere*. This is the result of an ambitious programme of the early eighties: to rebuild all the remaining trams – our name for what the more classical French call *vespasiennes*. There must be some problem with the profitability of running these places.

Prettiest Art Nouveau Façade: Former Parisiana Cabaret, now *Új Színház* (New Theatre), VI. Paulay Ede utca 35.

Best Swimming Pool: *Komjádi Béla Sportuszoda*, II. Árpád fejedelem utca 8. Not always open to ordinary mortals, i.e. non Olympic-level swimmers.

Most Traditional Shirtmaker: *Fleischer*, VI. Nagymező utca and Paulay Ede utca.

Best Non-naff Hungarian Style Restaurant: *Kéhli Vendéglő:* III. Mókus utca 22. (Open only in the evening.)

Most Accessible Upper Middle Class Home from the 1880's: *The Post Office Museum*, VI. Andrássy út 3., first floor. (Second floor for Americans.)

Best Button Shop: *Dénes Vándorfy*, V. Váci utca 75. (Only women's ones.)

Best Place to Look at Second Hand Furniture and Not Buy Anything: *Tűzoltó utca Furniture Store*, IX. Tűzoltó utca 14.

Newspaper with the Fanciest Name: Either *Hócipő* or *Magyar Narancs*, ask a Hungarian friend or a receptionist about them. (Sorry, it's a short list.)

The Ten Greenest Spots in Pest in May: The *southern slope of Gellért Hill*, the *top of XII. Martinovics-hegy*, *V. Szabadság tér* (at the weekend), *XIII. Margitsziget* (between the Grand Hotel and the Rose Garden), *IX. Népliget*, *XIV. Városliget* (except for the weekend), *The Botanical Gardens* (VIII. Illés utca 25.), *I. Vérmező* (or 'blood field', thus called because of the executions of 1795, which took place here), *'May 9th Park'* (on an island, north of Margaret island), *XII. Városmajor* (starting point for a cog-wheel railway that chugs out towards even greener spots in outer Buda).

Most Mysterious, Oversize Stone Lady: in the yard of the former Two Lions Inn, in *IX. Kálvin tér 9*. Originally in the middle of the square and the only bit that survived World War II. The whole statue re-carved and re-erected: V. Erzsébet tér. It's called the Danubius Fountain.

Nicest Modern Statue in the Castle: *The Knight and His Page*, on the wall overlooking Buda, at the bus parking lot, between Szent György tér and Dísz tér (Károly Antal, 1983). This is the enlarged 'copy' of one of the mid-15th-century statues excavated nearby in 1974. You have the impression of seeing a new and perfect statue, not just the fragments.

Funniest Classroom Slogan: *'Double-entry bookkeeping is one of the most glorious inventions of humankind and its use should be encouraged in each and every household.'* (Goethe). VII. Wesselényi utca 57, first floor, visible from the street.

Shabbiest Old Shop: corner of V. Hold utca and Aulich utca, an optician shares the space with a watchmaker. You can have black and white film printed here — a rarity in town.

THE UGLY

Biggest Bookshop in Town: *Fókusz könyváruház*, VII. Rákóczi út 14.

The Only Bookshop Open Until 11 p.m. Every Day: *Láng Téka*, XIII. Pozsonyi út 9. Open so late because it shares the space with a video rental outlet.

Biggest Residential Block: *III. Szőlő utca*, at the Buda end of Árpád bridge. A ludicrous, kilometre-long, ten-storey, pre-fab block.

Most Expensive, Most Extensive Scaffolding in Town: All over the *Institute of Sociology*, in VIII. Pollack Mihály tér, the former Festetics Palace. It's worth visiting: grand scale, oversize floor tiles inside, more or less preserved.

Most Unfinished Planned Avenue: *VII. Madách Imre út* — ends after 200 metres.

The Street Most Crowded with Fake Fin-de-siècle Lamps: *V. Váci utca*.

Aristocratic Palace in the Most Pitiful State: V. Reáltanoda utca 12. The former *Blaskovich Palace*, where 'Kincsem', the Miraculous Mare (1874-1887) used to live in the yard. She won all her 54 races. Have a look at the second floor.

Most Traditional Surviving Street Toilet ('Green Tram'): *VI. Nagymező utca*, at the corner of Paulay Ede utca. You should wear a gas mask on entering the premises.

Top Twelve Restaurants Taxi Drivers Take the Unsuspecting Moneyed Tourist, Where No Gourmet Ever Goes: *Császárkert, Kárpátia, Mátyás Pince, Margitkert, Ménes Csárda, Monarchia, Paradiso, Nautilus, Vasmacska, Új Sipos, Régi Postakocsi*, and … (You can fill in here the names of most of the Castle District restaurants.)

Most Intrusive Recent Public Building in Buda: *the extension of MTI*, Hungarian News Agency, the aerials even spoil the silhouette of the Royal Palace as seen from Pest.

THE NAFF

Cheapest Kitsch '*Antique*' Shop: VII. Hernád utca 7.

Most Traditional Looking, though Somewhat Posh Café in Buda: *Angelika*, I. Batthyány tér.

Most Elegant Gate Leading Nowhere: Opposite the back of the National Museum Garden, VIII. Puskin utca 8. You can't enter it, for two different reasons.

Best Steak in Naff Environment: *Fehér Bölény* (White Buffalo) restaurant, V. Bank utca 5.

Least Naff Danube Cruise: *Legenda Ship* at ten. With really nice student hostesses, who manage to behave with the kindness of a distant relative.

The Twelve Naffest Things you can Do in or After Budapest:
— to use a taxi from Ferihegy Airport to downtown Budapest,
— to go to a restaurant and accept a table near the gipsy band, because you can't get away,
— drop an extra piece of red pepper into your fish soup,
— to drink a lethal concoction for apéritif called 'Puszta cocktail',
— to ask a friend to tell the story of the National Theatre building,
— to go anywhere on bike except for Saturday and Sunday mornings, before 9.30 a.m.,
— to change money in Váci utca, and risk being outwitted by street moneychangers, when the profit is so small,
— to attend a so called Gulyás Party, a 30-year-old scam,
    a raid against the purse of lower middle class
    package tourists,
— to drive downtown,

- to pop into just any restaurant, without consulting a local friend,
- to quarrel with a policeman, one not wearing glasses,
- **not** to buy 'Paul Street Boys' by Ferenc Molnár in English and read it back home on the train or the plane,
- **not** to come back.

Naffest New Style Pastry Shop: *Perity Mestercukrászat*, VI. Andrássy út 37. Mirrors, white columns, Christ on the Cross, four TV sets with MTV on, plus a lot of gold and an ordinary telephone set.

Textile Shop with the Largest Number of Hungarian Coat of Arms Communist Style: *Merino Textile Shop*, V. Petőfi Sándor utca 20. Elderly people still call it 'The Brammer', with reference to the last pre-war owner. Watch out for the coat of arms on the ceiling, just by the columns.

Best Obvious Tricky Snapshot in Town: *Several bridges together*, from Castle Hill, from the front of the Royal Palace.

Second Best Obvious Tricky Snapshot in Town: *The Statue of St Gellért*, taken from the Pest side, through Elizabeth bridge.

The Naffest Lampshade Specialist: in *V. Molnár utca* at the corner of Irányi utca.

The Ghastliest Public Building: The *sixties office block* in Vörösmarty tér, a blatant contrast to everything that is precious in the very centre of the city.

The Copy of Palazzo Strozzi of Florence: on the Grand Boulevard, *off Oktogon square:* VI. Teréz körút 15. On the ground floor: one of the three 'central wedding halls'.

The Dumbest Thing to Have Changed in Budapest: the yellow colour they used to paint trams.

A CLOSING REMARK TO THE SHORTLIST

As is obvious from the proportions, it was written by a wickedly pessimistic Budapest person: the Good Things in Budapest easily outweigh the Bad, the Ugly and the Naff. So: it is worth coming here. And worth coming back, regularly.

A CITY INHERITED

THE WALLS

The following five walks try to show visitors
all the important sights of the city. My intention is to give you
a sense of orientation in Budapest, and to provide an image
in depth of the city.

FOR SHORT-STAY VISITORS: THE FIRST WALK The magnificent view from the top of Gellért Hill and the tour around the Parliament building are worth adding to this route. The route itself can hardly be made quicker by car: most of it takes us through pedestrianised areas.

FOR THREE OR FOUR DAYS: THE FIRST FOUR WALKS These routes include all the important sights. If you complete them all, you will have a clear idea of the structure of the city. Part of the routes can be done by car to save time.

AN INTRODUCTION TO EVERYDAY LIFE: THE FIFTH WALK There are few tourist attractions included in the fifth walk. It helps the visitor to glimpse the life of the districts along Grand Boulevard. This walk is, in a way, halfway between the first four walks and the chapter 'For Serious Addicts'. It makes no sense to follow this route by car.

THE BEGINNING AND THE END: VÖRÖSMARTY TÉR It was not difficult to choose Vörösmarty tér as the starting and finishing point of all our walks. It is right in the heart of the city, near the river, close to the big hotels and to the junction of the three underground lines. In the middle of the square is a statue, erected by public subscription to the memory of Mihály Vörösmarty (1800-1855), a major figure of romantic poetry. Carved from Carrara marble, it has to be covered in ugly canvas (more recently in transparent plastic) from late autumn until early spring to protect it from cracking. In winter the middle of the square looks as if Christo the packaging artist has been working here.

The poet himself is the centre of the composition, while the figures around him are reciting his famous patriotic poem, whose opening line is carved into the pedestal of the statue. (*'Be faithful to your land forever, O Hungarians.'*) Below this line the black, round spot contains the most precious of all the donations. A beggar offered the lucky coin he inherited from his mother towards the cost of the statue. Now you have to peer to find it among all the graffiti.

The dominant building of the square today is, unfortunately, a hideous modern office building.

There used to be a German theatre on the site capable of seating 3,500, and later there was a department store too. A photograph of these buildings can be seen on the thick poster-pillar behind the statue (the building with the pediment is the theatre, the department store was the building called Haas Palace). The present 'Palace of Musical Art' was finished in 1971 and reflects the bleak modernism of the sixties, a sort of parodic extension to the Vigadó Concert Hall, a sort of Budapest Barbican. The building has a highly indecent nickname, which does not translate into English. The middle part of the complex incorporates the rehearsal hall of the State Symphony Orchestra. Now they have to pay rent for the building originally erected for them — the complex now belongs to a foundation that supports informal education in the country.

The big window with various concert posters overlooking the square belongs to the ticket office, which can be reached through the main entrance to the building. It sells tickets for musical events. At least twice a year a long queue of patiently waiting people forms outside the front door. This is when the office starts selling tickets for various subscription concerts in spring or autumn.

When (in 1992) this block was donated to a then pro-government foundation, to provide income for cultural projects, they faced a difficult task: how to get the tenants to pay a fair price for this prime location. The large exhibition space on the Vörösmarty square front, for example, called Csontváry Hall, was trying to find the balance between prestige and sales, and the rent remained symbolic during the transitional phase.

Well, after many months of careful negotiations, the foundation closed the gallery and opened a glitzy new place called **Art Café**. They contracted the café operations out and now they are said to pocket 25 times more rent, a substantial sum for their cultural projects. Moreover, the café has 'real art' on the walls, i.e. authorised copies of Csontváry, the demon-driven, larger-than-life, eccentric Hungarian painter, one of the least known great forerunners of modernism in European art history. I mean authorised copies of Csontváry, by the staff of the National Gallery. And in this way they managed to preserve the spirit of the place.

(To know more about Csontváry see National Gallery, Walk One.)

The shop beside it is a busy record shop, once the biggest in the city, called the 'Hungaroton Szalon'. On the left is the classical music department, on the right everything else. The Hungarian classical music catalogue is also available here. It is worth having a look at recordings on this Hungarian label — the company was recently privatized and bought by a consortium of Hungarian business people, who pledged to revive it.

Opposite this modern building there is an Edwardian one. Its ground floor is occupied by the **Luxus** department store, for decades the only place to buy clothes of 'import quality'. Now it is just a string of smaller boutiques. The décor is unbelievably naff and ridiculous, using brass in every conceivable inch, and even more.

However, the greatest attraction of the square is the confectioner's **Gerbeaud**, which has been in this building since 1870. Apart from a terrace, the café has three separate shops. The one on the left (entrance from Dorottya utca) is a separate café which is not always open, and can be rented for special functions. The main shop opens from the square itself and is always full of tourists. The one to the right of the building lacks the original splendour nowadays: it is just a shop selling Gerbeaud delicacies — you can sit down or eat or drink in a hurry.

It is worth walking through all the rooms as the 19th-century decoration and furniture are quite remarkable and very varied. The German contractor added questionable pictures to the scene we liked for decades. But he also added a new toilet complex in the basement. A veritable feat of cleanliness. And the "globe clock" is there. Remember: it is naff to leave your coats in the cloakroom, like the others, the "tourists". After all, you are a "traveller".

The confectioner's occupies the ground floor of two neighbouring buildings, which is why the rooms are so different. If you can find a table near the corner window in the vaulted part to the right (when you are facing the café from outside), you will feel and hear the trains of the old underground line thundering underneath. In one of the high rooms, with a richly decorated flat ceiling, there is a portrait of Émile Gerbeaud, the Swiss confectioner who bought the shop in 1884. He started selling his cakes at reduced prices; until that time only the very well-to-do could afford cakes here. He was the one to invent **konyakos meggy**, this Hungarian bonbon speciality which is dark chocolate with a sour cherry inside, matured in cognac. The story goes that he himself smashed the punch cakes whose colour was not what he had prescribed. The service in Gerbeaud is still very polite, although a little impersonal and strikingly slow. The waitresses are too busy and they have no time to chat about the guests in code-language as their old-time counterparts did. The choice, however, is first class, unlike the layout of the menu. Apart from Hungarian specialities, all the classics of Viennese confectionery are available.

Kis Gerbeaud, the little shop in the right wing of the building, used to be a world apart: an eminent meeting place for the 'Gerbeaud-ladies', i.e. old ladies who used to live better lives, wearing a lot of jewellery and waiting for their friends with a cup of coffee with whipped cream on the table. This place has been converted into a cake-shop. You can't sit down any more. You can't even drink a cup of coffee. It is difficult for me to recognize the place where my ersatz-grandma aunt, Mrs Rudolf Bozóki, née Irén Engländer (1904–1976) dragged me to, almost every first Tuesday of the month, to boast about my reasonably good grades to her fellow Gerbeaud-lady friends, and invariably to stuff me with a cake called 'corner block' (sarokház), a chocolate cake with a lot of whipped cream. The ladies wore-heavy perfumes, had relatives in the States and Britain, and retailed bad news about every conceivable subject. And they had a terrific time, in the centre of this Central European city, one that had seen good days.

Some say that nearer and nearer the Millennium, the good days of another fin de siècle are on the horizon again. We'll see.

The Castle Area and Váci utca takes us across the river to Buda, looks at some houses from the Middle Ages and at a very old church, which King Matthias would not recognize, even though he was married there twice. We shall visit the Royal Castle, which, finally, has a proper dome. We cross back to Pest by a modern bridge and plunge in the busy life of the city centre. We shall even visit a charming flowershop.

Time: 7-8 hours. It's so long that every now and then I mention places to sit down for a coffee or a meal (but I only give the name — you have to find the address and comments at the back of the book).

THE PROMENADE (DUNAKORZÓ) When viewed from the river in the second half of the last century, neo-Classical Pest was hidden behind large hotels. Here, on the river bank stood the Carlton, the Bristol, the Hungaria and the Ritz; they were of the same height as the only building remaining from that period, the one on the corner of Vigadó tér, i.e. the Thonet House. (Only one of these hotels survived the war, but even that was later pulled down.) The space in front of these hotels, the Korzó, became popular for promenading when tram tracks were laid along the old walk.

This row of hotels contained no fewer than nine cafés, all overlooking the river, all of whose terraces merged into one another. People from everywhere in Budapest, of all walks of life, used to stroll here from spring to autumn. This was a tradition that had survived from the time when Pest was a small town, when there was always a place to go to meet friends and to socialize. Pest once had three such promenades but this was the most important and the busiest — it had no fewer than four rows of benches. (The other two were Váci utca and Bástyasétány, which will be visited later during this walk.) Dunakorzó relaxed the stricter rules: near strangers walked together or even talked to each other. There is a story of a famous bohemian writer who was once accompanied by a young man on the Promenade. They strolled along together chatting. Suddenly the writer was greeted by a passer-by. The young man asked who it was. 'How on earth should I know?' replied the writer. 'I do not even know who you are!'

Evenings were especially beautiful here when all the cafés were illuminated. There was music in all of them: the best Gypsy and jazz bands played here. At a safe distance from the bright terraces sat people who used to come in all the way from the suburbs to listen to the music here but who could not afford to sit in a café.

Now that a new row of hotels has been built, the promenade is beginning to come to life again after its apparent death. Although it is mainly tourists who stroll here, the locals seem to be slowly returning as well, especially the older generation. At night, however, sleaze dominates at the lower (Erzsébet híd) end, with all three sexes offering themselves for sale.

Copies have been made of the old-time 'Buchwald-chairs', although now you do not have to pay 20 fillérs to the 'Buchwald-ladies' with the big leather bag when you want to sit down. Hopefully, the money will be found to keep the chairs free of rust somehow.

THE CUTEST OF CUTE LITTLE PRINCESSES

The little bronze statue perching on the railing (by László Marton, 1990) has sat there for only a couple of years, though some tourists might think it a hundred years old. The statue made most sculptors furious. A lot of artists and critics have found it downright kitsch. Tourists, including Prince Charles, loved it. The latter did so much that he acquired a copy, and invited the artist to London, where a show was devoted to his work. (See his Liszt statue on Walk Five, p. 162.)

HOTEL INTERCONTINENTAL, HOTEL HYATT 1E, 1F

At the Pest end of Lánchíd. Both hotels were built in the early 1980's, almost at the same time, bringing the Danube bank back to life. What would the Prince of Wales have said? They are far too big, they have spoiled the inherent scale

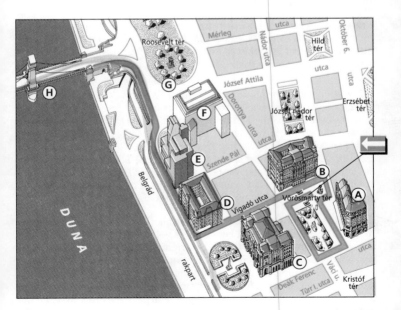

1 **A** Luxus Department Store **B** Gerbeaud confectioner's **C** Vigadó Concert Hall **D** Thonet House **E** Hotel Intercontinental **F** Hotel Hyatt **G** Statue of Ferenc Deák **H** Lánchíd — Chain Bridge

of the riverbank. They do not fit here. They do not even match the Marriott Hotel south of them (which was built fifteen years earlier — a long time, especially for Budapest hotel architecture). Not that they were unsuccessful buildings as such. I do not hold the common Budapest opinion that the Intercontinental, which has 408 rooms, looks like a tape recorder standing on its side; it reflects the afternoon sun from too many angles for that (József Finta, 1981). In the Intercontinental Hotel the salads of the Grill Bar and, especially, the cakes of the Viennese Patisserie on the first floor have gained the highest reputation. (And there is a large artwork on one of the walls, one that defies definition: a coloured wooden relief that evolves fully into three dimensions at some points. The figures are recognizable to Hungarians.)

The Hyatt, or more correctly, the Atrium Hyatt Hotel, has 356 rooms. The hive-like building reveals its true self from the inside. All its rooms open onto a circular gallery around a central courtyard, hence the name Atrium (Lajos Zalaváry, 1982). Over the atrium hangs a replica of the first Hungarian-built aeroplane. The café underneath is one of the coolest, most pleasant spots in Budapest.

At the entrance of the Intercontinental Hotel is a statue of József Eötvös, a 19th-century writer and politician. The inscription says: 'Erected by the Nation' and the small tablet was added by Hungarian secondary school pupils and teachers on the occasion of his centenary.

There was a pontoon bridge over the Danube from spring to autumn from the Middle Ages onwards. In winter the river froze up and even carts could pass across the thick ice. Of course, there were times when a large number of citizens got stuck in Buda when the thaw set in. In the winter of 1800 the entire magistracy of Pest went over to Buda for the wedding of the Austrian governor and were not able to return to their own city for weeks.

It was impossible to build a bridge of wood and stone over a river of this width. In 1820, a young captain of hussars, Count István Széchenyi, had to wait at the bank of the river for a week while travelling to his father's funeral. He decided to found a society for building a bridge. He sent to Scotland for an architect, William Clark, and a masterbuilder, Adam Clark, who in spite of their names were not related to each other. Even the iron was imported from Britain. After protracted and fiery debates, Parliament passed the law that even the aristocracy should pay the toll on the bridge. Some members of the Upper House declared that they would rather make a two-day detour to the south and cross the river by ferry, so intent were they on maintaining the noblemen's exemption from tax.

LÁNCHÍD 1H–2A Linking Roosevelt tér (Pest) and Clark Ádám tér (Buda). The bridge was built between 1842–49. The span between the pillars is 202 metres. The weight of the original structure was 2,000 tons. It was not quite finished when Austrian troops withdrawing to Buda towards the end of the Hungarian War of Independence tried to blow it up. They failed, however, to lay the charges properly and no damage was done to the bridge; on the other hand, the colonel who gave the order to set off the explosive charges was blown to pieces.

'When the bridge was ready, its creator was so proud of it that he declared he would drown himself if anyone could find any fault in his masterpiece,' begins

2 **A** Lánchíd — Chain Bridge **B** I. Fő utca **C** A café in the remaining part of a block destroyed during the war **D** Hunyadi János út 1. **E** The entrance of the Tunnel **F** The lower end of the Cable Car **G** The upper end of the Cable Car **H** Sándor Palace, **I** Várszínház — Castle Theatre **J** Ruins of the former Ministry of Defence, the future home of the János Neumann Digital Library, **K** Statue of a Hussar **L** Batthyány Palace

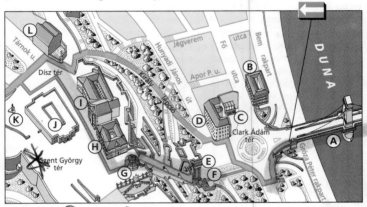

✶ archiological dig – very large!

an old anecdote. 'So the people came and examined every little part of it, but in vain. They could not find anything wrong with the bridge. Then one day an apprentice cobbler discovered that the lions at the end of the bridge had no tongues. And Clark committed suicide.'

In fact the lions were made later than the bridge itself, and the sculptor gave his word that the lions do have tongues; you can't see them unless you stand directly opposite them. In January 1945 German soldiers were, unfortunately, rather better at preparing demolition charges for bridges. They also pushed the button and dropped the central span into the Danube.

THE TUNNEL *under Castle Hill was built in 1857; the contemporary Budapest joke was that it was built so there would be somewhere to push the bridge into when it rained.*

CABLE CAR (SIKLÓ) 2F–2G

With a track almost 100 metres long, and a gradient of 4.8 in 10, the cable car was opened for service in 1870. The idea was to provide cheap transport for clerks working in the Castle District. It used to be operated with a steam engine. Its successor, completed in 1986, is powered by electricity, although it still uses a cable, with the down car counter-balancing the up car. It runs from 7.30 a.m. to 10 p.m., but is closed every other Monday. At the lower terminus there is a long queue during the daytime even out of the tourist season, so if you get off the bus here, try the Király lépcső steps. Castle Hill rises only 50-60 metres above the riverbank, so you can walk to the top in 5 to 10 minutes. If you make a little detour to the left at the first point where paths cross, you can admire the fine proportions of Lánchíd from above the Tunnel and you can also see the cable car from a little bridge over the tracks.

CASTLE HILL, this flat crag 1.5 kilometres long, packed with houses, could be compared to a floating stone gallery. At first sight the district may look poor and provincial compared to some old city areas in Western Europe that have remained substantially intact since the Middle Ages. Apart from some stately town houses, most of the buildings are simple plastered burgher's houses. The streets, all of which lead from the old gates, follow the shape of the hill. It was after an unexpected, devastating Mongol attack in the middle of the 13th century that the first citizens of Buda moved up the hill. Later the Royal Court was established on the hill, and with this began the quite lengthy Golden Age of the district. Buda became one of the most important cities in Europe in the 15th century. The number of its inhabitants is estimated to have been about 8,000. It was a melting pot of different nations: 'Pontiffs of Italian culture live in the neighbourhood of noblemen used to the rough life of soldiers. Republican Swiss ambassadors open their doors to Turkish aristocrats,' writes a historian. Buda started to decline under Turkish rule (1541–1686) but the siege and bombardment of 75 days before its liberation in 1686 left it in ruins. The Austrian authorities counted 300 inhabitants in the remains of the city. Reconstruction began, following the old street layout, but the houses were now only two storeys high, and not three as they had been before. A Baroque city slowly came into being, hiding the old ruins behind its thick walls. The Castle became a district of government. It was besieged again in 1849, and again reconstructed; later the ministries moved here. After a long period of peace, it was battered to pieces yet again in January 1945, before the eyes of the anguished civilian population. The German forces were completely surrounded, but held out here for almost a month. This was the city's thirty-first (!) siege.

The last reconstruction lasted for a long time — too long for the ministries, which moved out, allowing museums to take their place. Most of the houses of the district are still used as flats, some of them modernized only in the last few years. Cars have recently been banned from the area and now only people who live or work in the area, guests of the Hilton Hotel and taxis are allowed to drive here. The Castle has become quiet again. According to an architect-writer, the spirit of the city came here in its retirement. There is a peacefulness up here that cannot be found anywhere else in Budapest. The Venice Charter, regulating the reconstruction of historic buildings says, 'If a building has several architectural layers, the reconstruction of the remains of some earlier state can be permitted solely on condition that in so doing only parts of lesser value are demolished while the reconstructed part should be of great historical, archaeological or aesthetic value.' The whole city of Buda is a good example of such reconstruction. While the rubble was being cleared away after the war, many remains dating from the Middle Ages came into light and these were not covered up afterwards. From what we have left it seems certain that the walls were painted in different colours everywhere, with black, white and green patterns. Even the doorways of the ruined houses held surprises. Dozens of niches were discovered among the ruins whose function is still not clear to archaeologists. Some think they were resting places for nightwatchmen, others say they were used as stalls by broadcloth traders. In total, 63 such niches can now be seen in the Castle area. Apart from some other Hungarian towns, they are not found anywhere else in Europe. The oldest ones, from the 13th century, finish in a simple round arch; later they were more and more richly decorated. Perhaps there was some kind of competition between the residents of old Buda to have the most beautiful niche.

The great attraction of the Castle District lies so much in the unity of the place and in discovering it under one's own steam that I was very reluctant to be categorical about the route with the most interesting sights. The tablets on the walls of the buildings indicate which century they were built in (SZ.= 'century', after Roman numerals), or name any previous buildings on the site (HELYÉN = 'on the site of').

The walls of the Castle are well preserved almost everywhere. Except for some short sections, you can walk around on them. Let's start our walk here and see the part overlooking Buda. If we start from the gate called Fehérvári kapu to the round bastion nicknamed the 'Sour Soup Bastion' (Savanyúleves Rondella) we will be walking where the promenade of the Buda side once was. Nowadays it is fairly quiet.

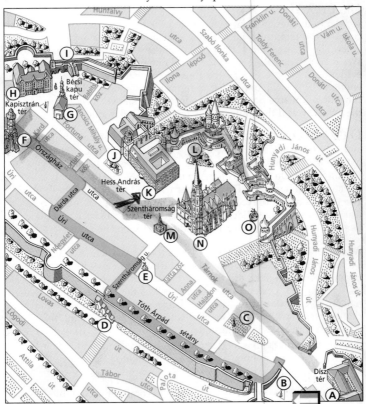

3 **A** Várszínház — The Castle Theatre **B** Statue of a Hussar **C** Memorial to the soldiers of 1848 **D** Way up to Castle Hill **E** Statue of András Hadik, general of the Hussars **F** Maria Magdalena Tower **G** Lutheran Church **H** National Archives **I** Vienna Gate **J** Statue of Pope Innocent XI **K** Hilton Hotel **L** Fishermen's Bastion **M** Holy Trinity Column **N** Matthias Church **O** Statue of St Stephen, First King of Hungary

Am. Express in Hilton Hotel.

THE STATUE OF ANDRÁS HADIK **3E** 'The most hussar of Hussars': that was the nickname of this daredevil general of humble origin (1710–1790), the commander of Buda Castle, and favourite of the Empress Maria Theresa. In the pediment there is a glass case with the names of the heroes of the Imperial and Royal 3rd Hussar Regiment. The statue (by György Vastagh Jr.) was unveiled in 1937. Experts say that it is a perfect image of the ideal, effortless, elegant cooperation between horse and rider. If you go very close, you can see that the testicles of the horse are shiny yellow. Generations of students of engineering have come and touched the parts on the morning of difficult exams. It allegedly brings luck.

A rest: Café Miro — Úri utca 30.

ÚRI UTCA **31.** A three-storey building, with an almost completely Gothic façade. In its present form it may date back to the second half of the 15th century, the reign of King Matthias, but the core structure may be even older. The façade, which had been rebuilt several times, collapsed during World War II, revealing some medieval remains. This building is the only evidence that there used to be three-storey houses in Buda. There was enough of the wallpainting left to reconstruct the original decoration. The function of the five protruding windows is unknown. There are niches in the doorway, and the staircase was restored in a Baroque style.

ORSZÁGHÁZ UTCA **18–20–22.** These three houses, built in the 14th and 15th centuries, show how most of the Castle District might originally have looked in the Middle Ages, and why this used to be called Olasz utca (Italian Street). On the gate of the house in the middle the initials stand for the name of Johann Nickl, the butcher who had the house rebuilt in 1771. The present tenant of No. 18 does not want to lean out of the windows, as was customary in the Middle Ages when there was a knock at the door, so he put a rearview mirror on his window and keeps his house locked.

MARIA MAGDALENA TOWER (MÁRIA MAGDOLNA TORONY) **3F**
On the corner of Országház utca and Kapisztrán tér. This 13th-century Franciscan church was in medieval times the church where Hungarian speakers worshipped. Under Turkish rule this was the only church allowed to remain in Christian use, all others being converted into mosques. The chancel was used by Catholics while the nave was Protestant. In the end, it too was converted into a mosque.

Both chancel and nave were destroyed in World War II and have not been rebuilt except for one stone window, as a memento.

'THE FLYING NUN' *On the corner of Országház utca and Petermann bíró utca.* Quite a few street names have become protected by the city. Recognized artists were commissioned to make allegorical figures to illustrate them. This one was by Miklós Melocco in 1977.

According to the memorial plaque next to the figure, the convent of the Order of the Poor Clares, in which Parliament at one time held its sessions, stood nearby (Országház utca 28.). The building is now used by the Academy of Sciences. Some further protected street signs are at Dísz tér 8. and at Fortuna utca 4.

4 **A** Maria Magdalena Tower
B Military History Museum
C National Archives **D** Vienna
Gate **E** Lutheran Church

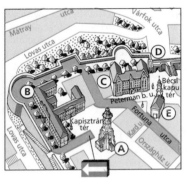

MILITARY HISTORY MUSEUM (HADTÖRTÉNETI MÚZEUM) 4B

I. Tóth Árpád sétány 40. This was built as an army barracks in the 1830s, with remarkable twin windows. On both sides of the gate some cannonballs can be seen in the wall; these have not been removed, out of respect for the Hungarian army, which liberated the Castle in the spring of 1849. On the round bastion, cannons from the Turkish era are exhibited, some of which have richly ornamented handles in the form of a bird's head.

This museum underwent some severe leadership crises in the early nineties. A professional military historian director was briefly replaced by a politician who had lost his job. Recently there was a brand new exhibition for the 1100 years commemoration, and there are regular concerts as well. I have only daughters, and they never drag me here, but it is a nice place for Sunday fathers with more than one son.

TOMB OF A TURKISH GOVERNOR Near the left wing of the museum there is a small tomb with the following inscription in Hungarian and in Turkish: IT WAS NEAR THIS SITE THAT THE LAST GOVERNOR OF THE 143-YEAR-LONG TURKISH RULE IN BUDA FELL IN A BATTLE, AT THE AGE OF 70. HE WAS AN HEROIC ENEMY. LET HIM REST IN PEACE.

Let's walk back into the centre of the Castle District past a modern building that is in ideal harmony with its surroundings (designed by Csaba Virág, 1979). The giant transformers of the National Electric Supply Board sub-station needed the hard rock of the hill — that's why it had to be located here. The next building, the National Archives (designed by Samu Pecz, 1913–20), does not give rise to such a question. The only question here is why it should be so big. Quite a few medieval houses had to be demolished to clear the site.

A rest: Café Pierrot — Fortuna utca 14.

VIENNA GATE (BÉCSI KAPU) 4D Bécsi kapu tér was called the 'Saturday Market' in the Middle Ages. This was the market at which non-Jewish merchants bought and sold. This is the northern gate of the Castle District on which all four streets that run the length of the hill converge. From this square it takes only a few minutes to walk to the busy centre of Buda, Moszkva tér. If a child answers his parent back, they usually scold him by saying 'Your mouth is as big as the Vienna Gate'.

You can walk up to the top of the gate. Enjoy the panorama of Buda and the view of the relatively new Lutheran church in the square, built at the end of the last century. Parliament can be seen from an unusual angle. To the right of the Gate, next to the bastion wall, there is a small grove of trees. This is called the Europe Grove because the mayors of cities all over Europe brought and planted rare trees here in 1972. There are sixteen types of tree here, among them a Turkish hazel, a Japanese cherry and a cherry laurel.

BÉCSI KAPU TÉR 7. The building, which stands on the site of a medieval house, was rebuilt in its present form in 1807 by a priest and teacher who lived here. He also commissioned the portraits of Virgil, Cicero, Socrates, Livy, Quintilian and Seneca. There are beautiful grilles on the windows and on the door of a staircase in the gateway. In the first half of this century this was the house of Baron Lajos Hatvany, an erudite patron of arts, who spent the major part of the profit of his sugar factory on art patronage. In 1935 and 1936 Thomas Mann was his guest here no fewer than three times.

MUSEUM OF COMMERCE AND CATERING TRADE (KERESKEDEL-MI ÉS VENDÉGLÁTÓIPARI MÚZEUM) *I. Fortuna utca 4.* The present building was built on the foundations of three medieval houses at the very beginning of the 1700's. It later became a hotel and later still an office building.

---

director's choice • director's choice • director's choice

DR. BALÁZS DRAVECZKY, DIRECTOR, HISTORIAN OF CIVILIZATION (59)

1. A specimen of the once abundant, but now vanished grape of Buda — in the courtyard of the Museum, the former 'Fortuna' Hostelry, on the right side of the entrance. 2. A faience ewer and basin from the Grand Hotel Hungaria, 1871. It's decorated with vistas of contemporary Budapest. (Gallery One, 'Be our guest in Budapest') 3. A bedroom from Hotel Gellért, 1918. (Gallery Three, exhibition 'Be our guest in Budapest') 4. Ceramic advertisement for mineral water from Margaret Island. (Introduction to the exhibition 'Hungarian Commerce in the first half of this century') 5. The title 'imperial and royal court supplier' was awarded to the most prominent manufacturers and merchants in the Austro-Hungarian Monarchy and it was advertised proudly on signboards, like the one you can see (Gallery One, 'Hungarian commerce in the first half of this century') 6. A provincial grocery store, complete with all fittings and accessories. (Gallery Four, 'Hungarian commerce in the first half of this century')

On the left there are three rooms used by the Museum of Catering Trades. Among the treasures there is a 40-centimetre-long, Easter-rabbit-shaped mould, an icebox with marble inside its lid and the complete shopfittings and equipment of a small confectioner's in Buda. One of the old attendants still remembers the shop in its heyday. 'There were not more than five tables in it. On Sunday at noon we streamed out of the church and dropped in for cake. Two ladies served the customers. They made their cream cakes in front of our very eyes. All these are gone now,' she says. I remarked that small confectioners' are now opening again one after the other but she demurred. 'I'm a merchant's daughter myself and my father always told us that you need a whole lifetime to establish yourself. These new ones want to buy a house and a car within four or five years. It's not the same.'

The new permanent exhibition, opened in 1996, for the Millecentenary celebrations, is called 'Budapest, Waiting for Guests'. It's not just a collage of objects and text, but a successful attempt to recreate a way of life. A room in the luxury Hotel Royal (now closed), a café whose billiard table has a reversible top for converting into a dinner table, and other interiors are recreated. There were more than 400 cafés in Budapest in 1900. There were distinct categories: café spectacle, café bar, café concert, café dance, boulevard café and café restaurant. There is a legendary table there from Café New York, with cartoons of many eminent writers, Ferenc Molnár among them. A very nice place with a very nice exhibition, exuding all the smell and atmosphere of the good old days.

A rest: Litea — in the courtyard of Fortuna utca 4.

RED HEDGEHOG HOUSE (VÖRÖS SÜN-HÁZ) *Hess András tér 3.* This is one of the oldest buildings of the district; its history can be traced back as far as 1390. The red hedgehog above the gate presumably comes from the coat of arms of its noble owner. After the Turks were driven out, the house was converted into an inn, where balls and even theatrical performances were held.

HOTEL HILTON 5B *Hess András tér 4.* This, the most elegant hotel in Budapest, was completed in 1976 and was given a warm welcome by both architects and experts on historic buildings. (It was designed by Béla Pintér.) At the opening ceremony the President of Hilton International called this hotel the most beautiful pearl in the whole string. One side of the hotel is the wall of the old Jesuit cloister, built in a late Rococo style and decorated with plaits. The Gothic remains of a Dominican church are enclosed by the modern hotel in such a way that they can be visited. There are open-air opera performances in the Dominican cloister in the summer.

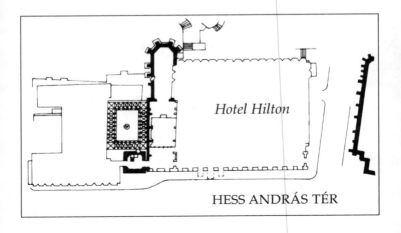

Hotel Hilton

HESS ANDRÁS TÉR

5 **A** Statue of Pope Innocent XI **B** Hilton Hotel **C** Fishermen's Bastion **D** Statue of Stephen, first King of Hungary **E** Matthias Church **F** Holy Trinity Column **G** Memorial to the Soldiers of 1848/49

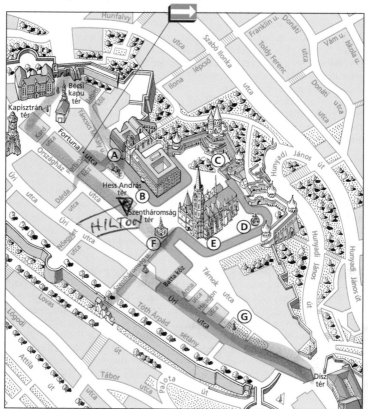

FISHERMEN'S BASTION (HALÁSZBÁSTYA) 5C

A look-out terrace, totally unfit for defence purposes, with five round towers and a main tower with several floors. It was built between 1890 and 1905. In the Middle Ages the fishmarket was nearby and this part of the wall was traditionally defended by the Guild of Fishermen, hence the name. We have just seen its replica at the confectionery exhibition, only slightly more sugary than the original. While the tourists are at the dinner table, Halászbástya is visited by teenage couples intent on a first kiss as soon as the musicians leave.

MATTHIAS CHURCH (MÁTYÁS-TEMPLOM) 5E

I. Szentháromság tér. The real name of the church is the 'Church of the Blessed Virgin in Buda', but it is universally known as the Mátyás (Matthias) Church. Its popular name derives from the fact that the great Hungarian king Matthias held both of his weddings here. Originally it was the church of the German burghers. The main eastern gate and the long apse are 13th century, the latter built after the French pattern and ending in a regular seven-sided polygon. The central part of the church was built around 1400. In Turkish times all the furnishings were removed and all the decorated walls white-washed. Later it was converted into a Baroque church and by the middle of the last century it looked rather miserable. Between 1873 and 1896 it was restored by Frigyes Schulek, who preserved all the original elements found as the walls were pulled down. His dream was a new building that would retain what was inherited from the past. The row of chapels along the north wall was added by him. The 80-metre spire has a rectangular ground and first floor, above which it becomes octagonal. Schulek kept the original tower intact up to the third floor, but from there finished it according to his own plan. It was also at the end of the last century that the walls were repainted on the basis of fragments found during the restoration.

There is a clash of opinion on the artistic value of the church. Some regard it as a masterpiece of European eclecticism, others claim that it is no more than overdecorated stage scenery. Both may be right. The building is evidence of all the knowledge the hardworking 19th century had of the Gothic period, but at the same time it is able to arouse emotions immediately, rather like a momentarily glimpsed set in a film. Anyway, the man in the street likes this church a lot.

HOLY TRINITY COLUMN (SZENTHÁROMSÁG SZOBOR) 5F *In the middle of Szentháromság tér.* The square is at the highest point of Castle Hill. The 14-metre-high monument was erected between 1710 and 1713 by the inhabitants of Buda to fend off another plague epidemic. There was no square here in the Middle Ages, only a street less than 10 metres wide.

THE HOUSE OF HUNGARIAN WINES ("Magyar Borok Háza", 1014 Budapest, Szentháromság tér 6.; Phone: 212-1031, 156-5367; Fax: 212-1032; Opening hours: Monday through Sunday 11 a.m. – 7 p.m.) was opened in September 1997, during the Budapest Wine Festival, an annual event taking place at Vörösmarty tér at the beginning of September and offering a unique possibility to get a first impression of regained diversity of Hungarian viticulture and wine making. Should you miss the festival, make sure you pop in the House of Hungarian Wines, beautifully installed in the cellars of the Neo-Gothic building of the pre-war Ministry of Finance. (Entrance for visitors is from opposite the Hilton Hotel.) Tasteful and informative *décor:* texts in 4 languages including English. For about 6 USD you will be guided around the cellar, see a representative selection (over 400 different items) of Hungarian wines from all 20 Hungarian wine regions, and be offered to taste 80 different wines. (Not necessarily the most precious bottles, of course.) All exhibited wines are also for sale.

If you happen to be a Hungarian-based (big) business, with frequent visitors from abroad, you might be tempted to rent some pretty storage space of your own, from where you can offer your own wine to those of your visitors you especially want to please.

On top of the immediate pleasure, you can have the good feeling that the profit you contribute to is spent on the cultural advancement of the Hungarian minorities over the border, by the owner of the building, called Foundation for Hungarian Culture. So buy there, and buy a lot.

The Old Town Hall of Buda — Collegium Budapest *I.*
Szentháromság utca 2. The first session of the Council was held here in 1710. The statue at the corner of the building represents Pallas Athene, the guardian of towns; it has been there since the end of the 18th century and was made by an Italian sculptor. (This is a copy.) The various alterations to the building were carried out by half a dozen contractors, ranging from local masters to internationally known builders. The prison was in the yard, a place with such a low ceiling that even the shortest man could not stand upright. In 1873, the year of the union of Buda and Pest, the building lost its function.

The building is much admired for the fine proportions of its windows and for its inner, forked staircase, trod these days by foreign scholars. The Collegium Budapest is an Institute for Advanced Studies, founded by and similar to the Wissenschaftskolleg Berlin. The scholars come for six months or a year. They work here in the house, but live elsewhere. Recently they acquired a site nearby, where they want to build an apartment house worthy of the Collegium. Once I was invited to have lunch with the Dean. I expected a sort of High Table, but found myself in a noisy, lively cafeteria – in the heart of an institution that looks really like some of the smaller Oxford colleges.

I. Szentháromság utca 1-3. In some places 'neutral' buildings were built on the site of buildings destroyed in the war, following a fashion adopted in some historical towns in Italy. Fortunately, before there were enough to make a collective impact, the trend was abandoned and today only 'non-polluting-modern' buildings, which harmonize with their environment, are permitted. The planning rules are strict: in the case of this corner house, the bulk, the height and even the roof structure were strictly prescribed (György Jánossy, László Laczkovics, 1981). Traditionally the aesthetic of Hungarian towns favours verticality, with lines running upwards. This explains why the architects omitted the third horizontal line under the roof. Thus the pillars in a way repeat the vertical directions of the church oppo-

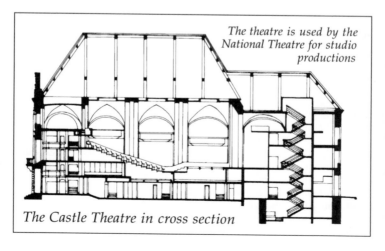

The theatre is used by the National Theatre for studio productions

The Castle Theatre in cross section

site, only on a smaller scale. The broken façade echoes the medieval site. (Other successful modern buildings in the Castle District: Úri utca 4., 10., 32.; Fortuna utca 16.; Tóth Árpád sétány 30.)

Tárnok utca was the site of the weekly market of the German burghers on Wednesdays. Ordinary bread was sold from tables, black loaves from mats. Until the middle of the 15th century bread was unleavened. There was a wide choice of game and fruit. Only live fish were sold; on the second day their tails had to be cut off to show they were not quite fresh. Peaches and grapes could only be sold by special permission of the Council, as they could be used to make alcohol.

THE HOUSE OF A MEDIEVAL WARLORD *I. Úri utca 19.* The house is presumed to have belonged to an infamous Italian aristocrat of the 15th century. It is here that the only street-bridge has survived, although various documents mention quite a few such bridges. It was rebuilt in its present form in the 1830's. In Turkish times it was occupied by monks. In the courtyard a tomb and a sundial can be seen.

ENTRANCE TO THE CATACOMBS — WAXWORKS EXHIBITION *I. Úri utca 9.* There is an underground labyrinth, about 10 kilometres in length, under Castle Hill. The caves were joined up by the Turks for military purposes. Today a section of about 1.5 kilometres can be visited. It has recently been occupied by a fancy waxworks exhibition — a memorial of Hungarian history which is both funny and serious. It is a completely private initiative which required a large bank loan; this is why entrance fees are considerably higher than in any museum subsidised by the state.

Guided tours in four languages start out every 10-20 minutes; visitors are not allowed in on their own because of the high risk of getting lost.

Water always drips in limestone caves and this one is no exception. After heavy rain the dripping resembles a shower in some places. The temperature is 14º Celsius, the humidity is about 90%, so making the figures of wax is out of the question; a plastic mixture is used instead. Meanwhile the clothes on the figures succumb very easily to mould. The show takes the visitor a long way back into the past of Hungary. It starts with the mythological beginnings and finishes in the flourishing Renaissance court of King Matthias. Nothing of more recent but less glorious times is shown. Only a street sign on the wall reminds us of the time during World War II when thousands of people lived through the siege down here; some say that the postman even came down here to deliver their letters for a while. *(The Waxworks Exhibition is closed on Monday.)*

A rest: Korona Patisserie — Dísz tér 16.

THE LAST RUIN: FUTURE HOME OF JOHN NEUMANN MULTIMEDIA CENTRE AND DIGITAL LIBRARY **6B** This was once the three-storey Ministry of Defence; it was reduced to a ruin at the end of World War II, during the siege of Budapest. Until quite recently, carpenters and electricians had workshops here, to serve the needs of the big museums in the Castle. By 2000, some new blocks will be built, to complete the square and make it similar to what it looked like before the war. The last blocks

6 **A** Batthyány Palace **B** Ruins of the former Ministry of Defence, the future home of the János Neumann Digital Library **C** Várszínház — Castle Theatre **D** Sándor Palace, formerly residence of the Prime Minister **E** The upper end of the Cable Car **F** Statue of the legendary Turul bird **G** Contemporary Art Museum/Ludwig Collection (Royal Palace Wing A) **H** National Gallery (Royal Palace Wing B) **I** Matthias Fountain **J** National Gallery (Royal Palace Wing C) **K** Statue of Eugene of Savoy **L** National Gallery (Royal Palace Wing D) **M** Lions **N** National Széchényi Library (Royal Palace Wing F) **O** Budapest History Museum (Royal Palace Wing E) **P** Gothic Great Hall **Q** Palace Gardens **R** 'War Hammer' Tower **S** Southern Round Bastion **T** Tower of the 'Gate of Sighs'

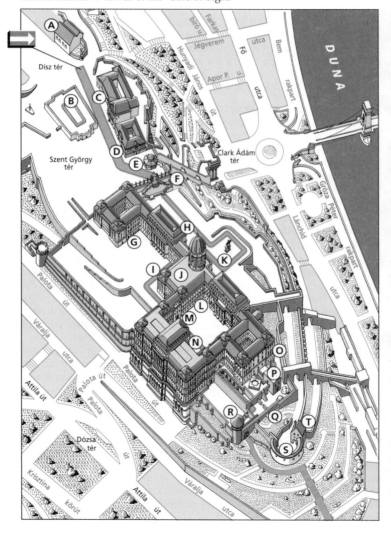

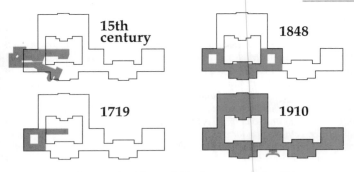

How the Royal Palace was built

ever built in the area, I hope. The Neumann Centre has already been set up in a virtual way. Have a look at www.neumann-haz.hu.

CASTLE THEATRE (VÁRSZÍNHÁZ) 6C I. Színház utca 1-3. The building itself was completed in 1736, as the church of the Order of Our Lady of Mount Carmel, in a late Baroque style. In 1784 Joseph II dissolved this order, just as he did most others. The monastery was converted into a casino, the church gave place to a theatre. The latter was designed by Farkas Kempelen, the inventor of the famous chess automaton. The theatre had a wooden structure and could seat 1,200. Performances were in German, but it was also here that the first play in Hungarian was performed. The theatre was rebuilt several times but the wooden structure remained until, in 1924, a part of the gallery collapsed. The next performance was not until 1978, when the new theatre, of marble and concrete, but seating only 264 (!) people, was opened. Unfortunately, the dress circle and the foyer are not separated so even the slightest sounds from outside can be heard. And there are always some sounds from outside.

Today it is the studio theatre of the National. Success is an infrequent visitor here, I am afraid to say.

Beyond Várszínház, restoration work on the old-time Sándor Palace is already nearing completion. Before the war, this building used to be the office and residence of the Prime Minister. The latest news is that it is going to house the János Neumann Library Multimedia Research Centre.

ROYAL PALACE (KIRÁLYI PALOTA) 6G–6M The history of the palace is very much like that of the Matthias church since this is also a mock-historic building with many original parts. However, it is even younger than the church: a Royal Palace whose royals have never been residents, only visiting guests.

The first, Gothic, Palace, which was built and added to for 300 years, was totally demolished. It was ruined by the Christian army which liberated Buda from the Turkish occupation in 1686. In 1715 work started on a completely new, much smaller Baroque palace. Its ground area was increased by 1779. After some minor reconstruction, the Palace was almost doubled in length at the end of the 19th cen-

tury (it is now 304 metres long) and a huge wing was added at the back. All the halls on the ground floor opened into one another. The neo-Baroque palace, which also had some art-nouveau elements, had a false dome, with an attic underneath. The reconstruction (by Miklós Ybl and Alajos Hauszmann) was finished in 1904 . At the end of World War II, it was the last redoubt of the besieged German troops. The roof fell in completely and most of the furniture was destroyed. At the end of the 1940's, experts on historic buildings decided that the palace should not be restored in its original form, although it would have still been possible to do so, using the remains and some of the plans. They declared that they wanted to return to an earlier, 18th-century form of the palace, but at the same time they wanted to retain the dimensions of the 1904 version. So finally they built a Baroque façade that had never existed before and added a newly designed, though pleasing, real dome to the building. The idea behind all this was that architects of the time saw no value in the eclectic style, even though this is now considered to be the richest aspect of architecture in Budapest.

The inhabitants of the city knew nothing of this dilemma, they were just happy to take possession of the Castle step by step again. Nowadays the building houses three large museums and the National Széchényi Library.

CONTEMPORARY ART MUSEUM – LUDWIG COLLECTION (KORTÁRS MŰVÉSZETI MÚZEUM) *Royal Palace Wing A.* When this *Wing A* of the Royal Palace reopened to the public, some twenty years ago, the sign over the entrance read: 'Museum of the Working Class Movement' — not exactly stylish up here. However, its exhibitions always focused on the history of Hungarian civilization as a whole. And when the totalitarian regime started to crumble, the museologists were busy collecting the leaflets that called for demonstrations. When the small, primitive stencilling machine — earlier confiscated by the police — was solemnly given back to the samizdatniks, the museum wanted to buy it. It was not for sale. Later, the first freely elected Mayor, Gábor Demszky, himself of samizdat fame, donated it to the Museum. Then the Museum's name was 'Twentieth-Century History Museum of the National Museum'. It was gradually swallowed up by the National Museum and had to vacate this building; by December 1996 it had left for good.

The nucleus of the new art museum was a large gift from the Aachen-based billionaire industrialist and art patron Peter Ludwig. The Museum of Contemporary Art exhibits works made since 1989, i.e. really recent art, art in the making. The director, Katalin Néray, and the Minister of Culture, Bálint Magyar, asked top Hungarian businesses to become co-funders of the Museum, and thirteen of them did. You can read their names on a tablet right by the entrance.

A very strong collection — occasionally entertaining and funny, sometimes even beautiful.

If only the awful red marble interior walls, originally designed for the Museum of Working Class Movement, could be changed. If not, at least the totally pointless oversize stairs, big enough for Broadway musicals, could be dismantled. Anyway, there is the long-awaited museum. Let's rejoice.

Katalin Néray is also the commissioner for the Hungarian entry for the Venice Biennale. Have you ever seen Hungary's beautifully restored pavilion, just to the right of Italy's? If not, don't forget to go soon.

Looking down from the western side of the Palace to the foot of the walls, you can see that archaeological excavations are still going on. They were, in a way, made possible by the devastation of the war and by the slow pace of reconstruction afterwards. Although archaeologists have not found the very first 13th-century palace, some very remarkable finds have been made from the time of the Anjou dynasty (14th century). The stripes in the pavement of the courtyard mark the courses of earlier walls.

THE STATUE OF EUGENE OF SAVOY **6K** Opposite the front entrance overlooking the Danube is the bronze equestrian statue of the famous general (József Róna, 1900). It was he who led the armies that liberated Hungary and expelled the Turks. The commission for the statue was originally given by the town of Zenta, the scene of a decisive battle; the town however went bankrupt and could not pay the artist. Hauszmann, the architect who directed the final work on the enlargement of the palace, discovered the statue in Róna's studio, and he persuaded the Prime Minister to raise funds and buy the statue with the help of the Emperor. Francis Joseph agreed to give the money and, what is more, he ordered that the statue be erected in Buda in place of an equestrian statue of himself that had previously been planned. After the restoration of the Palace it was doubtful for a while if the statue of the 'Austrian general' could be set up in Buda at all: it was rumoured that he could not abide Hungarians.

NATIONAL GALLERY (NEMZETI GALÉRIA) **6H–6J–6L** *Royal Palace Wings B–C–D.* The art of a small country is always a private affair and this is especially true of the art of the past. Still, those who spend half an hour strolling around the exhibition of **Hungarian Painting in the Nineteenth Century** will not regard it a waste of time. They should not bother about the names with strange spellings and historic figures unknown to them. The paintings in this exhibition, which takes up one floor of the gallery, breathe a definite awareness of life. There is a Hungarian word, *honfibú*, for this feeling but such a word seems to be missing from other languages. It can best be glossed as 'patriotic sorrow'. There is the grief of generations behind this word, the grief common to all for their ill-fated country. This short Hungarian word is one most frequently used in 19th-century patriotic poetry. Hungarian painting developed its unique character during the Romantic era. It is a deeply sentimental way of painting, and even has some elements of Romantic horror.

The painting of the late 19th century may seem familiar. Impressionism and other developments became popular in a rapidly developing Budapest, which, like Vienna, was a flourishing intellectual centre. Hungarian painting has one mysterious, lonely genius, three of whose major paintings can be seen on the staircase, on the landing between the second and the third floor, where the light is dim enough to conserve them. Tivadar Csontváry Kosztka (1853–1919) first took a pencil in his hand when he was 27. Outside a village chemist's shop, where he was working, an oxcart stopped and he made a sketch of the dozing oxen on the back of a prescription form. It was then that he started to draw and paint. He sent his first drawings to a famous art teacher in Budapest, and later studied in Rome, Paris and Munich. During these years he also opened his own chemist's shop to cover his expenses. He was already a

---

director's choice • director's choice • director's choice

LORÁND BERECZKY, DIRECTOR GENERAL: **1**. *Head of a King* from Kalocsa, circa 1200 (Ground Floor, in the Lapidarium, Wing D, left of the Main Entrance.) **2**. The Master MS: *The Visitation*, 1506. (Wing D, 1st Floor, opposite the stairs.) **3**. Pál Szinyei Merse: *Picnic in May*, 1873. (Wing B, 1st Floor, 19th-C. paintings.) **4**. József Koszta: *The Three Magi*. (Wing C, 2nd Floor, left of the staircase.) **5**. Csontváry Kosztka, 1902. (Wing C, 2nd Floor, left of the staircase.) **6**. Gyula Derkovits: *Along the Railway*, 1932. (Wing D, 3rd Floor, on the riverfront, in the middle.)

---

well-known artist at the beginning of our century, although he was frequently attacked for his style. He had four exhibitions in his lifetime. After his death, his family had already agreed with some carriers to sell his large canvases as tarpaulin, when suddenly a 24-year-old architect turned up and invested all his inheritance in the paintings.

In 1949 the Hungarian Embassy in Paris exhibited some of his work. When Picasso saw the paintings he asked to be left alone in the room with the doors locked for an hour. At a later exhibition he told Chagall, 'There you are, you old master, I bet even you could not paint something like this.' Most of Csontváry's paintings can be seen in a museum in the city of Pécs, about 200 kilometres south of Budapest.

MATTHIAS WELL (MÁTYÁS-KÚT) **6l** A bronze statue of King Matthias (Alajos Stróbl, 1904) as a huntsman, in the company of his shield-bearer, his chief huntsman and his Italian chronicler. On the right at the bottom, the beautiful Szép Ilonka ('Helen the Fair') can be seen, a girl of low birth who fell in love with the king while he was hunting, not knowing who he was. The nicest ears of any hunting dogs ever.

LIONS guard the entrance of Oroszlános udvar (The Lion Courtyard — designed by János Fadrusz, 1904). Two of them are trying to discourage visitors with their grim looks; the other two, inside the gate, roar angrily at those brave enough to enter. The huge door in the gateway between the lions leads to an elevator which will take you down to the bottom of the wing overlooking Buda, to the stop for Bus 16.

The entrances to the National Library, the Budapest History Museum and the National Gallery can be found in the courtyard. Visitors can get to some of the exhibitions from here as well.

NATIONAL SZÉCHÉNYI LIBRARY (NEMZETI KÖNYVTÁR) *Royal Palace, Wing F.* The inside of the building was restored only in the 1970's. The building itself has two floors above the level of the courtyard, but the ground floor is really the fifth floor of the library. This is the so-called Ybl-wing (added in 1890–1902), which extends over the edge of Castle Hill.

The library has about two million books and even more manuscripts, musical scores and newspapers. Among these are the few codices which have not been dispersed from King Matthias's celebrated library. (These codices are called Corvinas, after the bird on the king's coat of arms: *corvus* means 'raven' in Latin.) There are 70,000 books shelved in the reading rooms. The Main Reading Room, which consists of several smaller rooms is not very elegant, but is very spacious; working conditions are ideal thanks to the view from the windows. The lighting is all natural, and from above. The books are taken to and fro by small carriages which run between the glass roof and the mock-ceiling. They are rather noisy if they happen to be working.

BUDAPEST HISTORY MUSEUM (BUDAPESTI TÖRTÉNETI MÚZEUM) 60

Royal Palace, Wing E. A most carefully arranged, intimate exhibition, illustrating the 2,000 years of Budapest's history, with clear maps and a reconstruction of the medieval Gothic palace that took 40 years of hard work to make.

Recently the 'History of Budapest' Exhibition was extended to the present day, using the most modern display techniques, and drawing on help from stage designers and other visual artists. It puts the city's history powerfully into context, rather than just showing the objects; contrast the grand display of the National Museum.

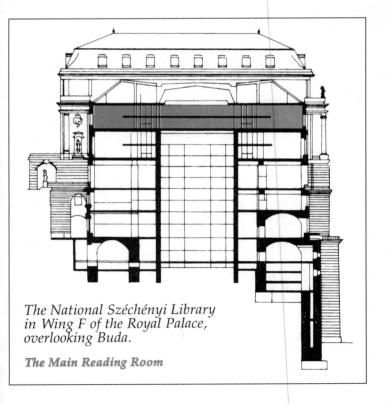

The National Széchényi Library in Wing F of the Royal Palace, overlooking Buda.

The Main Reading Room

director's choice • director's choice • director's choice

DR SÁNDOR BODÓ, DIRECTOR GENERAL 1. 'Boot-shaped Bizarre', sacrificial vessels ('áldozati edények') from the end of the Bronze Age. (2nd floor, in the staircase, Case V.) 2. The portrait of a man wearing a capuccio is one of the outstanding pieces from the collection of stone statues that once adorned the 15th-century palace. (Ground floor, Gothic Statue Find). 3. A painting depicting *Buda and Pest, with vineyards on Gellért Hill* (by János Szentgyörgyi, 1830, Modern History of Budapest, 1st floor, Room 3). 4. *The capture of King Porus,* a silver relief by József Szentpéteri, which was shown at the 1851 Great Exhibition in London (1st Floor, in the corridor). 5. An advertisement for the 'Telephone Courier', that predecessor of the radio, invented by Hungarian Tivadar Puskás. The ad encourages people to listen to 'broadcasts' from the Opera House. (1st Floor, Room V). 6. A view of the Bridges and the general panorama of the city. (From the windows of the first and second floor exhibition areas.)

After World War II excavations began around and under the ruined Baroque palace on an area covering 30 acres. In the basement front hall of the History Museum there is a good plaster model of Castle Hill, shown as if the Palace had been removed from the top. The several numbered trenches along which the archaeologists worked are shown, together with copies of what was found in them. Above this model there is a large drawing in white on black of the Gothic Palace as researchers believe it to have looked. The largest of its halls was 70×17 metres, big enough even for the tournaments that were held here.

Compared to this, the ten or so surviving rooms seem humble, but they are fascinating nonetheless. The palace from which they were resurrected was once famous all over Europe and praised in the writings of travellers and ambassadors. (In the second half of the 15th century, King Matthias had a larger income than either the English or the French kings.) Almost all of the restored rooms were outside the main building: a cellar, an ice-cellar, a cistern, corridors. Only two major sights can be found here: the Gothic Hall, which presumably used to be part of the Queen's apartments, and the Crypt. It is in these parts that the 'Gothic statues' are exhibited, which, after a very unquiet life, were found in 1974.

Sometime at the beginning of the 15th century, because of some hurriedly started construction work, about fifty stone statues were found to be surplus to requirements and thrown out into a yard that was later filled in. The statues probably portrayed the courtiers of the previous king, all dressed in clothes after the French fashion. (Playboys of the trecento, the archaeologist who led the excavations called them.) So it is only these 'dumped' statues that have come down to us; most of those which were held in high esteem did not survive Turkish rule. The secular statues are in the Gothic Hall (Room 11), the ones with religious subjects are exhibited in the Crypt (Room 16).

From spring until autumn visitors may go out to a small garden which is arranged in a medieval pattern and from there they may also get to the Castle walls.

The southern courtyard of the Castle may be reached by going through the front hall of the History Museum. From there we leave the courtyard through Ferdinand Gate.

DEER HOUSE (SZARVAS-HÁZ) 7G *I. Szarvas tér 1.* This triangular café was built at the beginning of the 18th century in a late Rococo style. The original café sign can be seen above the gate to this day. It houses the Aranyszarvas Restaurant, famous for its game dishes. Until the 1930's the northern slope of Gellért Hill was packed with small old houses with wine-cellars which became pubs. This was Tabán, a popular place of entertainment, the 'Grinzing of Budapest'. All of these houses were demolished for

7 **A** 'War Hammer' Tower **B** Southern Round Bastion **C** Tower of the 'Gate of Sighs' **D** Entrance to Royal Gardens **E** Casino and Restaurant **F** Medical History Museum **G** Deer House **H** The house of Benedek Virág, an 18th century poet **I** Tabán Parish Church **J** Rácz Baths **K** Statue of Queen Elizabeth, wife of Francis Joseph **L** Statue of St Gellért **M** Rudas Baths **N** Elizabeth Bridge

reasons of public health; Szarvas-ház and the yellow building opposite still preserve the atmosphere of the old district.

THE STATUE OF QUEEN ELIZABETH, WHO ALLEGEDLY LOVED THE HUNGARIANS 7K

The whole nation mourned the death of Elizabeth, wife of Francis Joseph, when she was assassinated in 1898. She was said to be a great friend of Hungarians and even spoke our language. This statue originally stood on the other side of the Danube. The people waited for forty years until it was set up again in 1986. Before the war there was another statue on this spot, that of the ultra-right wing leader whose policies led Hungary directly into alliance with Nazi Germany. This statue was blown up by Communist resistance fighters at the time of the German invasion. A tablet in the ground near the statue of Queen Elizabeth commemorates this.

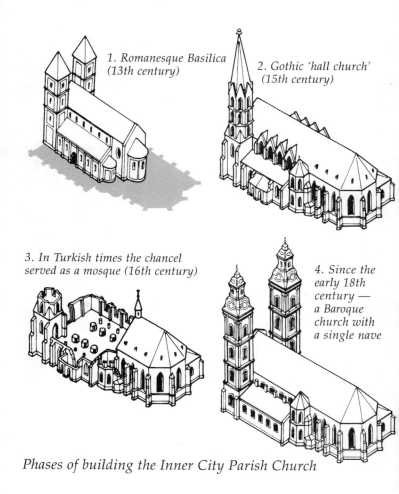

1. *Romanesque Basilica (13th century)*

2. *Gothic 'hall church' (15th century)*

3. *In Turkish times the chancel served as a mosque (16th century)*

4. *Since the early 18th century — a Baroque church with a single nave*

Phases of building the Inner City Parish Church

8 **A** Elizabeth Bridge **B** Inner City Parish Church **C** Faculty of Arts, **D** Entrance to Haris köz **E** Hotel Taverna **F** Fontana Department Store **G** Statue of Fisher Rézi, symbol of the fishermen's guild **H** Statue of Mihály Vörösmarty, romantic poet **I** Vigadó concert hall **J** Hotel Marriott **K** A detour to southern Váci utca

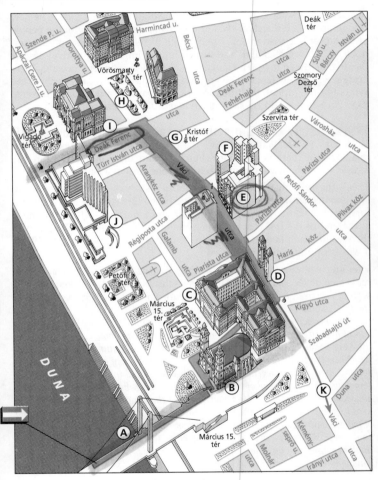

ELIZABETH BRIDGE (ERZSÉBET HÍD) 7N-8A *Linking Március 15 tér (Pest) and Döbrentei tér (Buda).* The predecessor of the present bridge was named in honour of Queen Elizabeth. Fifty-three (!) designs were entered for the competition, which was won by three German engineers. The plan, however, was rejected by the contractors as it was a suspension bridge and Hungarian factories could not produce cable of the required quality. Instead, a chain bridge was built between 1897 and 1903 using huge scaffolding all across the riverbed; but it did borrow the elegant arch from the prize-winning design, which echoed the late eclecticism of the centre of Pest. It was destroyed by the Germans in January 1945. The damage was more serious than for the other bridges and reconstruction would have cost too much. Its successor was a suspension bridge designed by a Hungarian engineer, Pál Sávoly (1964). The two towers are joined by suspension cables, each consisting of a bundle of 61 separate cables. The new bridge imitates the arch of the old one, which is perhaps why the people of Budapest like it so much. The opening of the bridge was on the afternoon of 21 November 1964 and turned into an impromptu festival despite the drizzle. (Even my piano lesson was cancelled — I went to see the new bridge, with my teacher.) The new Erzsébet híd has virtually become the symbol of the capital, the first modern yet beautiful attraction of the city. (See 'For Serious Addicts' for some remarkable modern buildings.)

INNER CITY PARISH CHURCH (BELVÁROSI PLÉBÁNIATEMPLOM) **8B**

V. Március 15. tér. Walking across the bridge from Buda, you would not imagine that there is a centaur-church behind the nondescript Baroque façade. From the waist down the church continues in a Gothic chancel.

This is the building with the most eventful history on the Pest side. There are remains here from as early as the end of the 12th century, and each century has left its mark on the building (it was a mosque in Turkish times); at the end of the last century, when the original Erzsébet híd was built, there were even plans to demolish it, as it was in the way. Until the 1930's it was surrounded by small shops.

Váci utca stretches from Vörösmarty tér to Vámház körút, that is, as far as Szabadság híd, to the south. In the Middle Ages this was the length of Pest. The two parts of the street, to the north and to the south of Erzsébet híd, are very different from one another. The northern part is an overcrowded, commercial, naff, touristy pedestrian zone; the southern part has also just been pedestrianised. According to a local history monograph, the two parts of the street resemble each other just as little as a famous over-adorned prima donna and her sober, humble, housewife sister. When the inhabitants of the city say 'Váci utca', they only mean the 'over-adorned' part with its legendary riches. It had developed into a highly fashionable shopping street by the end of the 18th century and was becoming richer and more handsome right up until World War I. Ten of the buildings still standing today used to witness mornings when the tenants were woken up by the loud gossiping of maidservants waiting for the horse-drawn rubbish-cart, and reliable 'civil servants' in uniform caps, that is, porters, stood on the streetcorner all day long waiting for custom. The shops were forever changing hands, as the landlords were continuously putting up the rent.

Today the same is done by the Municipal Council: the idea behind the ever increasing rents is that only quality shops should be found here. At the beginning of the seventies, the steam-roller of modernization hit the street: all the shops were given uniform 'modern' shop windows, regardless of the style the building itself was built in.

Recent features of the street include the ethnic Hungarian pedlars from Transylvania, dubious money-changers and even a wandering Chinese who will write your name in characters — the latter has been a great hit with school kids.

The southern part of Váci utca has still not adjusted to the new situation. There is a sort of Sleeping Beauty quality lingering here. You may meet the occasional deputy mayor, rushing to the Budapest City Council meeting (usually on the last Thursday of the month), Mr Vincze, the visionary designer/businessman/gallery owner, looking like a bespectacled Russian painter of the late twenties or a very corpulent, bearded Serbian literary historian, returning late from the Serbian Church sermon behind New City Hall (corner of Szerb utca and Veres Pálné utca).

MILLENNIUM COURT **8F** *(V. Pesti Barnabás utca 4.)* Ringing in the old and the new: this keeps us very busy in Budapest nowadays. The hotel follows a new luxury hotel trend, i.e. offering a home to people who do not wish to live in a hotel, but are not willing to buy or rent a flat of their own. The design (József Finta and Associates, 1997) preserves the original façade (over a hundred years old) of the former 'Iron Court', a mixed office and shopping complex. The management plans to have exclusive services for residents: they might one day be able to pick out and buy contemporary Hungarian art works they want to live with from the Millennium Court Collection. Adjacent is one of the very few remaining 18th-century secular buildings in Pest.

Opposite is the Faculty of Arts of Eötvös University. You can see some of the prettiest bluestockings in Central Europe from your bedroom.

THE FORMER SECOND-HAND BOOKSHOP (A VOLT ANTIKVÁRIUM)

V. Váci utca 28. The plans for this building were drawn up by the architect of the Parliament in 1877. There has been a bookshop in here for about a hundred years. György Lukács, the philosopher who lived nearby, went into the shop every day in the last years of his life to see if they had anything to interest him. He used to have a chat with the manageress who wore spectacles and had curly hair that was just beginning to turn grey. She has recently been forced to retire. My friends and I demonstrated against this — in vain. Then the shop was sold on condition it would go on operating as a bookshop. You can see the result.

HARIS KÖZ **8D** At the beginning of the century the owner of a piece of land in the neighbourhood of Váci utca had the idea of building a street on the site of his old bazaar. So as not to forfeit his ownership, he had to close his street every year for one single day. The last such occasion was in 1949. In that very year the piece of land was nationalised, together with the street.

THE FORMER QUEUE AT THE ADIDAS SHOP *V. Váci utca 24.* In previous times, if there was a queue in Budapest it was either bananas sold in wintertime or a famous novelist autographing his/her new book. Adidas is an Austrian sportsware brand, coined from the name of the owner, Herr Adi Dassler. The permanent interest used to be due to somewhat lower prices — the wholesale firm acts as a retailer here. But why not open another shop, and another and another — until there is no queue?

(I kept that sentence from the very first edition of 1989 — since then of course they opened another shop, interestingly enough, in Váci út, but the queue remained here for almost a year. Then it gradually disappeared. And now you

can buy everything on earth in Budapest — it has become a consumer's paradise, with new shopping malls opening every other month. The Forint even became convertible… An unbelievable thing. Since queues were obviously the consequence of unconvertible money, unconvertible money was the consequence of the Wall. Do you follow me?)

HOTEL TAVERNA AND TRADE CENTER 8E *V. Váci utca 20. and 19.* It took a long time for post-modernism in architecture to arrive in Hungary, although it fits into the eclectic townscape very well. On the small area where the hotel is situated the architect (József Finta, 1985) managed to find space for 224 rooms and catering for 600 guests. There is a café, a beer cellar, a confectioner's, a champagne bar, a sweetshop, a bowling club and a sauna. The façade gives the impression of permeability. According to an architectural magazine 'it is exterior and interior at the same time'. Opposite the hotel the International Trade Center (József Finta, Gyula Csizmár, 1985) was built on two neighbouring lots. The border was where the façade pillar can be seen. The passage is open to the public, and from it you can look into the pleasant, intimate hall of the building. The figure on the pillar of the façade (by Tibor Borbás) waves the flag of trade in his hands.

A rest: Café Zsolnay — Váci utca 20.

PHILANTHIA FLOWER SHOP *V. Váci utca 9.* The art nouveau decoration of the shop, although it does not suit the classical façade of the building at all, has miraculously survived various hard times. The shop name is the Greek for 'the love for flowers'.

Maybe one day the chandeliers will go. How could they do it to this interior?

THE SITE OF VÁC GATE *Next to the corner of Váci utca and Türr István utca.* The white line on the paverment marks the site where the medieval city wall once stood with its northern gate, Váci kapu. According to contemporary sources, there used to be a 'deadly bustle' around the gates. In 1789 it was quietly pulled down. (An event independent of the ones in France, of the same year.)

This has been a long walk. If you do not want to go back to Gerbeaud again, you can sit in Anna presso (Váci utca 7.) or Muskátli (Váci utca 11/a.). The latter used to be the haunt of young artists who wanted to save the world at the very beginning of the sixties, before the Hungarian beat-movement. They either do not come here any more or have become so conventional that you would not recognize them.

BUDAPEST BESTS : : BUDAPEST BESTS : : BUDAPEST BESTS
Mihály Ráday, television anchorman, councilman, crusader

'At Least Adopt a Horse!' — that was our publicity slogan in 1995. We tried to raise funds to give a facelift to the **Városligeti körhinta** with a nicely printed 4-page colour brochure. We managed to find some old pictures, so re-designing was well under way — that of the dome, which was pulled down after World War II, that of the almost entirely stripped façade, and we also planned to reproduce the carved gates which had been replaced by hideous ones made out of aluminium: an act worthy of a prison sentence for the perpetrator.

It was the then British ambassador who gave the campaign its first momentum. He told me one day: 'My mission in Hungary will be over in six months. Before I leave I would gladly contribute five or six hundred pounds to the restoration of something of value in Budapest. If you have an idea, don't hesitate to tell me.' Not much later I called him and asked if we could meet in the Amusement Park. And we could. His Excellency, Her Majesty's Ambassador to Hungary, got on the 'körhinta'. We had a great ride. I also told him that the old name of our Amusement Park was the 'English Park' until the Communist coup d'état in the late 1940's. Then I declared my claim. With the help of his one million forints we could start planning and the real work.

It was he who taught me the charming British word 'merry-go-round'. That's what he called it, not 'carousel' like the Americans. Hungarian anglophiles prefer the latter, since that was the title given to the American musical version of the celebrated play by Ferenc Molnár, originally entitled _Liliom_, a sentimental comedy about the love of a merry-go-round operator and a servant girl. Thanks to Sir John Birch and all the other generous donors, today the old **körhinta** is ready from the outside and just as beautiful as in 1906.

Have you already inspected the comely frescos of the **körhinta**? Have you noticed the hand-carved and hand-painted torch-bearing angels, the chariots, the ships, the fine 'magic steeds'? Have you noticed that every single horse has its own, distinctive face and features and their genuine leather saddles were made by craftsmen at the turn of the century? You haven't? It's high time you went to look.

Otherwise, if I'm asked what to see in Budapest, I tend to suggest two things. Two things not available to the west of us: Turkish baths and Hungarian art nouveau. So: visit the Király Bath, Rác Fürdő or Rudas, then off you should go to Pest, where you can admire Ödön Lechner's yellow ceramic bees on the walls of the former Post Office Savings Bank (today the National Bank), heading for their hives. ('Walk Two' in this book, I presume.)

By the way. You haven't been thinking of adopting a horse, have you? One, at least. _(Drop me a letter, addressed to City Hall Budapest, if so!)_

WALK TWO

The City and the Vízíváros Area walk takes us all around the city of Pest, passing behind the Parliament building. As the whole of the building can only be seen from a distance, we shall cross over to Buda, visit a Turkish bath and walk under the chestnut trees lining the river. We shall also look in through some gateways. Time: about 6 hours, refreshments included.

*József Nádor tér used to be one of the most attractive squares of the City before the advent of the motor car. It takes its name from Archduke Joseph, the seventh son of Emperor Leopold, who was the governor or palatine (**nádor** in Hungarian) of Hungary from 1796 for over fifty years. His statue is in the middle of the square. The original plan was that he should face in the opposite direction but, because of the great construction work he originated, it was decided that he should look towards the City. After so much reconstruction some now think he should look the other way.*

POSTABANK HEADQUARTERS *V. József nádor tér 1*. The Romantic-style building, originally a residential block (Hugó Máltás, 1859), was completely refurbished recently by the Postabank Corporation, an Austrian-Hungarian joint venture. The eccentric founder/CEO/chairman of the board/newspaper tycoon/art patron Gábor Princz has his spacious office on the top floor, which was built as an addition in 1922. The carefully furnished room includes some valuable rare books, Hungarian and foreign, and some excellent, three-dimensional artwork by the painter László Fehér. To make up for the lack of a panorama of the Castle, there is a large photograph of the view the inhabitant of the room would see — if the rest of the building were pulled down... There is a similar trick in the inner courtyard: a gigantic mural painting on the wall, the panorama of Váci utca as it would look if the adjacent building (Café Gerbeaud) were not there.

Obviously, you can neither visit the CEO's room, nor the inner courtyard, but as there is no underground garage under the building, you might glimpse Mr Princz himself, a somewhat stocky, black, curly-haired man in his early forties, entering or leaving his fortress. He wears a tie only if he absolutely has to. Otherwise in black, high-necked pullover. If he has to wear a tie, he often chooses blazing red ones. Or is it his celebrity prima-donna wife who chooses the colours? They can often be spotted together at first nights, concerts and openings.

GROSS HOUSE *V. József nádor tér 7.* A typical neo-Classical block of flats (János Hild, 1824). At the beginning of the last century it housed the famous Blumenstöckl pub where guests could choose from three set meals. The most expensive was two forints, and for that price you could eat as much as you wanted. (That was a different forint, of course. The present one was introduced in 1946.) Anyone who told a bad joke or argued loudly had to pay a fine into the Saracen-head money-box. At the moment the building is occupied by Postabank, and they have exhibited some photographs of lovely old relics along the arcade at the side of the building, documents that cant't reflect the bank's own history, since it was only established in the late 1980's.

CENTRAL EUROPEAN UNIVERSITY (KÖZÉP-EURÓPAI EGYETEM) 9H

V. Nádor utca 9. This neo-Classical masterpiece was completed by Mihály Pollack in 1826 for Count Antal Festetics. The street was called Tiger Street at that time. Pollack (1773–1855) designed no fewer than 186 buildings, among them the National Museum. You can walk in through the circular hall unhindered, at least as far as the receptionist. That is enough to see the secret of the inside: a recent extension that is much bigger than the original, and yet invisible from the outside.

Budapest-born George Soros spent his adolescent years in hiding in his home town, helping his father save Jewish lives. Later he emigrated, and was going to become a scholar and a philosopher; he was a follower of Karl Popper. He was well over forty when he found his real vocation as an alchemist: a prime mover in long term monetary markets. A passion for 'opening up' Central European societies — i.e. democratizing them — began to obsess him in the early eighties. It was in the mid 1980's that he set up his Foundation in Budapest, which was at first a joint venture with the Academy of Sciences and Letters. This University is said to be the biggest single long-term charitable commitment of his anywhere in the world. He hopes it will play a pivotal role in educating the future élites of East and Central Europe. Soros himself, now in his sixties (though he looks considerably younger) often comes to Senate meetings, which are held on the first floor, just above the circular entrance hall, with the statues that represent the four seasons. He still speaks impeccable Hungarian.

By the way the students do not live in the building, but five kilometres out of town, in Pest. CEU is slowly taking over the whole block. Deep inside it, a library is just being carved out of a big garage. And the excellent bookshop is obviously open just for you, even on Saturday afternoons between 2 and 5, highly unusual hours for an academic bookshop.

'PIRANESI HOUSE' – THE FAVOURITE BUILDING OF THE ILLUSTRATOR OF THIS BOOK

V. Zrínyi utca 14. The block was converted to its present form in 1879. Heavy, bombastic, but still somehow majestic. Cuts out the light, takes up a lot of space, rather attempts to impress the onlooker with a fireworks of forms and shapes, enough to fill two sketchbooks of any student of architecture. It inspired several of the artworks of András Felvidéki, the illustrator of this book. It reminds him of Piranesi. (The Museum of Fine Arts has hundreds of original Piranesi prints.)

OKTÓBER 6. UTCA 3. 9I The house with the passageway was built in 1844–45 and has recently been restored. If you include the two small spiral ones hidden at the sides, it has four staircases. The statue in the garden honours Béla Czóbel, a great post-impressionist painter.

BUDAPEST CATHEDRAL: THE 'BASILICA' 9J *V. Szent István tér.* The largest church in the city, it can hold 8,500 people. The dome is 96 metres high. The name may be misleading since, strictly speaking, basilica means a church of a totally different shape. (It has the rank of 'basilica minor', hence the name.) It took so long to build it that it is remembered in the saying 'I'll settle up when the Basilica is finished.'

Until quite recently there was no bishop seated here, but now that the Archbishop of Esztergom has been given a double assignment and a new title, Archbishop of Esztergom and Budapest, the church can properly be called 'Budapest Cathedral'.

The work on the building started in 1851, when Pest was still a small town. The designer, József Hild, died soon afterwards, and was succeeded by Miklós Ybl, the architect who later designed the Opera House. On examining the works he had inherited, Ybl was astonished to find cracks in the walls. He had a fence built around the half-ready church and set watchmen to guard it. Eight days later, in January 1868, the dome fell in. You can imagine how empty the streets were then, since the disaster, which happened in broad daylight, had only one eye-witness: a baker's apprentice. In the newspapers, he gave an eloquent account of what he had seen: 'I can see small clumps of stone starting to roll down from the top of the dome. As they are falling slowly downwards, tumbling in the air, a kind of groan-like sigh permeates the air, and the whole dome begins to tilt. First in absolute silence, then with a horrible roar.' More than 300 windows were broken in the area. Inferior building materials were blamed.

Ybl drew up new plans and work started again almost from scratch. But he did not live to see the church finished, since he died in 1891.

The Basilica was finished by József Kauser in 1906. Emperor Francis Joseph gave a speech at the opening ceremony and, it was rumoured, cast suspicious glances at the dome, which is 22 metres in diameter.

The general opinion is that the Basilica is too gloomy. Only mysterious patches and beams of light bring some life to the statues and ornaments at some lucky times of the day. Behind the main altar stands a statue of St Stephen, King of Hungary, (Alajos Stróbl), who is the patron saint of the church. There is another statue of him above the main entrance. The mosaics were designed by Hungarian painters and made in Venice. The neo-Renaissance ground plan is in the form of a Greek cross.

The main façade is not on the busy Bajcsy-Zsilinszky út but on the opposite side. The Basilica is a rare example in city planning in the sense that during the time it was built the structure of the city around it changed. When the second plan was made there was already a need for a 'second façade' and Ybl cleverly solved this problem by enriching the walls outside the chancel with an elegant Ionic colonnade and with statues of the twelve apostles.

9 **A** Luxus Department Store **B** Vigadó Concert Hall **C** Gerbeaud **D** József nádor tér 7. **E** Statue of József nádor, Habsburg Regent **F** József Attila utca 16. **G** Derra House **H** CEU Building **I** Október 6. utca 3. **J** St Stephen's Church, the 'Basilica' **K** Bajcsy-Zsilinszky út 17. **L** Bajcsy-Zsilinszky út 19/a. **M** Bajcsy-Zsilinszky út 19/c. **N** Bajcsy-Zsilinszky út 34. **O** Hungarian National Bank **P** Bank Center

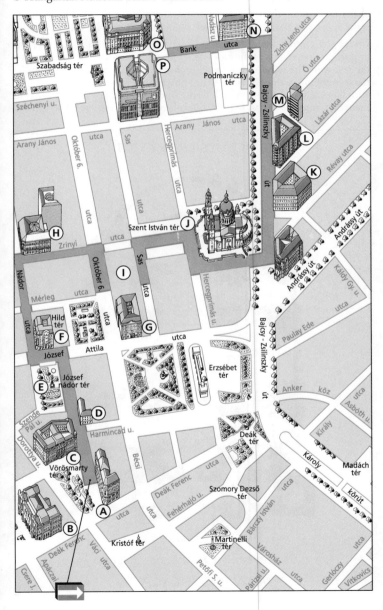

The Holy Dexter (Szent Jobb), allegedly the right hand of St Stephen (1000–1038), is the most revered relic of the Hungarian Catholic Church. Though there is a gap in the story of the relic, between the death of the king and the first time the relic appeared, it is relatively short. Historians don't say it's altogether impossible. It can be visited in a chapel to the left of the main altar. You drop a coin in the slot and the relic lights up. If not right away, the guard gives the case a knock, and behold, it does.

Under the church there is a large cellar; it was here that many of the important documents of the city and some valuable art treasures survived the last war. The windows of the church overlook Bajcsy-Zsilinszky út. In the second half of the 1960's some unknown student elements painted here with large letters: LENIN, MAO, CHE. Since they did not have spray cans then, they must have had to carry buckets of paint to the spot. You can still

BAJCSY-ZSILINSZKY ÚT

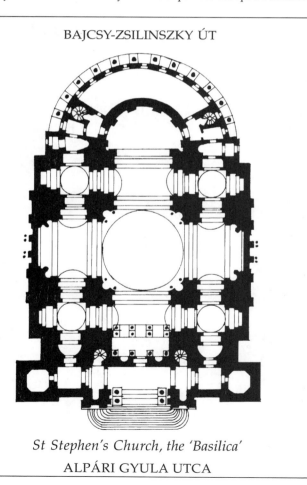

St Stephen's Church, the 'Basilica'

ALPÁRI GYULA UTCA

see the fading graffiti on the wall. (After he read these lines, a friend of mine, a well-known scholar and critic, called me and claimed responsibility.)

The chancel is worth looking at from the other side of the road as well, for example from the pastry shop. These few metres do make a difference. Or you can look at the Basilica again from an unusual angle, while sitting comfortably at the terrace of the small café (corner of Lázár utca).

To know why it is an absolute must to go up to the dome and look out from the terrace, turn to page 30, 'Finding Your Way/Viewpoints'.

A rest: Café Kör — Sas utca 17.

A Nice Block of Flats 9K–L–M *Bajcsy-Zsilinszky út 19/a, 19/b, 19/c.*

In the 1930's modern architecture made a breakthrough in Hungary (for the second time) and construction started everywhere in the city. The optimum use of space was combined with plans for healthy, cleverly arranged flats. This block is an example of how well this style could be fitted into surroundings 50-100 years older (Jenő Schmitterer, 1940). All three gateways have their own surprises. The 19/a building has lead glass windows on the ground floor and interesting lamps on the capitals of the columns. The gateway of the 19/b block has pleasant proportions, and, what is more, on the ceiling behind the entrance the present tenants have managed to solve the problem of squaring the circle. The third block is the one currently in the best state. This one has the best preserved lighting, and even the mosaic glass has survived, redolent of the atmosphere of old times. All the tranquility and elegance of this style is summarized in the stone giant, resting on the edge of the roof of the 19/b block. It can only be seen from a distance so do not forget to look back.

Podmaniczky tér was once occupied by houses but was cleared during the war. The square, housing a station on the Third (Blue) Metro Line, is becoming a new gateway to the city. At the request of the Budapest City Preservation Society, it was named after Baron Frigyes Podmaniczky, a leading figure in city planning during the last century.

The Most Complex Public Monument Ever — With a Bench and a Clock

That of Baron Frigyes Podmaniczky in the middle of V. Podmaniczky tér. The doughty 19th-century campaigner for new urban projects holds a statue of Pallas Athene that has become the symbol of the conservationists. Traditionally she has a lance in her hand. Ask a Hungarian friend why, he/she thinks Athene hasn't got it with her in this statue. (In case he/she doesn't know: this is the subtitle of a television programme by maverick politician/cameraman/journalist/mediastar Mihály Ráday, Pesident of the Budapest City Preservation Society: 'Our Grandchildren Will Not See It, OR THE LANCE IS SOMETIMES STOLEN FROM THE HAND OF PALLAS ATHENE, CITY DEFENDER'. I told you it was complex… (Mihály Ráday's 'Budapest Bests', see on page 77.)

Hungarian National Bank 10C *V. Szabadság tér 8-9.*

The stately bulk of the National Bank shows how eclecticism was already lightening up under the influence of art nouveau (Ignác Alpár, 1901). Between the first-floor windows a fine relief shows people working, from peasants through mint workers to a tycoon doing nothing more than sign a cheque. On the southwest corner, towards the square, you can see Hamlet pondering whether to be or not to be, with the skull of poor Yorick. The inside of the building can no longer be visited.

BANK CENTRE 10B *V. Bank utca/Sas utca/Arany János utca/Hercegprímás utca.* When the architect József Finta showed me around the Bank Centre, he said that it was the first building for which he'd been allowed by the developer to choose the quality of materials he wanted. Finta argues that the city should grow upwards by two or three floors in this area. The glass-walled higher levels are deceptive; this is a bigger building than it looks. Half of it is occupied by the headquarters of the National Savings Bank. You can walk through the building, with a detour via some fine shops selling Bang and Olufsen designer hi-fi and sweets. In the lobby you can have a look at the nicest wheelchair lift in Central Europe. This will take the handicapped down to the cafeteria/restaurant in the basement – which won't be built until an investor materialises.

A STATUE TO THINK ABOUT In front of Bank Centre, towards the National Bank there is an abstract statue in three parts by Ádám Farkas, Professor at the Academy of Fine Arts. If you come from the direction of Hold utca, the statue obviously forms a lion. But only from this direction.

I asked the sculptor if it was intentional. He said, with a characteristic, cunning smile: 'Yes and no.' He is the President of the Japanese-Hungarian Artists' Club. Maybe he was elected because of his calm, cunning smile. Or maybe he acquired it during his visits to Japan.

Szabadság tér (Liberty Square) is one of Budapest's hidden treasures — it is not along any major streets or boulevards, you just come across it, as if by chance. Until as recently as 1898 there were huge barracks here called the 'Neu-gebäude' or New Buildings; they covered the entire area bounded by Hold utca – Báthori utca – Nádor utca – Bank utca. The barracks were pulled down, and the square and neighbouring streets were built as a homogenous unit in its place.

Out of the eclectic palaces one art nouveau block sticks out: the American Embassy. That's where Cardinal Mindszenty spent the years from 1956 to 1975. The archbishop was imprisoned in the fifties (needless to say, under false charges). In 1956 he was freed, but the invasion of Hungary prevented him leaving for the West. There is the statue of a stocky man in front of the building. He is US General Harry Hill Bandholtz who, as an officer of the entente peace-keeping force in 1919, saved the treasures of the National Museum. He went to the building and 'sealed' the doors — with the only (paper) seals he had at hand: censorship seals. These had the US coat of arms, so they kept Rumanian soldiers from looting the building.

POST-OFFICE SAVINGS BANK (POSTATAKARÉK) 10F *V. Hold utca 4.* 'Hungarian style has no past but it does have a future', said Ödön Lechner (1845–1914), one of the most influential architects of Hungarian art nouveau. When he finshed this building (1901) it got a warm welcome from his contemporaries, who admired the simplicity of its handling of space and its use of Hungarian folk ornamentation. The beautiful plainness of the main walls give no indication how restlessly alive the building is inside and at roof level. You can walk into the main hall, where the cashiers work, during office hours (8 a.m. to 1 p.m. on weekdays). Torn banknotes are exchanged here for new ones. (By tradition you get back the same percentage of the value as the percentage of undamaged surface.)

The greatest attraction of the building is undoubtedly its roof of green, yellow, blue and brown hexagonal tiles, hidden behind the yellow majolica waves that crown the top of the main walls. The roof is full of flowers familiar from folk embroidery, angel-wings, Turkish turbans and scary dragontails. This, however, can only be suspected, even from further down in Nagy Sándor utca or opposite the market. A disciple of the architect asked Mr. Lechner, 'But tell me, Master, who will enjoy those wonderful ornaments on the roof, if they can't be seen from the street?' Lechner answered: 'The birds will.'

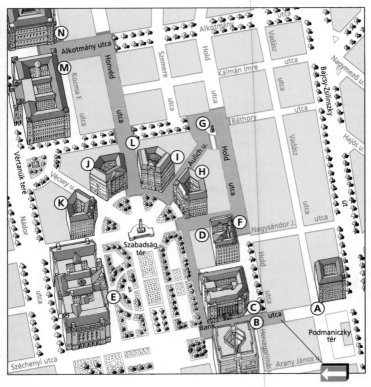

10 **A** Bajcsy-Zsilinszky út 34. **B** Bank Center **C** Hungarian National Bank **D** American Embassy **E** Hungarian Television (former Stock Exchange) **F** Post Office Savings Bank **G** Batthyány Eternal Flame **H–I–J–K** Office Blocks **L** Honvéd utca 3. **M** Ministry of Agriculture **N** Ethnographical Museum

When Lechner died, all unionised building workers stopped work for five minutes.

BATTHYÁNY ETERNAL FLAME (BATTHYÁNY ÖRÖKMÉCSES) 10G

At the crossing of V. Báthory utca, Aulich utca and Hold utca. On 6th October 1849, shortly after the defeat of the Hungarian insurrection against Habsburg rule, thirteen Hungarian generals were executed in a country town and the Prime Minister of the Revolutionary Government, Count Lajos Batthyány, was shot on this site, which, as we saw above, happened to be inside the big army barracks. Batthyány is commemorated by a permanent flame inside the red cup. (Móric Pogány, 1926.) Some years ago people living nearby were shocked to see that the flame had gone out and wrote indignant letters to a newspaper. The permanent flame has quietly been relit.

In the dying years of the old régime, police used force to break up some demonstrations here.

AN ART NOUVEAU BLOCK OF FLATS 10I *V. Honvéd utca 3.* There is

a bus stop outside the building but nobody is tempted to look up while waiting for the bus, as the ground floor is so unattractive, totally spoilt by reconstruction. The building has four floors, the long open corridor on the 'fifth floor' opening directly from the loft. Above that rises a steep, two-storey-high roof. From the other side of the street you can see that all the majolica is intact; only the plasterwork has been damaged. Here it is not enough to look into the gateway, you have to climb up at least as far as the first floor. Notice the tiles on the floor, the ear-shaped painted windows, the doorframes and the brass peepholes in the doors (Emil Vidor, 1904.)

The family of the one-time owner of the block still lives on the first floor, the 'piano nobile'. Though no compensation was paid in 1949, the family has just been offered the opportunity of buying the flat 'back' from the state.

This part of the Fifth District, called Lipótváros (after Leopold, an Austrian Archduke) swarms with people during daytime; in the evenings it is completely dead. Its main street, the broad, elegant Alkotmány utca, does not really lead anywhere and so has little traffic. But this is the route taken by all important guests when visiting the Parliament.

THE STATUE OF IMRE NAGY *V. Vértanúk tere, corner of Nádor, Vécsey*

and Báthory utcas. Imre Nagy (1896-1958) was a Communist all his life, who allegedly had a dark career in the Soviet secret police in the darkest 1930's. During the dark 1950's in Hungary, he was made Prime Minister in the very relative thaw in 1953. He was demoted in 1955, then during the 1956 revolution he was made Prime Minister again. But he was so used to greeting people as 'comrades', that he did so when talking to the revolutionary demonstrators here in this square, who did not really like it...

He became a symbol of freedom when forced into exile in Rumania, but was tried and executed in Hungary in 1958. During his trial he could easily have saved his life had he cooperated with the new régime — but he did not revise his opinions. He had become first and foremost a lover of liberty and independence, though he still considered himself a Communist.

11 **A** Ministry of Agriculture **B** Ethnographical Museum **C** Statue of Lajos Kossuth **D** Statue of Ferenc Rákóczi II **E** Houses of Parliament **F** Kossuth Lajos tér 13-15. **G** Statue of Mihály Károlyi **H** Szalai Confectioner's **I** A block inhabited by American diplomats **J** Playground **K** 'White House'

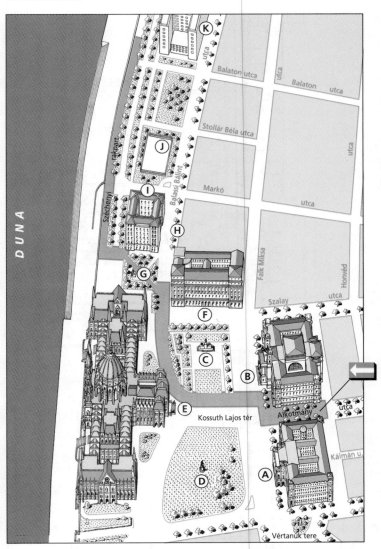

He was buried in an unmarked grave, later found only with great difficulty. As a matter of fact, he was buried face down, a real disgrace. His name was simply not mentionable in public between 1958 and 1988.

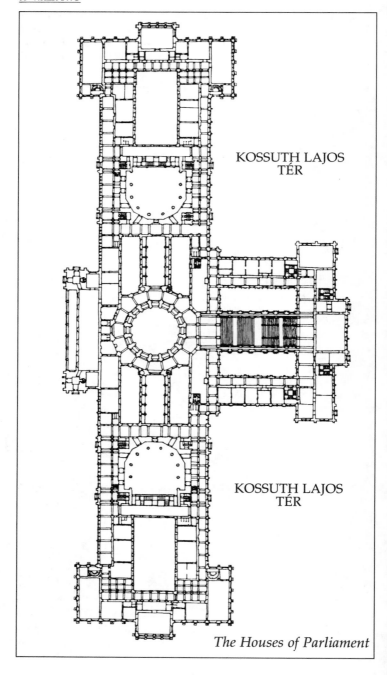

KOSSUTH LAJOS
TÉR

KOSSUTH LAJOS
TÉR

The Houses of Parliament

His reburial on July 1989 marked the birth of new democracy. Tens of thousands came to Heroes' Square, where two deconstructivist artists, Gábor Bachman and László Rajk, dressed up the Műcsarnok Exhibition Hall in black draperies.

Imre Nagy is buried now in Plot 301 of Rákoskeresztúr Cemetery, under the magnificent monument designed by György Jovánovics. (See 'Twelve Impressions'.)

This statue, erected on the centenary of the birth of Imre Nagy, was given little praise when unveiled. Critics found the symbolism — a bridge — cheap (it represents transition from totalitarian notions towards democratic ones), and everyone found the figure idealizing to the point of falsification. The martyr Prime Minister was a typical, stocky, overweight Hungarian peasant type, quite unlike this melancholic, café-type looking vaguely in the direction of the Houses of Parliament. (Tamás Varga, 1996.)

HOUSES OF PARLIAMENT (ORSZÁGHÁZ) 11E *V. Kossuth Lajos tér.*

'No more than a Turkish bath crossed with a Gothic chapel', scoffed Gyula Illyés, a great 20th-century poet. Work on the Parliament started in 1885 and an average of a thousand people worked on it for 17 years. Its designer, Imre Steindl (1839–1902), was originally an apprentice stone-carver, but went on to study architecture in Vienna and Budapest. He was 44 when this work started. By the time it was nearing completion he was already so ill that he could direct the work only from a chair carried to the spot. He died just a few weeks before the building was put into use.

Parliament is 268 metres long and 118 metres wide. The spire reaches 96 metres above the ground. There are 691 rooms, and the length of all the stairs together is about 20 kilometres. The building's structure is readily apparent, especially if seen from the river. To the right and to the left of the central hall under the dome, the council chambers of what were formerly the Commons and the Upper House are situated. 'I did not want to establish a new style with the new Parliament because I could not build a monumental building of this kind, one that would be used for centuries, with ephemeral details. My desire was to combine this splendid medieval style with national and personal features, humbly and carefully as is required by art,' the architect declared in his inaugural address at the Academy of Sciences. He must have meant Gothic when speaking of 'style' even though the ground plan of the building shows Renaissance features and the way space is organized inside is very often Baroque in character. It is thus a summary of Hungarian eclecticism.

Kálmán Mikszáth the novelist (See 'For Serious Addicts/Twelve streets and squares'), who went to the first session in the building as an MP, summarized his impressions by declaring, 'Dazzling, true, but still gaudy'. The writer said this about the inside of the building, the outside was covered with white, Hungarian limestone. As it turned out, the stone was not hard enough. Renovations began as early as 1925 and are still not finished. There are guided tours of Parliament for an entrance fee, but only for groups and only when there is no plenary session. Visitors are allowed in through Gate XII, the first gate to the left from the main entrance with the lions. You have to book in advance through the Office of Guides, T: 268-4000. Since that is a

Ethnographical Museum, formerly the Supreme Court

SZALAY UTCA

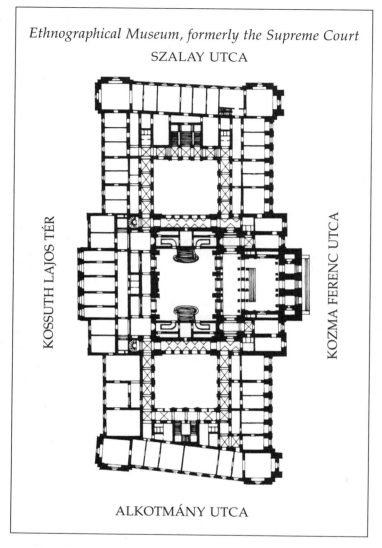

KOSSUTH LAJOS TÉR

KOZMA FERENC UTCA

ALKOTMÁNY UTCA

switchboard number, say: *'Keh-rem ahz eedegen-vehze-toeh-ket.'* 'Please, put me through to the guides.'

Since the first edition of this book, much has happened to this building. The red star (not part of the original design) has been removed from the spire. But more importantly, since the last elections there is real work being done inside — Italian style politicking. As there is only one chamber (no upper house), one of the two large halls is rarely used. Since five per cent of the popular vote is required to secure seats on the national list under our electoral system, it is unlikely there will be more than seven or eight parties in the House. (The system was copied from Germany, together with the 'constructive no-confidence vote' that assures stable government.)

LIFE IN THE PARLIAMENT BUILDING Life is quite busy in the House and the whole building except for January, July and August. You can get an idea from having a look at Kossuth square: only MP's can park there. It is the workplace not only of the 386 Representatives (half of them elected in constituencies, half of them on party lists), but also of the President of the Republic (see 'Crash Course' page 18) at the far left of the building, and of the Prime Minister at the other end.

The tone of the skirmishes reminds one of the British Parliament. An 'Immediate Questions and Answers' session was introduced in 1994. And opposition leaders often disrupt the work of the House with their belligerent 'before the agenda' speeches on Monday afternoons.

ETHNOGRAPHICAL MUSEUM (NÉPRAJZI MÚZEUM) 11B *V. Kossuth Lajos tér 12.* Showing a strong resemblance to the Reichstag in Berlin, although much more elegant than its German counterpart, this neo-Renaissance palace was built to house the Supreme Court and the Chief Public Prosecutor's Office (Alajos Hauszmann, 1893–96). Building another dome opposite the Parliament seemed out of the question. From the Ticket

---

director's choice • director's choice • director's choice

DR. TAMÁS HOFER PHD, DIRECTOR GENERAL 1. The main hall, the so-called 'aula', from the side of the entrance. The fresco on the ceiling, entitled the *Apotheosis of Justitia* recalls the original the building's original function as the Supreme Court (by Károly Lotz, 1896). **2.** The Gallery of Costumes. Twenty-five kinds of Sunday dress from all over 'Historical (i.e.pre-1914) Hungary', so including Hungarian, Slovakian, Romanian, German, Ruthenian, and Croatian clothes. (Second floor, permanent exhibiton, Room 1.) **3.** Two pottery brandy flasks in the form of a peasant couple. A potter's wedding-present for a friend. (Second floor, Room 10.) **4.** Scene of the display of the bridal trousseau in a farmhouse courtyard before the wedding (1898, Kalotaszeg, Transylvania). Bed with home-woven sheets, clothes in painted boxes, embroidered shirts, lead glazed pottery wine jugs in baskets, a woman is on guard with a stick. **5.** 'Christmas table' (Sárköz, South Danube region). On Christmas night, everything on or under the table will be blessed. On the table, there is a 'Christmas tablecloth', depicting a small church, and the Birth, and the small figures representing animals; apple, garlic, and, under the table, cereals, and corn. (First Floor, Room 14.) **6.** The panorama of the Houses of Parliament from the balcony of the Main Hall. This balcony is unfortunately not open to the public, except when there is a function in the Main Hall. (This selection was made in 1997, and so does not include any pieces from the non-European collections, which were not then on view.)

Office you enter an astoundingly huge and richly decorated hall where it is well worth looking around and up. At the back there are some chairs around a big table where you can sit down. From here you can admire the ceiling of the first floor, the large painted windows and the splendour of the staircase. The fresco on the ceiling shows Justitia, the Goddess of Justice, sitting on her throne among the clouds. The allegorical groups beside her represent Justice and Peace on the right, Sin and Revenge on the left. Károly Lotz worked on this fresco for ten months.

The museum is a very pleasant place, and has recently attracted much attention for its daring, unusual exhibitions, like the one that presented an ironic history of the pastoral image of Hungary propagated since 1896.

There are four statues in Kossuth Lajos tér, Kossuth and Rákóczi in front of Parliament and Attila József and Mihály Károlyi near the river on the right and on the left of the Parliament. (See 'Who was Who'.)

AN ELEGANT BLOCK OF FLATS 11F *V. Kossuth Lajos tér 13-15.* This was vacant land for a long time; the city authorities gave permission for a building, but with thousands of restrictions. All the measurements of the building, even the number of the windows, were prescribed to preserve the unity of the square. The building is a rare example of successful planning (Béla Málnai, 1929). The general conservatism of the 1920's changed the direction of the development of architecture: neo-Baroque became once again the most popular style.

The gateway is worth seeing even if this means climbing upstairs and looking down from above. The staircase is especially attractive from the bottom. The details of the doors to the flats are also quite remarkable. There used to be a row of cafés at the front of the building to which all the flats were connected with dumb waiters.

SZALAY CONFECTIONER'S 11H *V. Balassi Bálint utca 7.* Even during the time of the catch-all nationalization after the last war there were some confectioners in the city that remained in private hands. In time they earned a legendary reputation, even though all their proprietors did was to continue their trade like masters of the old school, wholeheartedly filling the pastry with custard and stirring the ice-cream. 'He leaves nothing out,' the older generation used to say. They used to know their customers personally and the staff did not change much either; in most cases relatives took over if there was a vacancy. The shop-fittings also remained the same and all these shops look movingly obsolete in spite of some efforts to modernize them. You would not think that this strict, tall, bald man, Master Szalai, is a living legend. Perhaps the legend is not really about him though, but his cakes.

Until 1949 he had a bigger, more elegant shop nearby. (V. Szent István körút 7.)

A PLAYGROUND 11J *Between Balassi Bálint utca and the river.* In the grim 1950's there were only two things in a playground, swings and a sandpit. Swings were always painted red. Parents were always arguing with their kids to get them to fasten the safety chain and not to stand up on the swings. There were usually some see-saws as well, which gave a chance for social activities. You could 'send your partner on a summer holiday', (which meant that you kept him in the air for a long time) or let him go down fast and so 'make him jump'.

But the real socializing area was the sandpit. Unfortunately the old park-keeper would not allow us to bring water. 'Watering again, are you!' he used to shout, waving his stick with the nail at one end for collecting dry leaves and litter. At that time there was much less for kids to do. And there was not even a single slide in town. Nowadays the best playground in town, according to my nine-year-old daughter, is in Margitsziget.

FALK MIKSA UTCA: ANTIQUE ROW It took about five years for this to become the right address for worthwhile antique shops in Budapest. It is just a short section of the street, between Szent István körút and Balaton utca. Ten years ago there was only one shop here, on the corner of the Grand Boulevard; then (as now) it belonged to a chain of second hand shops and pawnshops, called BÁV, that used the Venus de Milo as their trademark. Recently the old and declining shop was given a vulgar and tasteless facelift, since then no decent person has set foot in it. The excessive use of brass rails is an obsession with some nouveau riche owners of some middle size businesses. Maybe because it so much resembles gold?

NAGYHÁZI GALÉRIA V. Balaton utca 8. T: 131-9908, F: 156-9973. Open 10 a.m. to 6 p.m. Mon-Fri, 9 a.m. to 1 p.m. on Sat. The opposite end of the spectrum: the biggest shop in Hungary, with possibly the highest standards and quality, priced accordingly. Furniture, paintings, chandeliers, and all kinds of peasant textiles: blankets, skirts, folk costumes, old and recent. They are always friendly, even to obvious non-customers.

WHITE HOUSE 11K V. Széchenyi rakpart 19. For decades this building used to be the dreaded power centre from which the country was governed. The dictator/reformer/father figure János Kádár ruled from here for 32 years. Characteristically, we did not see the room he worked in until 30 of those years were up, in 1986, and then only because it was on the cover of Time Magazine. There was a large oil painting over his desk: 'Lenin, playing chess.' (Kádár genuinely liked the game and was a brilliant tactician in power struggles inside the Party.)

In an Orwellian way, there was the state coat of arms on this Party headquarters, and a large red star on top of the Parliament — not vice versa.

These days the White House houses the offices of MP's. But unlike Washington DC, there is no special underground train to carry MP's to the floor when there is an urgent vote.

You can't visit our plain and rather bleak White House. Even if you could, you wouldn't see the gigantic mural by a great Hungarian painter at the far end of the vast lobby, with its depiction of hard-working Hungarian comrades, since it is covered by the biggest curtain in Central Europe. (I peeped behind it once — the mural is still there.) And there is a really big state coat of arms hanging in the middle, made of iron and coloured enamel.

Parties move around the building every four years, according to where the political merry-go-round stops on election day.

You cannot imagine how good the feeling was to take a right turn straight away, after coming off the bridge from Buda — a privilege once reserved for higher party functionaries. This happened in 1989. Few people remember that happy moment any more.

MARGARET BRIDGE (MARGIT HÍD) 12C–13A *Linking Jászai Mari tér (Pest) and Germanus Gyula tér (Buda).* This was the second permanent bridge over the Danube, built between 1872 and 1876, designed by the Frenchman Ernest Gouin and built by a Parisian building firm. It turns at a 150° angle in the middle, partly so that all the piers should be at a right angle to the stream, partly so that the bridge should continue the line of the Nagykörút. The bridge has a branch that leads to Margitsziget (Margaret Island) starting out from the pier in the middle. This branch was included in the original plan but was only built in 1901. All that has remained of the original structure is this branch; for this reason we approach on the right side of the bridge so that we can look under the arch.

MARGARET ISLAND (MARGITSZIGET) *Between Margit híd and Árpád híd.* The island, now one of Europe's finest parks, was formed in the Danube over the last million years. With a length of 2.5 kilometres and a width of 500 metres at the widest point, it can be strolled through in about 2 hours at a leisurely pace. However, it is well worth spending half a day here.

A bridge connected the island with the Buda bank even in Roman times. In the Middle Ages it was called the 'Isle of Rabbits' and was a royal hunting reserve. The present name was given in honour of Princess Margit, daughter of King Béla IV; she lived in the nunnery on the island. During the Turkish occupation the whole island functioned as a harem.

There are more than ten thousand trees on the island, most of them plane trees, carefully planted by various Habsburg gardeners to counteract the ravages of floods. János Arany (1817–1882), one of the greatest poets of the last century, wrote his touching poems in old age, *Under the Oak Trees*, here. In fact, although there are some oaks on the island as well, gardeners say that the poet's favourite oaks were probably plane trees too. Up to the end of World War II the island was the property of a private company and maintenance was financed from the entrance fees paid by the public. There are various amenities on the island: a swimming pool, a lido, competion tennis courts, an open-air cinema and an open-air theatre, a smelly collection of exotic birds, and a rose, a Japanese, and a sculpture garden.

At the northern end there is the famous old Grand Hotel, which is now the Ramada Grand Hotel. The terrace is a pleasant place to sit and enjoy the shady trees, the tranquil and the elegant ambience — everything which makes the island worth visiting.

Access: Buses 26 and 26A, terminus at Nyugati Railway Station in Nyugati tér. They stop at the access road to the island from Árpád híd; trams stop at the equivalent on Margit híd. Cars are allowed access only from Árpád híd and only as far as the car parks around the hotel. There are minibus tours between 10 a.m. and 6 p.m. on Saturdays between 1 May and 30 September. Two enterprises hire out

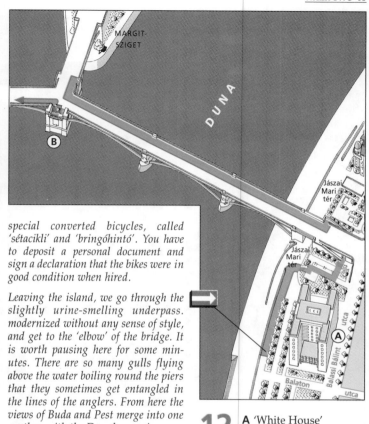

special converted bicycles, called 'sétacikli' and 'bringóhintó'. You have to deposit a personal document and sign a declaration that the bikes were in good condition when hired.

Leaving the island, we go through the slightly urine-smelling underpass. modernized without any sense of style, and get to the 'elbow' of the bridge. It is worth pausing here for some minutes. There are so many gulls flying above the water boiling round the piers that they sometimes get entangled in the lines of the anglers. From here the views of Buda and Pest merge into one another, with the Danube curving gently in the middle, embracing the City.

12
A 'White House'
B Margaret Bridge

This bridge was the scene of the greatest disaster in the history of Budapest. In November 1944, in the broad daylight of the afternoon rush hour, when hundreds of people were crossing the bridge on foot and by tram, the charges placed by the Germans on the section of the bridge between the island and Pest went off, presumably by accident. The number of casualties will never be known, but it ran into the hundreds.

THE PRZEMYSL MEMORIAL 13B *Left of the Buda side of Margit híd.* This, one of the most masculine lions in Budapest, symbolizes the Hungarian defenders of Przemysl, the fortress in Southern Poland. A Hungarian soldier modelled for it in 1932. Memorials to the Hungarian victims of World War I have been set up at various places of the city, most of them erected with donations.

Margit híd continues to Margit körút (Margaret Boulevard). After about 200 metres the road takes a sharp turn to the left, still further it turns right and

13 **A** Margaret Bridge **B** Przemysl Memorial **C** Statue of General Bem **D** Flórián Chapel **E** Király Baths **F** Military Tribunal **G** 'Point House'

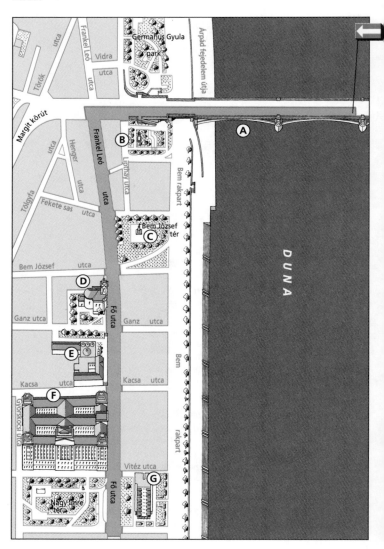

finally runs into busy Moszkva tér, the centre of Buda, which epitomises the traffic problems of the city. The winding Margit körút follows the line of a hill, Rózsadomb, on which first summer houses and later elegant villas were built. In the 1960's and 1970's hundreds of cube-like blocks were built next to the old, low buildings. The eastern slope of the hill is practically full. The other sides are also the scenes of busy construction work (Endrődi Sándor utca, Gárdonyi Géza utca, Törökvészi út). For Budapest residents, Rózsadomb is now a social category. If someone built a house or bought his own home in this expensive area, people just said that 'they moved up to the hill'. Rose Hill still remained the symbolic address associated with wealth, though it is common knowledge that real wealth has moved out to Adyliget and Budakeszi, the new suburbs.

A rest: Café Gusto — Frankel Leó utca 12.

To continue on Walk Two, you should turn left to Frankel Leó utca, a street which could just as well be on the Pest side. You can see a notice in one of the ground-floor windows of No 9., which translates as TROTTING ALL YEAR ROUND, FLAT-RACING FROM SPRING TO AUTUMN. It is one of the two dozen betting offices in the city. The two types of racing have two separate race-courses and two separate sets of followers.

At No 1. there is the small shop of a skate-grinder. The old-fashioned notice in the window says: 'Skates for grinding or assembly are welcome.' Opposite on the ground floor of No 2. is the 'Bambi' confectioner's just as it was in the trapezium-shaped cash desk and the figure of the (Disney) deer that inspired the name. The notice above the fridge containing soft drinks is seen in lots of other such places: DRUNK ELEMENTS WILL NOT BE SERVED. The other one above the cash desk reflects the spirit of the place better: ONLY FOOD SERVED TO THE TABLE MAY BE CONSUMED THERE. Which must mean that things sometimes happen differently here. Perhaps the old-age pensioners passing time at the 'Bambi' have been offering each other their home-made cookies; I wonder.

STATUE OF JÓZEF BEM 13C *II. Bem József tér.* Of Polish nationality, Bem was one of the most successful generals on the Hungarian side during the 1848-49 Hungarian Revolution and War of Independence, and was especially revered by ordinary Hungarian soldiers, who called him 'Father Bem' (Bem apó). The statue (János Istók, 1934) depicts the small figure of the general, wounded, his arm in a sling, commanding his troops into attack at the bridge of Piski. The inscription says: ~The Battle of Piski~. And underneath: ~I Shall Recapture the Bridge Or Die/Forward Hungarians/If We Do Not Have the Bridge, We Do Not Have the Country.~

The bridge was recaptured. As the saying goes: 'We won this battle, as usual, it was only the war we lost.'

After the crushing defeat of the revolution by the combined forces of the Tsar and the Habsburgs, Bem escaped to Turkey. He adopted Islam and became governor of Aleppo under the name of Murad Pasha. The statue has had an important role in anti-government demonstrations ever since it was erected.

FLÓRIÁN CHAPEL (FLÓRIÁN KÁPOLNA) 13D *II. Fő utca 90.* We are now entering Fő utca, which epitomises almost the entire history of the country. It was a baker who had the chapel built in the middle of the 18th century.

Before the quay was built the Danube several times burst its banks, and left its silt everywhere. As a result all the older buildings are considerably below street level. The church was bodily lifted 140 centimetres in 1938. A modern painter, Jenő Medveczky, painted all the fresco decoration in the same year. Now it is the parish church of the Greek Catholic community in Buda.

I saw a touching scene here, an old lady dusting the ceiling of the chapel with immense affection and thoroughness. She was using a long pole made up of several shorter ones joined together.

KIRÁLY BATH (KIRÁLY FÜRDŐ) 13E *II. Fő utca 84.* The part built by

the Turks, called the 'Bath of the Cock Tower', was built around 1570 inside the Víziváros town wall, so that the garrison could enjoy the benefits of a bath even during a siege. It was a smaller copy of the famous baths in Buda. The classical wings were added between 1717 and 1727. The baths took their present name (Király = King) not from some ruler but from the König family which owned them for a time. The steam bath is a fine spectacle. After buying the ticket, go up in the spiral staircase and follow the sign GŐZFÜRDŐ (steam bath). In the dressing room the attendant hands over a cotton apron which you take with you into any empty cubicle. After undressing, you lock the door of the cubicle with the key you find inside and tie it on a string on the apron. Pause to memorize the number of your cubicle and then you can go straight to the bath. Taking a shower is compulsory, the sauna itself is not. The actual Turkish bath is a pool under the octagonal roof that can be seen also from the outside; you get to it through a low door. There are mysterious beams of light of different colours coming through the hexagonal openings in the dome, illuminating the steam. Once you have been in and out of the steam of different temperatures and waters of 26-40° Celsius enough times, the next stop is the towel room. You leave your apron at the entrance, take a towel and dry yourself. You dump the wet towel, take a dry one and go up to the first floor **Pihenő** to have a rest. There are notices here on the wall saying 'Silence, please' and 'Time of rest: 15 mins'; the latter is never taken seriously. From here you go back to your cubicle, but you cannot open it with your key alone; like a safe it needs two keys to open and the attendant has the other one. It is customary to leave him or her a tip.

The bath is open for men on Mondays, Wednesdays and Fridays, and for women on Tuesdays, Thursdays and Saturdays from 6.30 a.m. to 7 p.m. (on Saturdays to 12 p.m.). It is closed for maintenance on every first Thursday of the month. Apart from a steam bath, you can use the bath tubs, the sauna and several other facilities. On one of the corridors there are some red scales, the sort that used to be everywhere in the streets of Budapest. In the beginning you had to drop in 20 fillér, then two 20 fillér coins. Not long after that, the scales disappeared.

Fő utca is the main street of the district called Víziváros (literally 'Watertown'). Looking up the streets to the right, for example, up Kacsa utca, you can enjoy a magnificent view of the slope of Castle Hill and you can get an idea of the poetic disorder of the district in the past. Imre Nagy tér, however, could well be a museum of modern architecture. The severe block at Fő utca 70-72 is the Military Court of Justice (13F), which perfectly exemplifies the primary aim of such buildings: to serve as a deterrent (1915). During the rebuilding of the façade it was perhaps felt that three revolving doors in the façade were too many and iron bars were placed on the ones at the sides; the one in the middle was replaced with a simple narrow door, which is not in the least in proportion with such a large building. It would seem truly impossible to slip out of this place unobserved.

The building opposite (Fő utca 69.) is a typical block of flats of the 1930's, while the red brick building opposite the side wall of the Court, on the other side of the square, was the first building in Budapest to have been built during winter — in 1941–42. After the last war, there were plans to develop the river bank with tall buildings. All that was realized of the plan was a famous high-rise block, the 'Point House' (Fő utca 61., 1948), so called because all the flats open from one single staircase in the middle of the building. But the rumour went around that the origin of the name was that there was no point in building it, as it cost twice the price of a traditional block (14A).

We have arrived at one of the finest spots of this walk, at Batthyány tér. Apart from some fine buildings, the attraction lies in the fact that it is opposite the main façade of Parliament. (A quite unusual view of the Parliament can be enjoyed from the first floor of the Market Hall, from the windows of the stalls hidden on the left.) The huge building seems to stretch calmly far into the distance. You can imagine the power of the explosion when a German ammunition store went up here on 2 January 1945, if all the windows of Parliament broke, even on the other side of the building.

The sleepy little square suddenly came to life in 1972, when this section of the Second (Red) Metro Line was opened. The terminus of the green suburban train (HÉV) is also here, under the square.

You can make a short cut here to the end of this walk if you take the underground in the direction of Örs vezér tér, the second stop is Deák tér, which is just three minutes' walk from Vörösmarty tér.

A WORLD FAMOUS LAVATORY (NYILVÁNOS VÉCÉ) *In the subway, Batthyány tér.* 'A little money takes away every smell,' to vary the Emperor Vespasian's famous dictum. This institution, which was always a busy but scruffy place, was leased out some years ago to a private entrepreneur, who imported the atmosphere of tropical countries, soft music and two chairs. The original owner in the mid-eighties was interviewed by journalists from almost every leading newspaper, as a symbol of New Hungary. Later on, he would have had to have a chain of video rental outlets to qualify as the beneficiary of privatization. Who cares about a private toilet when 70 per cent of the Hungarian economy has been privatized?

HIKISCH HOUSE *I. Batthyány tér 3.* The residence of an architect who lived at the end of the 18th century (the house was built in 1795). It is below the level of the square, as is every other old building here. There is a relief with four cherubs on the façade. They symbolize the four seasons.

THE FORMER 'WHITE CROSS' INN *I. Batthyány tér 3.* The Ballroom used to be in the prominent middle part, which also saw theatrical performances. The ironwork on the balcony on the left is Baroque, on the right Rococo. Joseph II (1780–90), called the 'King with a Hat' since he was never crowned, stayed here twice, rather than in a palace, to emphasize his puritanical character. You will be surprised at the large and wonderful courtyard hiding behind the gate. The Casanova Piano Bar entices those who

14 **A** 'Point House'
B St Elizabeth Parish
Church **C** Statue of Ferenc
Kölcsey, a romantic poet
D Market hall **E** Church of St
Anne **F** Calvinist Church

like that kind of thing. They say
Casanova himself put up at this inn.

To the left of the back gate of the
building is the tradesmen's
entrance to the Market Hall.

CHURCH OF ST ANNE 14E *I.*

Batthyány tér. Finely proportioned
in every detail, this to my mind is
one of the finest buildings in town.
(Kristóf Hamon and Máté Nepauer,
1740–1762). Inside, the Italianate
nave is in the shape of an elongat-
ed octagon. One of the builders was
Kristóf Hikisch, who used to live in
this square, and whose house we
have already seen. Over the years
the church has been the victim of
earthquakes, floods and wars.

One of the pleasantest cafés in
Buda, the Angelika, opened on the
ground floor of the vicarage at the
beginning of the 1970's. Under the
vaulted ceiling, most of the regulars are from the traditional middle
class of Buda, attracted by the
slightly snobbish decoration and
the pleasant staff. A place where
ladies wear their hats as they take
their coffee — and where the wayward boss takes the secretary.

*Further down Fő utca, we pass a neo-Gothic Calvinist church with an extreme-
ly complex ground plan on the left (Samu Pecz, 1896), and soon arrive at
Corvin tér, which is surrounded by a concert hall (the so-called Vigadó of Buda),
some charming Baroque blocks of flats (Corvin tér 2., 3., 4. and 5.), a church of
medieval origin, rebuilt in Romantic style, and the hillside. We turn left into
Halász utca and leave the Víziváros district to the right. On the corner of Pala
utca and Fő utca there is a late Baroque building which used to belong to a Greek
merchant.*

*From here you can see, and this is the only place you can see it well from,
Roosevelt tér at the Pest end of Lánchíd. The square is enclosed by the
Hungarian Academy of Sciences, the 'Spinach-palace', Gresham Palace, the
Ministry of Home Affairs and the Hyatt Hotel. Naturally the Roosevelt*

memorial tablet on the wall of a building in the square cannot be seen from here.
The inscription on the tablet says: 'FDR, 1887–1945, who, in the last war
between the peoples of the world, fought for the freedom of the oppressed and for
the victory of human rights. He helped democracy to win a final victory.'

A rest: Café Angelika — Batthyány tér 7.

THE FRENCH INSTITUTE (INSTITUT FRANÇAIS, FRANCIA INTÉZET)

15E *(I. Fő utca 17. T: 202-1133, F: 202-1323)* When this chic institution
moved to this prime location from its former, tucked-away, Theresa Town
small palace, its weight quintupled in Budapest cultural life. (Apparently,
its budget had too.) Designed by George Maurios (1992), the building is
an exemplary addition to the riverfront, which its proportions successfully
respect. Its style, however, was something never yet seen in Budapest. All
this originality was designed to house the French School, that's why it is
cut into two, with separate entrances. (The Fő utca façade was designed for
the school, and the rest for the Institute.) The silver cylinder is a boastful
allusion to the auditorium inside.

Apart from the fact that it is a premier cultural location, host and co-host of
everything from Baroque music festivals to jazz events and philosophical
talkshows, I like going to the French Institute for two things.

Number one is the panorama from the library — an entirely new one on
Pest. You can enjoy it from 1 p.m. to 7 p.m. on weekdays except for
Monday. There are wonderful lamps on the table. And yes, the books. It's
a three-level space, with a lot of books out of the stacks, displayed on a
shelf on the platform railings. There are incredibly helpful and proud
librarians (a lot of them, I gather). Proud of their library, the one they like
to call 'le petit Beaubourg'.

What seems to be even more promising is the new community space that
will now be open from 9 a.m. to 9 p.m., or to the end of the last programme
of the day. They decided to call it 'Café l´Orient Express', though the terminus of the famous train since it was re-started is Budapest, and it does
not go as far as the Orient.

The ladies who serve the ultra-strong espresso are nice and they whisper
in awesomely fluent French. The plexiglass dome of the café space gives
you a different kind of panorama: different from the library's. It overlooks
the courtyard of a typical Budapest block of flats. There are iron-railed
gangways on every floor. So you can sip your coffee, read your paper and
see the postman going around to distribute pensions. And see the teenag-
er coming home, bumping into Mrs. Kovács straight from the Batthyány
tér market. This is a space that teaches you how to be inquisitive, without
looking like a voyeur. No small feat.

Quite recently a monument was erected at the Institute, by Pierre Székely
Péter (the artist insisted on carving his name in that multilingual, double-
decker way). The statue, which fits into the grid of the pavement in a nice
way, is about the flawless Hungarian-French friendship. On the western
side there is a French word: 'affinité', on the southern surface, the
Hungarian counterpart: 'rokonszenv'. On the northern side it commemorates the wartime anti-fascist activities of the French embassy, and the inau-
guration of the new Institute by the Hungarian President.

CHAIN BRIDGE (LÁNCHÍD) 15J–16A

We have already crossed this bridge on the First Walk. In its present form, this is the third bridge. During the renovation in 1987, sixty tons of paint was used and most of the 100,000 rivets replaced.

GRESHAM PALACE 16D

V. Roosevelt tér 5. The design (by Zsigmond Quittner, 1904–6) of this headquarters building for an English insurance company was approved in London and does not harmonize with the rest of Lánchíd. Despite the art nouveau style its proportions are surprisingly

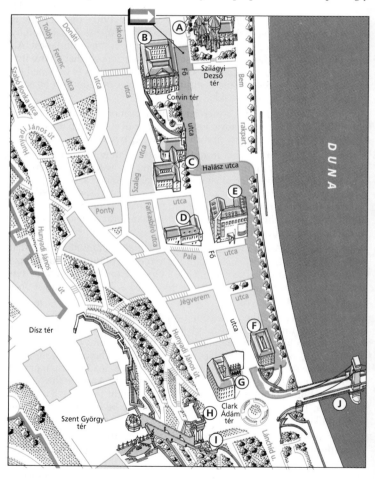

15 **A** Calvinist Church **B** Buda Vigadó **C** Church of the Capuchins **D** Fő utca 20. **E** The French Institute **F** Fő utca 1. **G** Café in the remaining part of a block destroyed during the war **H** The entrance to the Tunnel **I** The lower end of the Cable Car **J** Lánchíd — Chain Bridge

16 **A** Lánchíd — Chain Bridge **B** Hungarian Academy of Sciences **C** Statue of István Széchenyi **D** Gresham Palace **E** CEU Building **F** Statue of Ferenc Deák **G** Hotel Hyatt **H** Gerbeaud **I** Vigadó **J** Luxus Department Store

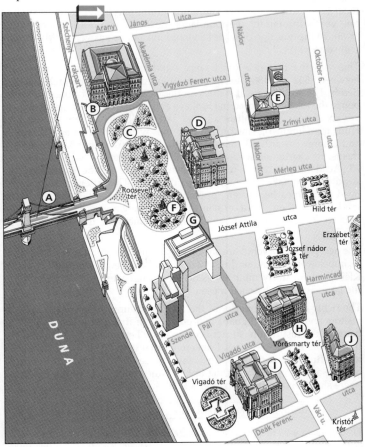

peaceful, and as one would expect, its surface is richly decorated. Gresham himself, the founder of the London Stock Exchange, stands in a gold setting so dominant that it can be seen even from the other end of the Tunnel. At sunset the portrait and the golden tiles of the façade, which at other times of the day are very pale, seem to glow. It makes a striking photograph if you can set it up from the Buda side of the bridge. The figures above the windows of the first floor illustrate the working life and the carefree life, the latter undoubtedly the result of buying a good insurance policy.

A rest: Mérleg étterem — Mérleg utca 6.

HUNGARIAN ACADEMY OF SCIENCES AND LETTERS (MAGYAR TUDOMÁNYOS AKADÉMIA) 16B *V. Roosevelt tér 9.* This institution,

like many others, was founded in the second quarter of the last century, in what is called the Reform Age. On the wall facing Akadémia utca the large relief immortalizes the moment when Count Széchenyi, in 1825, offered one year's income for the foundation of the Academy (Barnabás Holló, 1893). To the question of what he would live on, he answered: 'My friends will support me.'

This was the first neo-Renaissance building in the city and was built between 1862 and 1864, to the plans of Friedrich Stüler, an architect from Berlin. The six allegorical statues on the façade at second floor level symbolize the sciences studied in Hungary at the time. On the same level there are six statues of scientists: Galileo and Miklós Révai (an 18th-century Hungarian linguist), Newton and Lomonosov near the river, and Descartes and Leibniz towards Akadémia utca. Today the Academy has ten departments. Its charter allows for up to 200 academicians, who must be under 75. Academicians get a monthly salary, receive all the journals of the Academy and have their taxi fares paid as well. This latter tradition developed from an earlier system, operating in the fifties, following the Soviet model, when there was a car pool at the Academy, a sort of private taxi service. A recent innovation is the establishment of the Széchenyi Art Academy.

The acceptance speeches are major events in this building. Last time Mr Zsámbéki, of the Katona József Theatre talked about *The Broken Jug* by Kleist, not for thirty minutes, as he should have, but for a hundred. But the large audience listened mesmerized.

The richly decorated interior of the building is unfortunately not open to visitors and the armed guard will politely but firmly warn them off. The name of the institution is inscribed modestly between the second and the third floors in golden letters. I remember that in my childhood there used to be a full stop at the end. Then this last-century full stop disappeared because according to the orthographical rules published by the Academy 'there should be no full stop after a title'.

A rest: Restaurant Lou Lou — Vigyázó Ferenc utca 4.

The Academy used to dominate the square but lost its primacy at the beginning of this century with the construction of headquarters buildings for two financial institutions. Its status fell even further with the arrival of the 'Spinach-palace', so nicknamed because of its colour (Miklós Hofer, Tibor Hübner, 1979). Its weight is carried on steel spheres. Two foreign trading companies started this expensive office building, but ran out of finance. The building was finished by the state and finally three ministries moved in. There is also a canteen on the top floor for the staff – a rare luxury for Hungarian civil servants.

The Gresham Palace was built of durable materials, and its façade has resisted the ravages of time. The T-shaped passageway, however, has given up the struggle. The glass ceiling, which was once painted, was replaced by plain glass after the war. Only some fragments remained at the bottom. Relics of old decencies, as they say in Dublin.

Here we suddenly seem to arrive at a rundown district. From the passageway you can see the back door of the Gresham Casino, all sorts of office windows where the lights are always on, and an old-fashioned hairdresser's. Here is the entrance to an office with a frequently changing name plate. It has been a lonely hearts agency, an agency for the building industry and a shoeshop; a modest, hidden reminder of our age of entrepreneurs. There are offices, as here, in many residential blocks in the City area, often in the most inappropriate premises. Their staff, especially the women, do their very best to decorate these offices, keeping postcards sent to each other over the years on the wall or under the glass sheet on their desks.

The staircases have their own names (Gresham, Kossuth and Andrássy stairs). At some places here some of the old glass windows have been preserved. The walls of the inner courtyards are white or covered with light blue tiles.

Everyone agrees that the decline should be stopped some way or other. There seems to be no other way but to turn the block into a hotel. But the tenants — under the leadership of the grande dame of the Hungarian stage — are protesting. They want to stay.

By the way: the Roosevelt tablet disappeared during the recent renovation. A shame.

On the way back to Vörösmarty tér you can find some more information about the walk you have just taken, by browsing in the newly set up Info Touch system. Or stop for a moment at the tiny Dorottya utca Gallery. Its big windows keep prospective visitors away. Passers-by all cast a single glance, and feel that they have seen it all. No secrets, no longing to get in.

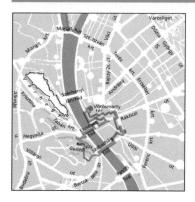

Gellérthegy and the Old City This walk leads through a district built at the end of the last century. We shall go over to Buda and climb a 141-metre-high hill, then come back across another bridge to Pest to have a look at some buildings put up at the beginning of the last century. And we might have some sausages on the way.
Time: about 6 hours.

VIGADÓ 17C *V. Vigadó tér.* This single word is the full name of this romantic concert hall and ballroom. It means something like 'merrymaking', a place for entertainments. When the hall was first opened, it was intended to have Hungarianized Italian name, though there were several other suggestions too, ranging from 'Gondilla' to 'Búfúdda'. It was planned as a concert hall and a ballroom and took seven years to build, beginning in 1859. It took so long partly because the builders needed several attempts to cope with the unusual task. The designer, Frigyes Feszl, was a demanding man and stuck to his guns, meticulously specifying even the smallest details. When the building was finished in 1865, it was received with unanimous obtuseness. Some found it to be too unusual, others to be too Hungarian. Still others criticized the lack of uniformity and also said that the main façade was 'bare' and the height of the main hall was monstrous (22 metres). An architect from abroad said, and perhaps not quite in mockery, that the building was 'auskristallisiert Tschardasch'.

In its present form, rebuilt after the war, it re-opened in the winter of 1980. Music lovers could hardly wait to experience the Large Hall, which seats 640 people. To improve the once notorious acoustics, special pyramids were suspended from the ceiling. The musicians were disappointed in spite of all that, but the audience was dazzled by the amazing variety of colours. Restoration work has been done very carefully, using the original plans to get the colours right, and consulting photographs for other details.

Unfortunately, the Large Hall and the equally luxurious staircase can only be seen during a concert, and the foyer is open only after 12 p.m. when the ticket office opens. (The show-cases on each side of the main entrance were thought at first to be a bad practical joke, but later it turned out that they were meant to be set up there, so they stayed.) The Söröző Restaurant and the Gallery, which does not sell its paintings, are in a style different from the rest of the building. The Vigadó can be rented for balls or receptions.

The building is anything but uniform, the façades at the side are much simpler, and they cleverly hide the fact that the building is not straight but follows the line of the site which breaks at a slight angle.

Vigadó tér used to be the busiest square in Pest. Before the permanent bridges were built, this was where the pontoon bridge was moored. Once Lánchíd was opened, calm fell on Vigadó ter.

A rest: Amadeus — Apáczai Csere János utca 13.

THE MARRIOTT HOTEL 17D *V. Apáczai Csere János utca 4.* The hotel was opened in 1969 (designed by József Finta and László Kovácsy). All its 39 suites and 349 rooms overlook the Danube. About a hundred years after the scandal that broke out about the Vigadó, a new one started over this hotel. It is generally held that it is too high, its proportions are different from those of the city; what is more, it turns its back on the capital, looks like a fortress and at least the back, windowless side is, quite simply, ugly. As the comment goes, if you stay at the Marriott, at least you can't see it.

The lovers of the Duna-korzó would like to drive the noisy Tram 2 underground and have the promenade widened. As this plan would be expensive, there is no sign of it being adopted.

Had dinner here one night over looking Tram #2 [handwritten annotation]

GREEK ORTHODOX CHURCH (ORTHODOX TEMPLOM) 17E *V. Petőfi tér 2.* The large group of Greek merchants formerly in Budapest were enthusiastic patrons of architecture, and they commissioned this baroque church from the architect József Jung (1791–94). Its southern spire was demolished in World War II. Nowadays services are usually conducted in Hungarian, and

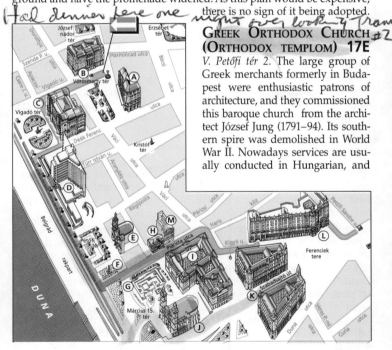

17 A Luxus Department Store **B** Gerbeaud **C** Vigadó **D** The Marriott Hotel **E** Orthodox Church **F** Statue of Sándor Petőfi **G** Contra Aquincum **H** Péterffy Palace **I** Faculty of Arts, Eötvös University **J** Inner City Parish Church **K** Klotild Palaces **L** Paris Arcade — Párisi udvar **M** Millennium Court Executive Residences

are always accompanied by singing (at 6 p.m. on Saturdays; at 10 a.m. on Sundays and some other times as well on public holidays). The building is open to visitors from spring to autumn between 10 a.m. and 5 p.m.

STATUE OF SÁNDOR PETŐFI (PETŐFI-SZOBOR) 17F *V. Petőfi tér.*

The statue is a bit far from the taste of our times (Miklós Izsó and Adolf Huszár, 1882). It shows the poet at the age of twenty-five, reciting his most famous patriotic poem, beginning 'Talpra, magyar!' (Rise up, Hungarians!).

Petőfi (1823-49) started life as a poor student and strolling player but soon became the most popular poet of his time, though his work was also praised by literary circles. He was a genius, and a master of poetic form. He introduced the vernacular into Hungarian verse, and so inevitably acquired the title of the Robert Burns of Hungary. His short life was the full one of a man whose love was requited, who took part in a victorious revolution and who became a soldier in order to fight for his country. He was killed in one of the last battles of the Hungarian War of Independence. After his death the rumour that he was still alive circulated round the country for many years. It was followed up very recently by a self-made millionaire, who sent a team to Siberia to dig up a grave. The corpse they happened to unearth later proved to be that of a young lady.

Petőfi is the first poet Hungarian children study in detail at school. Despite various attempts at translation, he is virtually unknown abroad.

Today there are eighteen different streets and squares named after Petőfi in Budapest. (This large number is partly due to the creation of Greater Budapest in 1949, enclosing a number of suburbs within Budapest.) There are lots of other things named after him: a museum, a bridge, an army camp, a radio channel, to mention just a few. His was the portrait on the 10 Forint banknote.

By the way, the self-made millionaire has since gone bankrupt, not because he wanted to find the body of Sándor Petőfi, people say.

THE RUINS OF CONTRA AQUINCUM 17G *V. Március 15. tér.* An

open-air museum, with the remains of the old Roman fortress. The eastern border of the Roman Empire was the line of the Danube, which means that only the Buda side was within the province of Pannonia.

From the end of the 3rd century this fortress, which was 84 x 86 metres across, and had walls 3 metres thick, served as an outpost situated opposite the nearby town of Aquincum, as the name indicates. Documents mention that it was visited by the Emperor Julian and even by Constantine the Great. There are other and more important Roman remains in much better preserved surroundings in the Aquincum Museum, in the IIIrd district. From spring to autumn Contra Aquincum is a popular place for the students of the Faculty of Arts, the building that overlooks the square. They call the place the 'concrete castrum', or at least they did in my time. Also frequented by students are the steps by the river between Erzsébet híd and Lánchíd, which are popular suntraps and ideal for sunbathing.

FACULTY OF ARTS 17I *V. Pesti Barnabás utca 1.* The university moved

into this building, (originally a Catholic monastery and school – *gimnázium* – built by Dezső Hültl in 1915-18), in the early 1950's. The university is named after Loránd Eötvös, the famous physicist. It also has a Faculty of Natural Sciences and a Faculty of Law. The real main entrance of the building is not in Pesti Barnabás utca, but through the famous 'Gate B' in the narrow passageway between Váci utca and the bank of the Danube. This area is very busy during term time, from the beginning of February to the middle of May. The corridors on the ground floor and on the first floor are almost totally covered with posters advertising various meetings and amateur performances, university magazines and university clubs. The most crowded place is the small, smoke-filled canteen on the first floor. It is invaded by the students in the breaks between lectures (usually between 9.30 and 10 or 11.30 and 12) for a cup of coffee or for the notes of a missed lecture. The current word is that the building will most probably be given back to the Piarist Fathers.

PÉTERFFY PALACE 17H *V. Pesti Barnabás utca 2.* The university building dwarfs this little house, which looks even smaller as it is below street level. When Pest was still enclosed by walls all the houses were this size; this one was probably designed by András Mayerhoffer in 1756. The restaurant situated in the palace is actually much older than its name indicates; it is not 100 but at least 150 years old.

PÁRISI UDVAR 17L *V. Ferenciek tere 5.* This block was built in 1909 (designed by Henrik Schmal) and the bank which commissioned it had offices on the ground floor (now used by the IBUSZ Travel Agency). The arcade has recently been enlarged by a new passageway that branches off and opens into Haris köz. The block is well worth exploring. If you take the lift between the bookshop and the leatherware shop and go up to the top floor, you can walk over to the other staircase and down the stairs again. The lift used to be in the middle of the staircase. From the windows between the first and the second floor you can look down on the witty roof structure of the yard.

FRANCISCAN CHURCH 18A *V. Ferenciek tere 2.* The church shows the influence of Italian Baroque and not that of the Austrian version, which gave us yellow churches with 'radish helmet' towers. It also follows the medieval Franciscan pattern of having a separate bell-tower-cum-vestry. There was a Gothic church on the site in the 13th century. The present building was finished in 1758 and dedicated to St Peter of Alcantara (1499–1562), who founded a branch of the Franciscan Order. His statue is in the niche in the middle, above the window of the choir. Above the front gate is the crest of the Order: two arms whose hands show the Stigmata (Jesus and St Francis of Assisi). On the left-hand wall of the church a large memorial tablet can be seen. This commemorates the catastrophic flood of 1838, when the whole of the present-day inner city was under water. In some districts 90% of the buildings collapsed. Count Miklós Wesselényi, 'the sailor of the flood', portrayed in action, was a hero of the rescue efforts.

KLOTILD PALACES 18C–18C *V. Szabadsajtó út 5. and 6.* These twin palaces were built at the same time as the original Erzsébet híd. They are almost mirror images of each other (Flóris Korb and Kálmán Giergl, 1902). In the old days, one of the most conservative cafés of the city was here.

18
A Franciscan Church of Pest
B 'Royal Block of Flats'
C Klotild Palaces **D** Párisi udvar **E**
Faculty of Arts, Eötvös
University **F** Inner City
Parish Church
G Elizabeth
Bridge

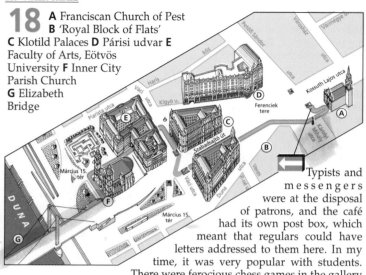

Typists and messengers were at the disposal of patrons, and the café had its own post box, which meant that regulars could have letters addressed to them here. In my time, it was very popular with students. There were ferocious chess games in the gallery all day long. The students disappeared when an expensive self-service restaurant opened up. And then a posh, tourist-oriented restaurant-cabaret.

On the other side of the building there is an expensive furniture and fittings shop. Several dozen such shops have opened in the last few years. It is very difficult to find good modern furniture.

A rest: Osiris Book Club — Veres Pálné utca 4-6.

PHOTOGRAPHS BY GYÖRGY KLÖSZ *In the subway between the two parts of V. Váci utca.* In the pedestrian subway under the Pest end of Erzsébet híd you can see photos taken by a famous photographer who lived at the end of the last century. The originals were taken on 18 x 24 cm glass plates. Klösz's studio was nearby, on the first floor of the first building after the Franciscan church. The photos exhibited in the subway portray the area around Erzsébet híd, before and after the reconstructions made necessary by the building of the bridge. It is mostly Klösz's photographs that make up a recently re-published illustrated book (*Budapest Anno...*, see the chapter 'Reading'). The graffiti and the beggars show how far we have come since then.

INNER CITY PARISH CHURCH (BELVÁROSI PLÉBÁNIATEMPLOM) 18F
You may remember this church from the First Walk. Then we did not pause at the statue on the outer wall of the chancel. This is the statue of St Florian, the saint who protects us from fires. It was erected in 1723, after the great fires in Pest.

ELIZABETH BRIDGE (ERZSÉBET HÍD) 18G–19A A suspension bridge,
built between 1960 and 1964. (More thoroughly covered in the First Walk.) The vertical suspenders are not fastened to the cables, but kept in place by the weight of the bridge.

The beautiful location of Budapest is largely due to a 140-metre-high dolomite rock which descends steeply into the riverbed. The underground part of this rock is 1,000 metres under the surface at Városliget. The western slope is much more gentle. Its area, together with its northern slope, the Tabán, is almost 60 hectares. Naturally, the city tries to protect every single one of the 5,766 trees here. (Some of them are fig trees planted by the Turks.) According to the legend, the hill was the dwelling-place of witches, who arrived here every night, riding on the back of a human being, to get their daily wine. Nowadays there is no wine produced here — but it really was once covered in vineyards.

St Gellért Monument 19C *Facing the Buda end of Erzsébet híd. The* bronze statue surrounded by a colonnade (Gyula Jankovits, 1904) is interesting not so much for its own qualities as for its location. St Gellért (or Gerald), Bishop of Csanád, was put into a nail-studded barrel (according to legend: most historians say it was a wheelbarrow) and pushed over the edge of the hill by pagan Hungarians in the struggle against Christianity in 1046.

It takes 20-25 minutes to climb to the top of the hill. The trees hide the city on the way up so the panorama appears suddenly as you get to the top.

a climb ~ worth it !

The Citadel 19E *On top of Gellért Hill.* The grim stronghold on the top of Gellért-hegy was built after the Revolution of 1848–1849; its military

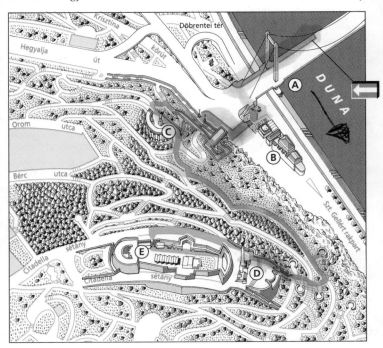

19 **A** Elizabeth Bridge **B** Rudas Baths **C** Statue of St Gellért **D** Statue of Liberty **E** Citadel

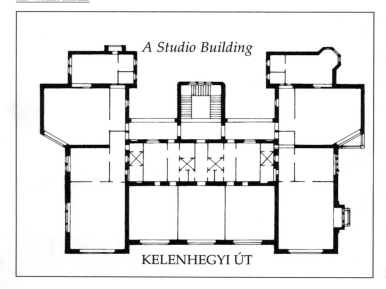

A Studio Building

KELENHEGYI ÚT

purpose was to control Castle Hill. It became municipal property in 1894, when parts of it were symbolically demolished. There have been plans to set up a Hungarian Pantheon or to make a relief map of Hungary here. It has been a prison camp, temporary accommodation for the homeless, the site of an anti-aircraft battery and finally, since 1961, a tourist attraction.

It is worth walking this far, if for no other reason than to hire a telescope to look down on the city. On 20 August, Gellért-hegy is the site of the great fireworks display, with the rockets released from various parts of the hill. The 14-metre-tall statue of the woman holding a palm leaf in her hands (1947, by Zsigmond Kisfaludi Strobl) is the Statue of Liberty, and commemorates liberation from Fascist rule, though it is said that she was originally designed as a memorial to the son of Regent Horthy, the ultra right-wing leader of the inter-war years. Liberty can be seen from all parts of the city; she has become the symbol of Budapest abroad and so is unlikely to be removed, unlike the Red Army soldier in bronze who used to stand guard at the base.

Instead of the usual path leading to the foot of the hill, let me recommend an even more pleasant route, threading between the villas of the hill. Find Verejték utca, then follow Kelenhegyi út down to the Gellért baths.

A STUDIO BUILDING *XI. Kelenhegyi út 12-14.* An art nouveau building made of traditional materials in a bold, functional way (Gyula Kosztolányi Kann, 1903). Painters and sculptors live here even today. Its architect is better known as a painter. Of his many building designs, few were actually built.

HOTEL GELLÉRT AND GELLÉRT BATHS 20C *XI. Kelenhegyi út 4.* If you follow the route I recommend, you first see the open-air part of the baths which has recently been enlarged. The new part is uncommonly well made; the post-modern softness matches the heavy bulk of the art nouveau building (by Ármin Hegedűs, Artúr Sebestyén and Izidor Stark) which was completed in 1918. The open-air swimming-pool stretches over to the other side of Kemenes utca and is connected to the main area by a subway.

'The Gellért Hotel looks like a huge white gem, and unlike other buildings, which go black with time, it grows whiter and whiter,' claims a friend of mine, who is also the illustrator of this book. The hotel, together with the baths, was built by the city as part of a conscious policy to make Budapest into a city of baths. If you cannot spare the time to swim, at least walk into the hall through the entrance at the side of the building for the sake of the mosaic floor and the glass ceiling. From the back of the hall you can look into the roofed-over part of the swimming-pool. Try to slip in — you are supposed to have a swimming-pool ticket. Hotel guests have a separate lift at their disposal to come down to the baths.

The main entrance of the hotel looks over the Danube. The lobby was rebuilt at the beginning of the 1960's, in the so-called 'Old Modern' style. Now it is beginning to look elegant in the same way as the 1965 Opel Rekord that fascinated me in front of this hotel one autumn day a long time ago. For this was the hotel where we could see all the latest models; for all I know Budapest schoolboys still go there to car-spot.

A rest: Grand Café Gellért — in the hotel

20 **A** Citadel **B** Statue of Liberty **C** Gellért Baths and the Hotel **D** Pauline Monastery **E** Liberty Bridge

PAULINE MONASTERY 20D *XI. Szt. Gellért rakpart 1/a.* This is another pseudo-historic building that fits wonderfully well in the surroundings. No one would think that it was built as late as 1932! (Károly Weichinger). It used to have a grotto chapel too. For forty years it was the student hostel of the Ballet Institution. I am not sure that the students felt at home in here.

The grotto that opens from the balcony nearby has recently been reconsecrated.

LIBERTY BRIDGE (SZABADSÁG HÍD) 20E–21AF *Linking Gellért tér (Buda) and Fővám tér (Pest).* The third permanent bridge (originally Francis Joseph Bridge) was opened on the occasion of the Millennium celebrations in 1896. Francis Joseph himself hammered in the last silver rivet. Not by hand, naturally: he pushed a button in a tent on the Pest side to operate the 45 ton hammer. There are very few things around which give a better example of how much the people took pleasure in ornaments. It would be difficult to imagine what the bridge would look like if the designers (Virgil Nagy and János Feketeházy) had not stuck to the following principles: 'When designing the bridge, we had to obey the requirements of beauty, simplicity and economy.' The bridge has a modular structure; that is, if the central part were removed, the rest would still stand firmly.

On top of each pillar, standing on a golden ball, is a 'Turul bird', the mythical bird of the Hungarians, stretching its wings, preparing to take off. Some would-be suicides still climb up here — most of them are rescued by the fire brigade. The famous silver rivet with the F. J. initials was stolen during World War I. So was its replacement. Today the rivet can be seen under a glass sheet. This one is not silver.

UNIVERSITY OF ECONOMIC SCIENCES 21B *IX. Fővám tér 8.* This neo-Renaissance building, originally the Main Customs Building, proved to be a trend-setter (Miklós Ybl, 1870–74), influencing construction all along Andrássy út. It has housed the university (formerly the Karl Marx University) since 1951. As an historic building it is protected; when the university wanted to add a floor to the old building, the request was rejected and they were ordered to restore the building. Starting either to the left, or to the right from the main entrance, you come to an inner courtyard, which is now covered with a glass roof, under which there is Karl Marx himself sitting in bronze. A bridge arches over the courtyard, commonly known as the 'Bridge of Sighs'. The cast iron pillars are still inscribed 'Ganz und Co. Ofen', the last word being the German name for Buda. It is well worth walking up and down the elegant staircases.

Various beams of light break through the windows at the most surprising places.

This university has an especially lively jazz-life; concerts are held not here but in the Közgáz Klub.

CENTRAL MARKET HALL (KÖZPONTI VÁSÁRCSARNOK) 21C *XI. Vámház körút 1-3.* At the end of the last century the city had five large, covered markets, all of which were built in a very similar style. All five were opened on the same day; the other four are in Rákóczi tér, Klauzál

Incredable !

tér, Hunyadi tér and in Hold utca. This one, designed by Samu Pecz, is the largest, and has six aisles along the sides of the 150-metre-long hall. The structure, the lighting and the coldstore were very modern in their time and are still in use. Formerly, laden barges sailed right into a special entrance; above its opening a notice says: 'TUNNEL INTO THE CENTRAL MARKET HALL'.

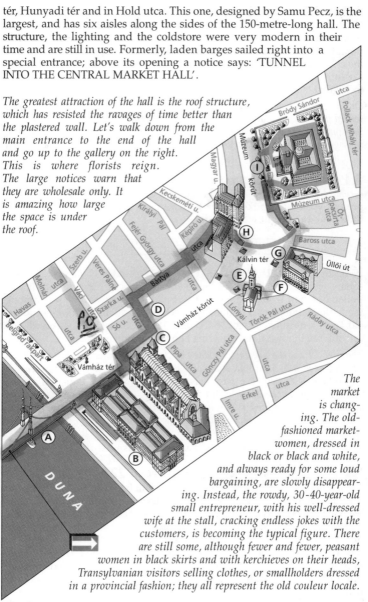

The greatest attraction of the hall is the roof structure, which has resisted the ravages of time better than the plastered wall. Let's walk down from the main entrance to the end of the hall and go up to the gallery on the right. This is where florists reign. The large notices warn that they are wholesale only. It is amazing how large the space is under the roof.

The market is changing. The old-fashioned market-women, dressed in black or black and white, and always ready for some loud bargaining, are slowly disappearing. Instead, the rowdy, 30-40-year-old small entrepreneur, with his well-dressed wife at the stall, cracking endless jokes with the customers, is becoming the typical figure. There are still some, although fewer and fewer, peasant women in black skirts and with kerchieves on their heads, Transylvanian visitors selling clothes, or smallholders dressed in a provincial fashion; they all represent the old couleur locale.

21 **A** Liberty Bridge **B** University of Economic Sciences **C** Central Market Hall **D** A part of the Medieval City Walls **E** Calvinist Church **F** Former 'Two Lions Inn' **G** Headquarters of an Insurance Company **H** Hotel Korona **I** National Museum

Burger King in a Butcher's Shop in the Ex-Hotel Nádor

V. Vámház körút 2. The building took its present form in 1840 and is now a residential block. There are quite a few neo-Classical buildings, even though the others may not have such fine proportions, in the quiet parts of the city, that is in the area between the Danube, the inner boulevard and Kossuth Lajos utca. This area is more or less as the Reform-Age city used to be (that is, before the 1848 Revolution).

On the ground floor, towards Vámház körút, there is a butcher's which has preserved its hundred-year-old, painted tiles. Here you can try the typical lunch of the simple clerks and old age pensioners in the area: have 100 grams of cooked sausage at the counter. Take some mustard or horse-radish and a slice of bread with it.

A Part of the Medieval City Wall of Pest 21D

V. Bástya utca, corner of Veres Pálné utca. The wall stretched in a semicircle from about the present Vigadó tér to Fővám tér. It was almost two kilometres long and a little more than eight metres high.

A rest: Fatál Restaurant — V. Váci utca 67.

Kálvin tér and the Eastern City Gate

V. Kálvin tér. This square was the site of one of the medieval gates of the city until it was pulled down in 1796. As many as five buildings survived the war, among them: the Calvinist church (József Hofrichter, József Hild, 1813–51) and the old Two Lions Inn, which operated until 1881 (Kálvin tér 9.), survived. You can still see the two lions cowering above the main entrance.

The silhouette of the city gate is hidden by the much-debated new hotel. You can have a look at it in New York-style café/salad bar/community space at the back of the section on the left. The gate is also recalled by a marble statue suffocating in the subway, at the Kecskeméti utca end. The statue, some people feel, is an attempt to represent the birth of the city, or rather a mother's lap, symbolically. For others, it is an all-too-convenient public convenience.

A rest: Korona Passage Pancake Bar

National Museum (Nemzeti Múzeum) 22A

VIII. Múzeum körút 14-16. The largest museum in the country, built between 1837 and 1847, to the plans of Mihály Pollack. At that time this was so far from town that the weekly fair was held in Kálvin tér and cattle sometimes wandered into the museum. It is almost 8,000 square metres in area, and has five independent departments: the Archaeological Collection, the Medieval Collection, the Modern Collection, the Numismatic Collection and the Historical Portrait Collection. A slow, painstaking reconstruction gathered momentum in 1994–95, in order to house the new 'History of Hungary' permanent exhibition.

It is a must for serious travellers. Despite the high standard of design, the bilingual inscriptions, the occasionally very imaginative multimedia programmes, the display is quite old-fashioned. It tends to induce a feeling of awe rather than to make people think. Some critics say that it fails to explain context. But it has meant that hundreds of objects could be restored, and properly and safely exhibited. In due course it could all be made livelier with programmable audio guides, (which might include minority opinions).

My absolute favourite is in the long 19th-century room: the full display of all the screws made by a particular factory, lovingly arranged on a large board. Look! We can produce all this!

My other favourite is a hidden part of the Exhibition, in the circular middle room. It is an unwanted memory of the Dark Fifties, when there was a temporary exhibition here promoting the eternal and unceasing (North) Korean-Hungarian Friendship. The decorators could not find a better technique for mounting the hundreds of letters than to drive them into the stone. Now, despite the hundreds of millions of forints invested, these scars are still there, even the

22 **A** National Museum **B** Eötvös University **C** University Church **D** Károlyi Palace, now the Museum of Literature **E** Hotel Astoria **F** East West Center **G** Headquarters of the World Alliance of Hungarians (former House of 'Soviet Culture and Science') **H** Block of flats **I** Synagogue

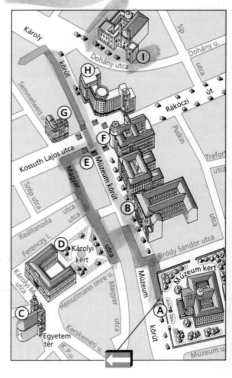

outlines of the letters can be made out. Can you see them?

The reconstruction of the National Museum is due to be completed in 2002, when the institution will be 200 years old. Currently a request to roof over the yard has been turned down by the Monuments Authority. And they failed to rechristen the nearby Kálvin tér metro station 'Kálvin tér — National Museum'. No big deal, they thought. It turned out to be impossible.

The museum played an important role on the first day of the 1848 Revolution. On 15th March a huge crowd of demonstrators gathered here to listen to the speeches of 'the Youth of March', their leaders. The speakers were standing on the wall left of the stairs while the crowd listened to them, clutching their umbrellas. Not everyone recognized the importance of the day; the director of the museum wrote in his diary: 'Some noisy mob had their hurly-burly outside which disturbed me in my work so I went home.' To the left on the ground floor are displayed the Crown Jewels of Hungary. They have a particularly spectacular history, having been lost, stolen or misappropriated at various times in history. The crown was made in the early Middle Ages, but has probably nothing to do with the one that was placed on the head of King St Stephen, the founder of the Hungarian state, in the year 1000. The last Hungarian king crowned with it was the Habsburg Charles VI, in 1916.

After World War II the crown was taken out of the country by escaping Hungarian fascists. Then it was held in the United States for decades until President Carter decided to return it to the Hungarian state. Secretary of State Cyrus Vance brought it back to Budapest in 1978, escorted by a large American delegation.

There are more than ten statues in the Museum Garden. There is even a column straight from the Forum Romanum, given by Italy in 1930. The garden is locked at 9 p.m.

And one more thing, on top of all: You should now return to Room 1, and have a quick look at the brick with an inscription, the one that marked the tomb of a 13th-century monk. It reads: 'Why are you staring at me? The way I look now, that's your future fate. You had better say an Our Father.'.

Around the Museum Garden *the aristocracy of the last century built their most beautiful town houses. Some of them are still standing, like the one at Ötpacsirta utca 2., which is now the headquarters of the Association of*

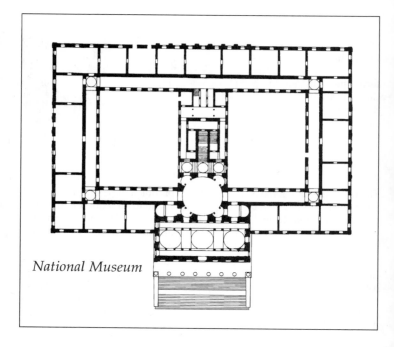

National Museum

director's choice • director's choice • director's choice

DR. FERENC SZIKOSSY, DEPUTY DIRECTOR GENERAL

1. The Hungarian Coronation Regalia — because it is one of the oldest of its kind in Europe — from the end of the 1200's to 1916. (Exhibited in a purpose-built room.) **2.** A Gothic stall from St Egidius' Church, 1483, with the coat of arms of King Matthias and his wife Beatrix. The other heraldry shows how lively foreign affairs were then. You can spot the Swedish, Norwegian, Spanish, English, French, and Cypriot coat of arms. (Room 5) **3.** A tablet to invite people to join the Silversmith's Guild of Brassó (now Brasov, Romania) 1556. A miniature tour de force. (Room 7) **4.** The Liberation of Buda: a wallcarpet, beginning of the 18th century. One of the very few pieces to depict an actual event from the history of Hungary. (Room 8) **5.** Lajos Kossuth's formal Governor's Costume. Following family traditions, I am biased towards Kossuth. (Room 12) **6.** A piece of the Iron Curtain, once in Hungary, because it was here in Hungary that this awful symbol of captivity was first breached.

Hungarian Architects, or another building on the corner of Múzeum utca and Pollack Mihály tér in line with the garden. Somewhat to the left of the latter there is a beautifully restored iron fence, which, however, hardly compensates for the sight of the glass blocks behind it. That is Radio Budapest.

At Múzeum körút 15. is the largest second-hand bookshop in Budapest. It has a wide range of antique books and foreign books. You may be lucky and find some surprising treasures, especially in German. Let's go back a couple of houses and go into No 21. It is a building with a passageway leading right through it and in the courtyard is part of the old city wall. On the other side there is a garden, Károlyi kert, where 15-20 years ago there used to be concerts in the summer. People could hire cushions to put on the uncomfortable chairs. The garden used to belong to a palace which was under reconstruction for years, but when it was ready, the tradition of the concerts was not revived. The streets around were already too noisy for music.

Behind Károlyi kert, Egyetemi templom (University Church) stretches its chubby spires. Since it has been surrounded by larger buildings, its fine proportions cannot be enjoyed. The best place to look at it is perhaps exactly here, at the entrance to the building we have come through. The peculiarity of the church is that it does not face east.

KÁROLYI GARDENS used to belong to an aristocratic family. It became a public park after World War I. It was not as nice as now, there was not even a fence around it. As I attended a nearby elementary school, we often came to play here, and to watch the chess players and the pigeons playing all kinds of games. It was here, mid-April 1966, that I was beaten up for the first (and last) time because of a girl. At the hands of a much smaller boy. And a much stronger one. I did not cry there and then, just round the corner. (By the way, I was beaten up two other times, but not because of a girl, or a woman.)

THE BACK YARD OF THE AUTHOR'S SCHOOL *Ferenczy István utca, the back of V. Reáltanoda utca 9.* When I was at that school, there were no cars in the back yard. None of the teachers had a car. We had endless long jump practices there instead. The favourite quip of the old PE teacher, called Yousouf, who led generations of students to victory in highschool championships (in basketball, not long jump, and not with me) was: 'My son, it's not worth running after a bus or a woman: the next one will be along soon enough.'

KÁROLYI PALACE: FUTURE HOME OF THE HOUSE OF HUNGARIAN LITERATURE *V. Károlyi Mihály utca 16.* Count Mihály Károlyi lived here, before he had to emigrate for the first time in 1919. It was confiscated from him for his alleged high treason. He became ambassador of Hungary to France after World War II, but resigned and stayed in France when the totalitarian madness took hold in 1949. Now the building houses the Museum of Hungarian Literature, and will undergo a thorough renovation by 2000 and all kinds of writers' associations, except for the most powerful, the Hungarian Writers' Union, will move in. Also, there will be a café and a bookshop, and a state-of-the-art library.

A rest: Café Talk Talk — Magyar utca 12-14.

HOTEL ASTORIA 22E *V. Kossuth Lajos utca 19.* This busy crossroads of the city has taken its name from the hotel which was built with an old fashioned touch (Emil Ágoston and Artúr Hikisch, 1912–14). The lobby of the hotel is luxuriously elegant, as was the café before reconstruction.

Astoria divides the inner boulevard road, Kiskörút, into two halves, which means that if you look towards the city, you will get to the Danube, no matter which direction you start walking, to the left, to the right or forward. The busy thoroughfare leading out of the city is Rákóczi út, a shopping street which goes as far as the yellow façade of Keleti Railway Station, visible in the distance. On one of the corners of Astoria there used to be a large empty site: only one half of the complex was ever completed (VII. Rákóczi út 4.: Béla Barát, Ede Novák, 1935; Rákóczi út 1.: Dezső Hültl, 1940); the war absorbed all the time and energy needed to finish the second half. The recent development doesn't really suit the surroundings — it's far too big and obtrusive, though it does try to echo the block opposite (Lajos Zalaváry, 1991).

This is where the National Theatre once stood — it was pulled down in 1908. The Astoria metro station on the Second (Red) Line can be reached from the subway although access is becoming more and more difficult, thanks to the crowds of street-vendors. The people wearing folk costumes are from Transylvania; they are Hungarians living in what is now Romania, who sell things they have brought from their villages. The men can easily be recognized by their straw hats, blue broadcloth jackets and black boots.

BROADWAY CINEMA *VII. Tanács körút 3.* This is the former cinema of the Institute of Cinematography, which has recently become a commercial outfit after many years of serving worthily as part of the education of Hungarian film buffs. There were always between six and eight films on at any one time, more even than advertised, in a complicated but logical

23 **A** Headquarters of the World Alliance of Hungarians (former House of 'Soviet Culture and Science') **B** Block of flats **C** Great Synagogue **D** Pest County Hall **E** Former Design Center **F** Budapest City Hall, former hospital for aged soldiers **G** Main Post Office **H** Servite Church **I** Parking block **J** Lutheran Church **K** Blocks of flats, the beginning of a never completed avenue

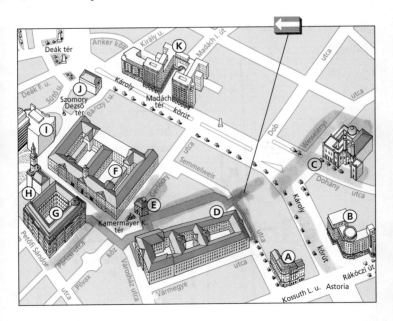

order, on the façade. Above the ticket office a display showed when and for which films you could get tickets. Unfortunately it did not compare with the Cinemathéque in Paris or the NFT in London in range of programming.

THE GREAT SYNAGOGUE 23C *VII. Dohány utca 2-8.* This is one of the largest synagogues in Europe (Ludwig Förster, 1844–59). The two onion-shaped domes are 43 metres high. Above the main entrance the Hebrew line reads: 'Make me a sanctuary and I will dwell among them' (Exodus 25, 8).

The building, which has three naves and a flat ceiling, holds almost 3,000 worshippers: 1,497 men on the ground floor and 1,472 women in the gallery. The 12-metre-wide central nave is built with cast iron in a single span. Both Ferenc Liszt and Saint-Saëns played the famous organ on several occasions.

The synagogue was originally built in a built-up area. One of the buildings inside the compound was the birthplace of Theodor Herzl, writer and journalist, who founded the Zionist movement (memorial tablet in the staircase of the corner building).

The arcade and the Temple of Heroes, which accommodates 250 people and is used for religious services on weekdays, were added when the building was enlarged (László Vágó and Ferenc Faragó, 1931). Outside hours of worship, the synagogue is open to visitors between 10 a.m. and 6 p.m. (3.30 p.m. in winter) on weekdays. *Not open when I walked by.*

The Holocaust Memorial *in the back garden (Imre Varga, 1989) stands directly above the mass graves dug during the 1944–45 Hungarian Fascist period. Each leaf of the tree carries the name of a martyr.*

In 1944, after the Nazi occupation of Hungary, Budapest Jews were forced to move into a ghetto (they had never lived in one before) as a preliminary to deportation. That finally — miraculously — didn't happen. But many died because

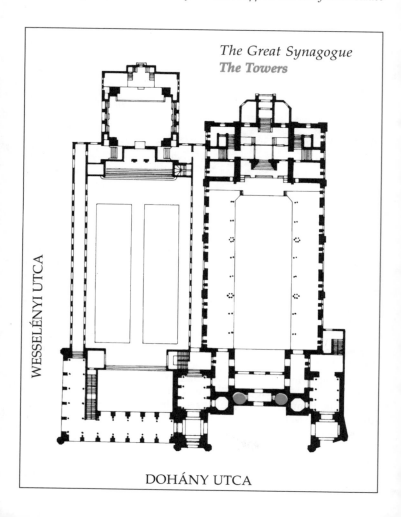

The Great Synagogue
The Towers

WESSELÉNYI UTCA

DOHÁNY UTCA

of ill health and starvation, or were randomly murdered. Before the war 5% of Hungary's population was Jewish; after the war it had dwindled to 0.5%. Practically all of them live in Budapest.

A rest: Fausto's — Dohány utca 5.

RÖSER BAZAAR *V. Károly körút 22.* In Farsi the word 'bazaar' means marketplace, a broad street. In Budapest, it is usually a building with a passageway full of shops and workshops. They have recently begun to come to life again.

COUNTY HALL (PEST MEGYEI KÖZGYŰLÉS) 23D *V. Városház utca 7.* If you follow the route in this book, you can go into the County Hall from the back, between 6 a.m. and 5 p.m. on a workday. You should pretend that you belong here — then you will not be stopped. The three-part building was completed in 1811, 1832 and 1841. This surprising oasis also contained the county prison and the prisoners'chapel. If you find the near gate locked, walk round the building from the right, via Vitkovics Mihály utca.

A rest: Galleria Drink — Vitkovics Mihály utca 6.

BUDAPEST CITY HALL (POLGÁRMESTERI HIVATAL) 23F *V. Városház utca 9-11.* Construction of this building started in 1711; it was to have been a home for disabled soldiers covering an area of 189 x 189 metres. In the end only the east wing was built (Anton Erhard Martinelli, Court Architect, finished 1747) and this housed two thousand soldiers. Maria Theresa found it more beautiful than her own palace in Vienna. The rest of the building was never built, simply because permission was not given to break through the city wall. Later it became the Károly Army Barracks, and it has been the Town Hall since 1894. There are 47 windows in each row of the façade. The statues above the main entrance are new.

MERLIN THEATRE AND CLUB *(Entrance from V. Gerlóczy utca 4.)* Originally conceived by City Hall masterminds as a drama school and English speaking theatre, the latter working only during the summer and providing an income for the school, which would run all year long... Then the two founders quarrelled, and only the drama school remained. A very lively egghead hangout, a club and a restaurant, with sophisticated video screens so that everything is visible from all tables simultaneously.

Actor/director/teacher/fundraiser Tamás Jordán originally trained as an engineer before spending almost two decades as the ever more brilliant star of a successful theatre company in Kaposvár; he came to Budapest less than ten years ago. It is his radiant personality that lures people here, his fun and amiable character. Until quite recently you could see his breathtaking one-man show: *The Apology of Socrates* by Plato.

Plays are occasionally given in English, but rarely the lighthearted, funny entertainment tourists or even travellers might get hooked on.

MAIN POST OFFICE 23G, 24A *V. Városház utca 13-15. Back door V. Városház utca 18.* This is the building that blocks the view of the Town Hall (Antal Skalniczky, 1875). Let's walk through it on the ground floor. As soon as I entered I could count four types of marble and six types of painted

24 **A** Main Post Office **B** Hotel Taverna **C** Fontana Department Store **D** McDonald's **E** Hotel Marriott **F** Vigadó **G** Gerbeaud **H** Luxus Department Store **I** Office block **J** Parking block **K** Servite Church **L** Budapest City Hall **M** Lutheran Church

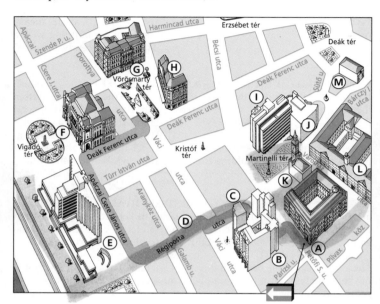

marble at the foot of the stairs. This is where Poste Restante letters are held. Since the post office bought a Japanese lettersorting machine a few years ago, non-standard envelopes need more stamps. Not surprisingly, the standard formats are $1/4$ and $1/3$ of the A4 format.

A BLOCK OF FLATS FROM THE EARLY FORTIES *V. Párisi utca 6.* Only a few inhabitants of the city raise their heads to inspect the vivid, elegant façade of this building from Párisi utca. It was built in the middle of the war (Gedeon Gerlóczy, 1942–44).

HOTEL TAVERNA 24B *V. Váci utca 20.* We saw the façade on the First Walk. Now let's walk just as far as the crossing in the inner yard, and there, at the small clock tower, we turn right. On the four sides of the tower, four little statues with marvellously liquid lines show the pleasures of relaxation (Géza Stremeny, 1985).

A ROW OF LAMPS *V. Régiposta utca 10., between ground floor and first floor.* Art nouveau neglected the cult of lions in Pest; these lamps are a rare exception. Rescue teams have been organized to save and repair the old lamps. In Váci utca there are too many of them — too much antiquarianism is as bad as none.

A rest: Pierrot in Pest — Aranykéz utca 2.

ARANYKÉZ UTCA 2. *The corner of V. Régiposta utca. Th̲* native design recalls the Vigadó (Miklós and Ernő Román̲ ground floor is occupied by offices, the lift starts from the level o̲ zanine. The City Protection Association has a special task force spec̲ in old lifts, in an attempt to save as many as possible.

Apáczai Csere János utca was on the river before the building of the quạ̲ now it is overshadowed by the back of the Marriott Hotel. The street is homogeneous, all neo-Classical buildings, all built with taste and all with their own surprises. At No 3. there is a half-naked beauty in marble, musing in the staircase, trying to hide one of her breasts behind a colourful and inadequate bunch of flowers. (Her name is Persephone.) At No 5. there are some exceptionally pretty iron grilles, as well as wooden and stone ornaments to protect the corners of the building. A building company has moved into No. 7. Behind the gate the surprise is another door and some fine statuary.

This walk took me four and a half hours and that was without going into the National Museum. I collapsed on the terrace of Dunacorso. This café existed at the time of the old Promenade. Then I went to the Hyatt hotel to inspect the aeroplane. I would have liked to go to the top floor by lift, but now this is only for hotel guests. Even the price of the cheapest room seemed to be too much for a ride in a lift.

WALK THREE 125

...s boldly imagi-
..., 1930). The
...f the mez-
...ializing

*Andrássy út
and
Városliget* This walk follows the
'Radial Avenue' at first. We shall look
at two apartments here, get a bird's-
eye view of Városliget and if we like,
row on the lake (or skate if it is
winter-time). We shall visit a castle
that is not part of the Amusement
Park and return by the underground
built for the Great Exhibition. Time:
approximately 5 hours.

'MERINO' TEXTILE SHOP *V. Petőfi Sándor utca 20.* The older generation
simply call it 'Brammer's'. Ödön Brammer, a textile merchant, built the
shop in 1924, when he had to move from a shop which he had been running successfully for years. His materials with their red, white and green
labels were to be found in most large department stores in Western Europe
at the beginning of the century. The English mahogany decoration of the
shop is under a preservation order which means that not even a single nail
can be hammered into the walls. During the decades of state ownership,
the restorer wished to emphasize this by adding the state coat of arms in
several dozen places on the old plaster decoration on the ceiling.

FORMER TÖRÖK BANK BUILDING *V. Szervita tér 3.* The façade is an
architectural battle field between art nouveau and modernism (designed by
Ármin Hegedűs and Henrik Bőhm, 1906). This building is typical of the
city, with offices on the first two or three floors and flats above that. The
title of the large glass mosaic is *The Apotheosis of Hungary*. The modern elements seem to dominate now, perhaps because the astonishingly heavy
Atlas statue, which used to crown the building, has been removed.
Unfortunately the bank's owner was not a relative of mine.

RÓZSAVÖLGYI HOUSE *V. Szervita tér 5.* The building (Béla Lajta, 1912)
was commissioned by a tailor. 'In Hungary the buildings speak French,
German, Spanish, English but not Hungarian,' the architect declared. Few
were able to find such a modern way of speaking Hungarian! The building takes its name from the music shop, established in 1850 and still there.
The original interior was destroyed by fire on 14 August 1961, as pointed
out by a little inscription, in Hungarian only and placed almost invisibly
high. A marvellous range of scores and old records.

*Unfortunately the new buildings in the square look out of place with the old. A
government building and a multi-storey car-park, which criminally make the
square smaller, and a telephone exchange that clashes with the church, were all
built in the 1970's.*

IN MEMORIAM CAFÉ QUINT *V. Bárczi István utca 1.* Behind the modest sign and the shopwindow there used to be a uniquely preserved interior. It probably dated from the end of the fifties, but the style was not so different from that of pre-war Budapest. You could drink one of the best coffees in Pest here, which was made with the antique instruments displayed on the counter. Even the waitresses were conservative in their dress and manners. The caricatures on the wall commemorated the fencing victories of the proprietor, Mr. Kovács, world champion and Olympic medallist. In the middle there were plastic boxes with transparent lids — good cookies in boxes made for sewing machine spare parts. The cham-

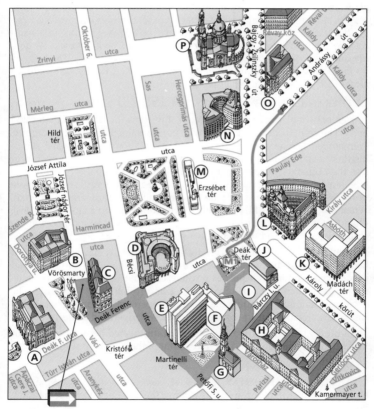

25 A Vigadó B Gerbeaud C Luxus Department Store D Grand Hotel Corvinus Kempinski E Office block F Parking block G Servite Church H Budapest City Hall I Lutheran Museum J Lutheran Church K Block of flats L 'Anker' palace, former Insurance Company M Coach station, the most recent of Hungary's listed architectural monuments (1949), building site of the new National Theatre N Trade Center O Office block P St Stephen's Church.

pion died soon after the shop was sold. After a ludicruous year, the café was given a Miro-inspired face-lift. It has become a pleasant place, especially the upstairs part.

Stop here for a moment to think about vanishing Budapest. Inside the café, after a horrible year, there is life once more. The recent redesign has given the place some originality again. It might even get to attract a clientèle of its own.

There are not as many types of coffee in Budapest as in Vienna; people simply ask for 'kávé', 'fekete' or 'dupla', which all refer to exactly the same thing: black espresso coffee. (The word 'dupla' has survived from about twenty years ago, when 'szimpla', a smaller portion, still existed.) For a cup of strong, Italian espresso-type coffee, about 6 grammes of pure ground coffee are used, and people drink it with or without sugar, milk, cream or whipped cream. In larger cafés you can order two different types of white coffee: one is made with real black coffee, the other with coffee substitute. Decaffeinated coffee is increasingly available, especially in hotels. Most Hungarians still think it an affectation. We only live once, they think, and then Hungarians don't live very long. The best coffee these days is to be found in the tiny shops of the COQUAN'S chain, in Nádor utca or Ráday utca, for instance.

LUTHERAN CHURCH AND MUSEUM 25I, 25J *V. Deák Ferenc tér 4.*

A memorial tablet says 'Sándor Petőfi, the romantic poet, was educated here.' The church attracts attention with its unornamented, spireless dignity. I remember there was a gigantic bust of Luther in the tiny courtyard, standing there as if it had grown out of the ground. It is not here any more. I went into the Lutheran Museum to ask about it. In the classrooms of the former school a touching exhibition has been arranged. Old clergymen, now pensioners, show visitors around and answer questions (in German as well). When examining one of the treasures of the collection, an altar-cloth of 1650, I had two questions put to me. Why do the disciples have red noses in the embroidered cloth and which of the disciples is missing?

The church (Mihály Pollack, 1799–1808), did originally have a spire but it had to be pulled down when the roof structure, which the Lutherans had been forced to build as cheaply as possible, could no longer carry it. The interior of the church is amazingly simple, even by Lutheran standards. The choir was built only to muffle the echo. It is open only during services. The church is a vigorous musical centre, with concerts advertised on the front gate.

The Luther statue, I learned, had been left unfinished because of the war. Recently it was finished and set up in front of the Theological Academy in the XIVth district.

UNDERGROUND RAILWAY MUSEUM *In the subway at Deák tér.* When

building the metro station, a short section of the first line became redundant. Some old carriages are exhibited here beside the old platform — and that is the whole museum. A tablet in four languages near the entrance gives a short history of the 'Francis Joseph Underground Railway', which was opened in 1896. There are more than the usual number of mistakes in the English version. If you walk to the end of the museum, it is there that the story really begins. The little museum has preserved the smell of the old line as well. Unfortunately, you cannot go into the old carriages. (I've seen rare exceptions made, however.) Entry into the museum is by tram ticket.

After the museum, let's go one stop by underground, which is now the First (Yellow) Metro Line (or, as people refer to it, the 'little metro'), in the direction of Mexikói út.

May 16 1997 was a historic day in Hungarian theatre and architectural history alike, for it saw the announcement of the winner of the competition for the new National Theatre. Fourteen members of the fifteen-strong jury voted for the design of Ferenc Bán, chief architect of Nyíregyháza. Neither the second nor the third prize was awarded, just the honourable mentions. Altogether there were 72 entries, and all kinds of ideas. One experimented with pieces from the facades of temporary homes of the National. (The company is in its fouth temporary home; 'she' has never yet played in a theatre specifically built for her.) Another suggestion was to put the stages and auditoria together under a gigantic, transparent Holy Crown of Hungary.

Controversy almost killed this idea off too. Opinion-makers hated the idea all along. They tend to think that Hungary has too many (almost 50) permanent repertory theatres and that to have a few less of these would make more sense than setting up a big new one. But polls steadily showed that people love the idea. Maybe not this particular idea for a building... But people hated the Beaubourg in the beginning, too.

Mr Bán's highly original design will rejuvenate the area just as the Centre Pompidou did in Paris. Come back and have a look at it in October 2000.

When you come up out of the station, you can see Andrássy út, originally Sugárút, or 'Radial Avenue', in front of you, a masterpiece of the bold city planning of the last century. It was finished in 1885 after fourteen years of building, in the course of which 219 houses, mostly one-storey, had to be demolished. Although few of the individual buildings stand out from the homogeneous ensemble, it is one of the finest streets in the eclectic style in Europe. Not that everyone shares this opinion: an American guidebook claims that the buildings of the road are 'an architectural hodgepodge, although most of them are described as neo-Classical'. I would call it neo-Renaissance (or eclectic), and not neo-Classical, which is called Classicist in Hungary.

The city was so anxious to preserve the character of its beloved Sugárút that no form of public transport was allowed to ruin it, though eventually they did allow a three-kilometre long underground line beneath it. This was built between 1894 and 1896, and was the second underground railway in Europe after the Metropolitan Line in London. The terminus at the other end was not where it is now, but above ground, in Városliget. Long ago, there used to be a lamp at the entrances to the stations that lit up when a train was coming.

The name changes of Andrássy út are instructive: Sugár (Radial), Andrássy (after the 19th-century statesman), Stalin (after the wise father of the world's proletariat), Hungarian Youth (in the days of the Revolution of '56), Népköztársaság (People's Republic, 1957-89) and now again Andrássy — the name that real Budapesters never stopped using.

AN UPPER-UPPER MIDDLE CLASS APARTMENT — THE POSTAL MUSEUM *VI. Andrássy út 3. First floor.* The building used to be a residential block (Győző Czigler, 1886), and is typical of the more decorative buildings on Sugárút. There are frescos on the staircase (Károly Lotz).

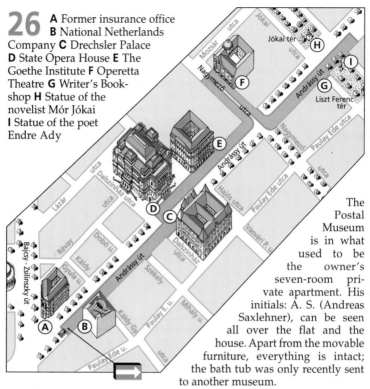

26 **A** Former insurance office **B** National Netherlands Company **C** Drechsler Palace **D** State Ópera House **E** The Goethe Institute **F** Operetta Theatre **G** Writer's Bookshop **H** Statue of the novelist Mór Jókai **I** Statue of the poet Endre Ady

The Postal Museum is in what used to be the owner's seven-room private apartment. His initials: A. S. (Andreas Saxlehner), can be seen all over the flat and the house. Apart from the movable furniture, everything is intact; the bath tub was only recently sent to another museum.

The individual items of the collection can be put into operation by the attendants. You can see a section of a pneumatic exchange. There is a good view of the dome of the Basilica from an unexpected angle.

DUTCH INSURANCE COMPANY HEADQUARTERS (HOLLAND BIZTOSÍTÓ SZÉKHÁZA) 26B *VI. Andrássy út 9.* The unusual outcome of the recent renovation cannot be seen from street level. As if the Lord Almighty had left a huge drop on the roof, to make room for the Board of Directors. You can walk up, and look up at the covered courtyard. The basement is painted black: a sort of Hades.

The block behind was pulled down, and an entirely new building was erected.

By the way, I have been cold-called by the firm at least four times, very aggressively. But considering all the new construction, this technique must work with certain people.

ÚJ SZÍNHÁZ (NEW THEATRE) *VI. Paulay Ede utca 35.* The pre-World War I cabaret (by Béla Lajta) has been modernized a couple of times since it opened in 1909. During a recent facelift, the façade was restored in an exemplary way (Kőnig & Wagner Associates, Budapest, 1990.) As

the designer explained at a press conference, the restoration of the façade cost only 1/75th of the total budget. The foyer is somewhat controversial, reminding some of us of Trump Tower, New York City. The auditorium is marvellous, though. After the first three years the general director's appointment was not prolonged, though theatre people wanted him stay on.

State Opera House

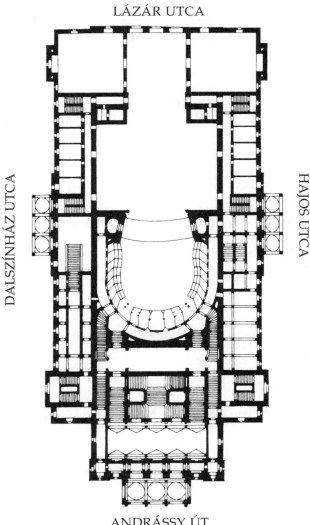

LÁZÁR UTCA

DALSZÍNHÁZ UTCA

HAJÓS UTCA

ANDRÁSSY ÚT

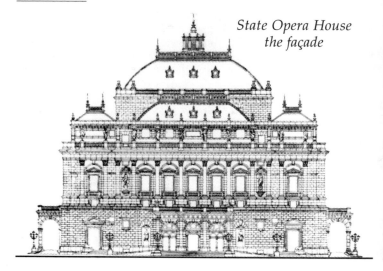

*State Opera House
the façade*

A rest: Picasso Point — Hajós utca 31.

STATE OPERA HOUSE 26D *VI. Andrássy út 22.* This is the most important building on this walk and one of the most important buildings in the history of Hungarian architecture (Miklós Ybl, 1884). Work on the building lasted nine years; the architect, who also directed the construction work, is said to have checked every cartload of bricks.

The huge building, perhaps because of its nature, does not look that large at all, except perhaps when viewed from Gellért-hegy. On the right there is the stage-door, on the left the carriage-way and entrance to the Royal Staircase. The auditorium seats 1,289 people. It was lovingly restored in the 1980's.

Both inside and out the building is decorated with hundreds of statues and paintings. In the niche to the right of the carriage entrance is a statue of Ferenc Liszt, to the left one of Ferenc Erkel, the father of Hungarian opera. In the niches at the corner of the building at the first-floor level are statues of the muses of opera: Terpsichore, Erato, Thalia and Melpomene.

On the stone cornice of the terrace above the second-floor level are the statues of (from left to right) Monteverdi, Alessandro Scarlatti, Gluck, Mozart, Beethoven (on the left); Rossini, Donizetti, Glinka, Wagner, Verdi, Gounod, Bizet (in the middle); Mussorgsky, Tchaikovsky, Moniuszko and Smetana (on the right).

The Opera House quickly became one of the leading musical centres of Europe. Gustav Mahler was the director here for three seasons and personally directed two Puccini operas. Otto Klemperer was briefly director here after the war. At present they have a repertoire of about ninety operas, more than any other company in the world. The Erkel Theatre, seating 2,400 people, also belongs to the Opera.

The box-office is on the left-hand side of the building and is open between 10 a.m. and 7 p.m. from Tuesday to Saturday (lunchbreak between 2 and 2.30 p.m.) and between 10 a.m. and 1 p.m. on Sunday. The decoration of the box office is in keeping with the rest of the building. The brass railings are intended to ensure civilized queuing. There are nearly always some tickets available on the day of the performance, albeit for the worst seats. When I last went to buy a ticket on a November morning I had no difficulty in getting one for the same evening. However, stamped on the ticket was: 'Warning! The stage cannot be seen from this seat.'

Seats like that (all in the upper circle) are accessible from a separate staircase through a side entrance. In fact I could not see anything of the stage although I could hear everything perfectly. I was sitting quite close to the fresco on the ceiling showing Olympus and all the Greek gods (by Károly Lotz) and closer still to the stalls. You can usually go down and take one of those seats in the interval.

There is an Opera Shop to the right of the main entrance, with very good books, collectibles & CDs. You can shop during the interval and then go back to pick up your purchases after the performance.

DRECHSLER HOUSE 26C *VI. Andrássy út 25.*

The apartment block opposite the Opera House took its name from a large café which used to occupy the ground floor (Ödön Lechner and Gyula Pártos, 1882). Six successive owners went bankrupt or committed suicide; this may not necessarily be the reason why the café disappeared.

Now the building houses the State Ballet Institute, whose students are on the move in and out at all times of the day. You can walk through the inner courtyard of the building which has an enchanting atmosphere (in winter time only one of the gates is open). The BREAKDANCE graffito gives you an idea how long it is since the building was last redecorated.

GOETHE INSTITUTE 26E *VI. Andrássy út 24.*

A plaque at the gate commemorates the fact that here stood, to the right of the gate, the Café Three Ravens (Három holló), where that genius of early twentieth-century poetry, Endre Ady, spent most of his evenings. The Hungarian government offered the premises for use as a Romanian Cultural Centre, to be opened on the same day as a Hungarian one was opened in Bucharest. But all that was kept in secret, and nothing happened for fifteen years. The ground floor meanwhile was vacant. The Goethe Institute then bought the space and launched their very attractive programmes. Cafe Eckermann was recently opened inside, with free Internet access in the afternoon. (One of the best kept secrets of the city.)

MŰVÉSZ CONFECTIONER'S *VI. Andrássy út 29.*

It opens early in the morning, at 8 a.m. (10 a.m. on Saturday). This intimate middle-class place is rather noisy early on because of the staff but later their chatter is drowned out by the hum of the customers. I like sitting in the inner room, left of the marble lady, who has an intense charm from the front. At around 9 a table of old show-business hands come together. At around 10 a very old, solitary man arrives and sits at his 'törzsasztal' (table reserved for a regular customer), in the right-hand corner. He is the doyen of men of letters, a prolific author responsible for dozens of historical novels. The ancient wooden coathanger in the self-service cloakroom, with the initials E. J. on it, is his. Don't use it.

Fresh pastry arrives around half past eight. I usually order a white coffee, a French brioche and the chandelier. They are reluctant to turn on the chandelier in the middle. Closed on Sundays.

Andrássy út is cut in half by a market place, which used to be at Nagymező utca. The part which is now to the left of the road is nicknamed the Broadway of Pest. It has three theatres, a nightclub and the famous former Arizona nightclub, hence the name of the theatre next door. The short section to the right has a theatre, a cinema, an exhibition hall and a 'little green house', an old public lavatory.

A con-man at the end of the century one morning started taking measurements at the upper end of Váci utca, attracting a great deal of attention. Finally a shopkeeper came out of his shop and asked him what he was doing. He replied that he was going to put up a 'green house' there. The shopkeeper gave him some money to build it ten metres down the street, away from his door. There another shopkeeper came out and the whole story started all over again.

MANÓ MAI HOUSE *VI. Nagymező utca 20.* The future home of the House of Hungarian Photograpy was originally built for Manó Mai imperial and royal court photographer in 1894. Photograpy was then a craft of high prestige — this building is one of the few purpose-built elegant sunlight studio complexes that survived. It has had an adventurous life since the original owner died: there was a cinema, then cabaret, later the Hungarian Automobile Club owned it. The House will be fully operational by 2000. You can visit the tiny second-hand photograpy bookshop on the mezzanine on all weekdays. Look at the little cherub with old fashioned camera at the right side of the ground floor. A great building to be filled with interesting life soon — a reason in itself to return to Budapest again.

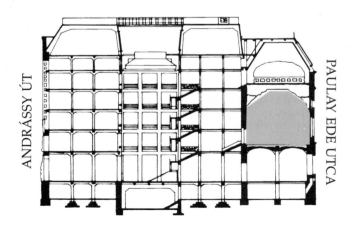

Divatcsarnok Department Store Lotz Hall

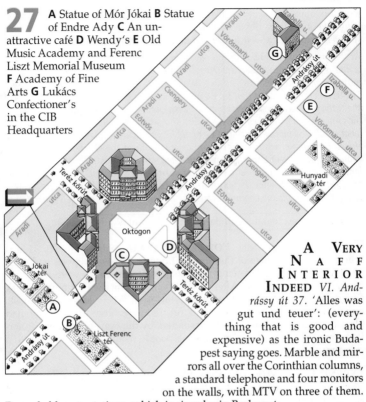

27 A Statue of Mór Jókai **B** Statue of Endre Ady **C** An unattractive café **D** Wendy's **E** Old Music Academy and Ferenc Liszt Memorial Museum **F** Academy of Fine Arts **G** Lukács Confectioner's in the CIB Headquarters

A VERY NAFF INTERIOR INDEED *VI. Andrássy út 37.* 'Alles was gut und teuer': (everything that is good and expensive) as the ironic Budapest saying goes. Marble and mirrors all over the Corinthian columns, a standard telephone and four monitors on the walls, with MTV on three of them. Remarkably ostentatious; which is singular in Budapest.

The cakes are outstanding, despite the heavy hand with the sugar. Service is attentive and quick. For the sake of American readers: 'naff' in British English means something like 'tacky'. In Hungarian: 'ciki'. A word that spread like prairie fire in the seventies.

DIVATCSARNOK DEPARTMENT STORE *Andrássy út 29.* This seven-storey building, built for the old Parisian Department Store, opened its doors in 1911. Before that there had been a casino on the site. The architect succeeded in persuading the owners to preserve the large ballroom, which is now called 'Lotz terem' (Lotz Hall) and can be seen at the back of the department store between the first and the second floors. Sales and Christmas toy sales are held there. The roof garden, however, can no longer be visited, which is a pity since it had a splendid view. Now there is nothing to recall the slogan that appeared on handbills the year the department store was opened: 'The oldest European-standard department store in the country'.

At the crossing of Andrássy út and the Nagykörút, the buildings form an octagonal square, hence its name, Oktogon, used during all those 40-odd years when the signs showed 'November 7 Square'. There is an old café in the square, rebuilt in appalling taste, a shop where you can buy various drinks, a Burger King (the biggest in the world) which is one of the most refreshing modern spaces in town today — it would make a perfect Amsterdam-style 'grand café'.

At this point the road widens and makes room for four rows of trees. Where there is now a pavement, between the trees, was once a riding track. The road was paved with wooden cubes to absorb the noise of cartwheels and hooves. The trees were planted at that time and were undisturbed for about 90 years, until about ten years ago some men appeared with chainsaws one morning and removed the crown off most of them. This shocked the people of Budapest, who were somewhat comforted by the Parks and Gardens Department's explanation that it was a choice between pruning the trees or watching them die. It didn't prove to be enough, and most of the trees have since had to be replaced. The new-old, recast lamps have recently been set up, paid for entirely by donations. The big ones cost 150,000, the small ones 45,000 forints. (About 9000 and 3000 dollars, respectively.) A small plaque commemorates the donors' names — mostly corporate.

A rest: Falafel Faloda upstairs — Paulay Ede utca 53.

THE FORMER SECRET POLICE BUILDING *Andrássy út 60.* This is where the secret police of the ultra-rightwing inter-war régime had their headquarters. Many left-wing activists and Communists were detained, beaten and tortured here. After World War II, during the Communist 'dark fifties', their secret police kept the premises on. Many left-wing activists and Communists were detained and tortured here. Some of those who had already been there. They were 'persuaded' by the same equipment, inherited from the previous régime... Some people would like to turn it into a museum of Stalinism.

FERENC LISZT MUSEUM AND MEMORIAL BUILDING 27E *VI. Vörösmarty utca 35.* It is only in our own time that Ferenc Liszt has gained recognition as a composer, although he always had a cult following in Hungary; despite not speaking the language, he always declared himself to be a Hungarian. His concerts at home were great events. After his years in Paris, Weimar and Rome, he settled in Pest in 1875, partly because he wanted to found a Hungarian Royal Academy of Music in his own house. He moved into this building in 1879, occupying the first floor, where the museum is now housed. In the hall you can see the copper plate which was on the door of one of his apartments. The inscription says in Hungarian and in German: 'Ferenc Liszt is at home between 3 and 4 p.m. on Tuesdays, Thursdays and Saturdays'. Visiting hours are now longer: between 10 a.m. and 6 p.m. from Monday to Friday and between 9 a.m. and 5 p.m. on Saturdays. Most of the pieces in the apartment are original. There are many portraits, beautifully decorated rare musical instruments, even Liszt's travelling keyboard and his glass piano. Andrássy út can be viewed from the window.

At the entrance Liszt records and various editions related to the composer can be bought. There are several small concert and rehearsal halls in the building and the sound of rehearsals can usually be heard. The building resounds with music. Through a window on the ground floor you can peep into a wind instrument workshop where the students' instruments are repaired.

The Old Exhibition Hall (Képzőművészeti Főiskola)

VI. Andrássy út 69. This building, which was erected by public subscription, tries to summarize all of architecture (Adolf Lang, 1877).

Now it houses the offices of the School of Fine Arts, and has recently started to organize exhibitions again. Everything inside, even the ceiling, is of marble – some genuine, some faux. The State Puppet Theatre gives performances in the basement.

Café Lukács and Cib Bank Headquarters 27G *VI. Andrássy út 70.* The imaginative conversion of this building put an end to a decade of stagnation in the life of this nicest of the handful of truly grand cafés. It once belonged to the Lukács family. It was confiscated in 1949 and closed to the public — it became the cafeteria of the secret police.

When I was a student, you could choose between the Baroque splendour upstairs and the 1930's elegance on the ground floor. Service was considerably slower upstairs but one could admire the naked porcelain lady combing her hair on the marble fireplace. You can still buy a copy in most large souvenir shops, in different sizes. The lower floor used to have some furniture in the corridor leading to the service area, that evoked the times of Jean Cocteau. This is all gone now. But

there is new life. The times they are a-changing... we sang with Bob Dylan, when I was twenty. But changes then in Hungary changed nothing. Now they do, at a Chicago pace again, in this, the second exuberant fin-de-siècle in Budapest's history.

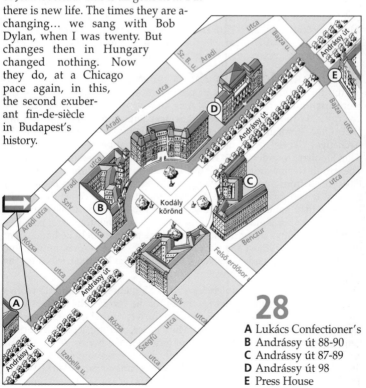

28

A Lukács Confectioner's
B Andrássy út 88-90
C Andrássy út 87-89
D Andrássy út 98
E Press House

The new café is a typical showcase.

Kodály körönd *is one of the finest circuses of the city. It is made up of four town houses whose shape forms the circle that gives the circus (körönd) its name. Of the four, architectural experts usually prefer the one at No. 88-90; my own favourite is No. 87-89, perhaps because of its rambling turret-rooms. One of them was the studio of Jenő Barcsay, the recently deceased master of modern Hungarian painting. The same block has a Zoltán Kodály museum in what used to be the composer's rooms.*

Further along from the Kodály körönd, the road becomes even more airy. The houses are further apart and hide behind front gardens. Further still the road is lined with detached villas. Unfortunately permission was given after the last war to build four modern buildings on this stretch. Two of them are especially out of place and of strikingly inferior quality.

HUNGARIAN PRESS BUILDING **28E** *VI. Andrássy út 101.* The plans for this fine example of an art nouveau villa are missing from the archives; all we know is that it was built sometime between 1900 and 1903 for the 'Timber-king of Szolnok' (a country town) and that for a short time it housed the Turkish Embassy. No two windows are the same. My favourite ornaments are the birds under the windows on the first floor and the stairs to the twin chimneys. Above the birds you can see some strange, totally non-functional iron consoles. They used to hold up a large sign saying 'Huszonötödik Színház' (25th Theatre), which was the 25th professional theatre company in Hungary. In the early seventies I often came here to watch their progressive, modern performances.

MILLENNARY MONUMENT **29E** *XIV. Hősök tere.* Erected in 1896 to celebrate the 1000th anniversary of the arrival in the Danube Plain of the Hungarian invaders from Central Asia, this was designed by the sculptor György Zala and the achitect Albert Schickedanz; and not completed until 1929. On a 36-metre pillar, exactly on the axis of Andrássy út, stands the Archangel Gabriel, who, according to legend, appeared in a dream to King Stephen, founder of the Hungarian state, and offered him the crown. The group was awarded the Grand Prix at the 1900 World Exhibition in Paris. Seen from opposite the angel, it looks a bit rigid and theatrically solemn. If you face the statue, the wings will seem to cover the angel's hands as they hand over the crown. But if you stand to the side, or even on the steps of one of the museums, you will see how the angel balances on a ball, nearly floating in the air, and how affectionately he hands over the crown, with almost the whole of his body. The figures around the pedestal are the legendary 'Seven Chieftains' who led their tribes on the conquest of present-day Hungary.

The colonnade has two semicircles and is 85 metres wide and 25 metres deep. Notice the symbolic figures on top of the corner pillars. The two in the middle are especially remarkable. On the left War whips his horses into an even more frantic gallop; opposite him Peace, carrying a palm leaf, rides gently out, his calm apparently communicated to the horses. At the far left are Work and Welfare, and at the far right Knowledge and Glory. Some of the statues of kings on the colonnade were changed after World War II. Those of Habsburg rulers (Ferdinand I, Charles III, Maria Theresa, Leopold

29 **A** Press House **B** Museum of Fine Arts **C** Tomb of the Unknown Soldier **D** The Archangel Gabriel and the Seven Chieftains **E** Millennary Monument **F** Restaurant Gundel **G** Zoo **H** Palm House in the Zoo **I** Bird House in the Zoo **J** Exhibition Hall

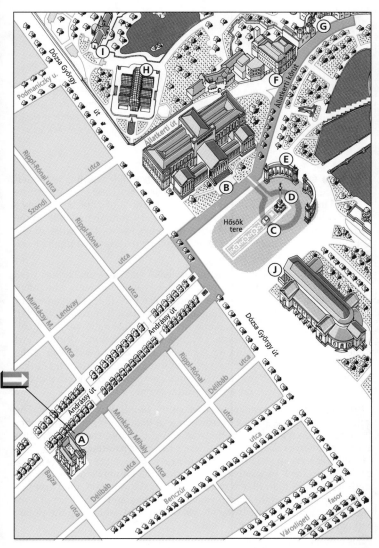

II, and Francis Joseph) were replaced by heroes of the Hungarian struggle for freedom. Here also is the Tomb of the Unknown Soldier. The pavement was recently relaid and made as smooth as glass; the square turned into a meeting place for skaters and skateboarders.

director's choice • director's choice • director's choice

MIKLÓS MOJZER, GENERAL DIRECTOR *(no directions given, since the collection is being moved around in the wake of extensive renovation. Find them...!) The dual main staircase, with the Marble Hall between them: a formidable and authentically original space by Albert Schikedanz.*
• *Ionic Hall — the most cheerful space of the building, a reminder of the fact that the building was also intended as a showpiece of architectural styles.*
• *Lombard Renaissance Hall, with the Madonna of Lod altarpiece by Boltraffio, and a series of outstanding pieces from Leonardo's immediate circle.* • *The Apostle James defeating the Moors by Tiepolo. There is not a single more triumphal piece in the entire Italian collection.* • *The small bronze equestrian statue of Francis I by Leonardo. The high point of the Renaissance collection.* • *Mary Magdalene, by Greco. One of the painter's undoubted masterpieces.*

MUSEUM OF FINE ARTS 29B *XIV. Hősök tere.* The building to the left at the end of the square was completed in 1906 (designed by Albert Schickedanz and Fülöp Herzog), with the purpose of housing the city's fine art collection, which by that time was already quite remarkable. In the pediment above the main entrance the relief shows the battle of the Centaurs and the Lapiths. The scene is a completed copy of a fragment on the Temple of Zeus on Olympia.

Behind the attractive façade, the monumental staircases and spaces were laid out without any heed to the practical needs of the museum, which consequently had to be rebuilt several times. Since 1957 the National Gallery has been responsible for the Hungarian Collection. It has the following sections: Egyptian Collection, Antiquities, Old Masters (a very rich collection), Old Master Sculpture; Hungarian Collection, Graphic Art Collection and Modern Paintings and Sculpture. After World War II the walls of the right-hand side museum building were so full of holes that kids could easily climb in. They could not get through the internal doors, though. (By courtesy of my editor, who was one of the kids.)

At the moment large-scale renovation of the building is under way. The 'art robbers of the century' took advantage of this. One night in November 1983, the thieves climbed up the scaffolding and into the museum, disabling the primitive alarm system. Seven priceless paintings, among them two Raphaels, were stolen. It took ten weeks to trace the paintings to the garden of a Greek monastery and to arrest the criminals in their homeland, Italy. Since then they have been sentenced to prison, the paintings have come home and the alarm system has been modernized. These paintings were restored before being shown at a special exhibition; the public had never before shown such interest.

Városliget, with an area of about one square kilometre, is the largest park of the city. It does not take long to walk across it. Our route takes us down Állatkerti körút, past the Gundel Restaurant (one of the most venerable in Budapest), past the Zoo (full of small buildings in a Hungarianized version of art nouveau) and past the Circus.

30 A Zoo: main entrance B Artificial Cliff C Elephant House D Municipal Circus E Carousel in the Amusement Park F Amusement Park: main entrance G Széchenyi Baths H Vajdahunyad Castle I Statue of the medieval chronicler Anonymus J Ice Rink K Exhibition Hall L Millennary Monument

GUNDEL RESTAURANT 29F *XIV. Állatkerti körút 3.* T: 321-3550, F: 342-2917. Open 7 p.m. to midnight, every day. 'The awareness that one has finally arrived at a setting designed primarily to minister to one's every need, a bright palace of rendered attention.' This phrase from the British writer John Lanchester's *The Debt to Pleasure* comes to mind whenever I enter this place. Now 102 years old, Gundel has regained its unprecedented leadership since reopening in 1992. The Budapest-born restaurateur George Lang (of worldwide fame) spared no effort in finding the materials that might suit the best traditional restaurant between Paris and San Francisco (this is an authentic guest statement — mine). What is really unusual is the first-rate collection of Hungarian masters on the walls. The last page of the menu tells you about the collection, and gives an exact location with a ground plan of the room. So you can just have a look from the corner of your eye. Mind you, the new logo and the stationery are by one of the most famous designers in the world, Milton Glaser. (See his posters in the bar, reminiscent of the Art Deco 1920's in Chicago.)

Mr Lang told me that the raised section in one third of the main room has no structural raison d'être: it is just a trick to create some intimacy in what is a basically very large room. Above the Dining Room are the Elizabeth Room and the Andrássy Room, the setting for the most elegant banquets of Budapest (a maximum of 260 people can be seated in the two rooms). Mr Lang, or when he is away, his right hand, Mr Gábor Budai, expect a lot from the 120-odd staff. Gundel now has its own wine list, and a very serious wine-cellar in the building — which you might well be invited to inspect after dinner.

By the way, when Mr Lang invited me to dinner, he asked for Table 8, a strategically located table, from where you can see everything. He knows best. This must be the best table.

THE ZOO (ÁLLATKERT) *Officially called the Municipal Botanical and Zoological Gardens — Fővárosi Állat- és Növénykert (XIV. Állatkerti körút 6. Open 9 a.m. to 6 p.m., closes 4 p.m. in autumn and winter.)* Originally established as a private corporation, it opened in 1865 on 16 hectares of land donated by the municipality of the (then still independent) city of Pest. At first it showed only animals, but by 1872 it was also exhibiting plants. From the 1880's it hosted peculiar 'live shows' — red Indian, black, Tamil and Arctic aboriginal families were invited to live in the Zoo for some months, to show how they lived.

In the early 1900's the Zoo went bankrupt, and the city took it over. It was reestablished in 1907 and a great number of new buildings – the ones we like so much today – were added by architects of the trend-setting National Romantic school, such as Károly Kós, Kornél Neuschloss and Dezső Zrumeczky. It reopened in 1912. Its musts are obvious: the main entrance, with the stone elephants at street level, and the twelve polar bears around the top, the Elephant House, the Bird House, Palm House, and other characteristic buildings. Kids always enjoy the 'Animal Kindergarten', where newlyborn animals are kept together (at least those ones who do not eat the others).

The energetic and conspicuously young general director Miklós Persányi, the first *non-biologist* in the job for many decades, managed in 1977 to have the National-Romantic buildings listed as **monuments**. (Mr Persányi, an economist, read the job advertisement abroad where he had been working for years. He confessed to me that to become the director of the Zoo was a childhood dream for him. Generally speaking, Hungary tends not to be the land of childhood ambitions fulfilled.) The general director and his staff work in the painfully obtrusive 1960's Bison House, a blatant example of the modernist craze raging then, so insensitive to the immediate (and larger) environment. But it is not just the Communists who made such things.

The Zoo is quite often the venue of fundraising events — I once attended a concert *inside* the Big Rock. Outside the big gate at the corner of Dózsa György út and Állatkerti körút, there is a very funny but obviously untranslatable slang slogan: 'Állati jó hely!' Literally: This is an 'animal-ly' (i.e. terrifically) good place. You can adopt all kinds of animals, and support the place in many imaginative ways. After many aborted attempts, the adjacent Amusement Park may finally be relocated to the Xth district of Pest, and the Zoo could then double in size relatively easily.

AMUSEMENT PARK (VIDÁMPARK) 30F *XIV. Állatkerti körút 14-16.* This incredibly worn-down, ramshackle fun-fair is a sympathetic, sad place for those of us who cherish happy childhood memories of it. A full view of Városliget can be had from the FERRIS WHEEL. It is very wise to hold on tight when the creaking construction starts moving. If there are only a few visitors, only every second gondola can be used. There is always a very long queue for the ROLLER COASTER, but you should not have to wait more than 20-25 minutes for your turn. Almost one third of the wooden structure is replaced every year.

The SLOT-MACHINE HALL has probably the most worn out American and Soviet machines in the world. If one breaks down, you have to turn to one of the gentlemen wearing a blue coat, chatting in the middle of the hall. They will open the machine but usually just shake their heads and say 'Play it on the other one', and point to a similar machine. Near the entrance is the octagonal building of the CAROUSEL. Children, some not so young, go mad with indecision over the ride to choose: the fiery horse, the luxurious triumphal coach or the spinning box. There is a fresco above and the operator peeps out from behind the organ. The other treasure of the fun-fair, the ENCHANTED CASTLE, was set on fire by an employee some ten years ago. His explanation was that he wanted to gain distinction by reporting the fire quickly. Only the exit of the castle, the 'Barrel', survived. Its totally modernized successor naturally lacks the old atmosphere.

(From 1 October to 1 April the Amusement Park is only partially open. Most of its attractions, like the Roller Coaster or the Ferris Wheel, are closed.)

SZÉCHENYI BATHS 30G *XIV. Állatkerti körút 9-11.* This, one of the largest public baths in Europe, is visited by two million people annually. It has two separate parts, two different worlds of architecture that attract two different types of regulars. You have to go round the building to see the Medicinal Baths, which were the first to be built (Győző Czigler, Ede Dvorzsák, 1909-13). It is one of the most relaxed buildings of the turn of the century. The dome of the main entrance, which looks so light from the outside, has a huge art nouveau mosaic inside; visitors will be kept busy admiring it for quite a time. The tiles on the floor, the lights, the door-frames, every fitting was made with exceptional care. You may also walk a bit to the left or to the right, as far as the two side-domes. This is where guests can have a thermal bath in a tub, in a very luxurious environment. The numbers chalked on the doors show what time the guest started his bath.

Of the flood of notices in the entrance hall, those written only in Hungarian tell guests where to find the Complaints Book, or specify who can use the baths through the National Health Service, and on what conditions.

The northern wing (by Imre Francsek) was opened in 1927, and its neo-Baroque interior already shows a very modern use of space. The entrance hall is largely in its original condition; the additions (such as the soft drinks machines) would seem to be glaring mistakes; they only emphasize the charm of the original. The atmosphere, always busy, is quite different here from that of the other wing. Behind the entrance hall there is a battered but lively restaurant, from which you can see the pools.

In winter the pools are reached through a heated corridor. The water temperature in the large pool is 27° C, in the warm-water pool 38° C. A unique local sport is featured here: water-chess, which is played on floating cork chessboards but which follows the normal rules.

The millennium of the Hungarian state was celebrated in 1896 with a huge exhibition, which took up the whole area of Városliget. A popular attraction of the Millennary Exhibition was a group of temporary buildings, set up with the purpose of showing the various architectural styles of those 1,000 years. Some of these were copies of real buildings. This mixture of buildings, however absurd the idea may now seem, met with such success that the city authorities commissioned a stone version to be built after the exhibition. Its popular name is:

VAJDAHUNYAD CASTLE 30H *XIV. Városliget.* Part of this was modelled on a Transylvanian castle of that name by the architect Ignác Alpár (finished by 1904). The complex consists of four main parts: the Romanesque, Gothic, the Transitional and the Renaissance/Baroque.

This bizarre notion was carried out by an architect of exceptional talent and imagination; the impression is fairy-tale rather than kitsch. Naturally, no two turrets are the same, yet the many contrasting forms seem to work together as a whole. In winter the boating lake is turned into an ice rink. The permanent stone building was built for the Agricultural Museum, which still occupies the Castle. Opposite the main entrance is one of the most popular

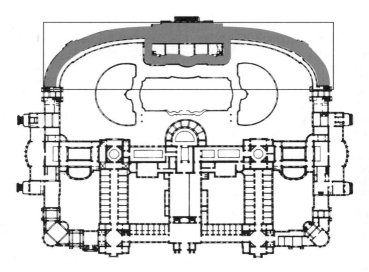

Széchenyi Baths

31 A Vajdahunyad Castle **B** Petőfi Csarnok — Metropolitan Youth Centre **C** *Fuit* stone **D** Former Metropolitan Museum (1885) **E** Statue of George Washington

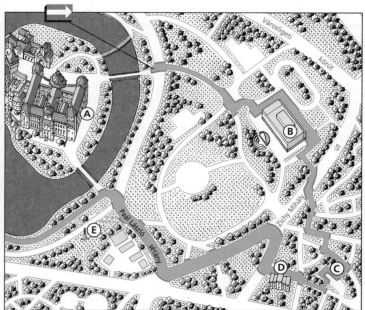

statues in Pest, that of Anonymus; he was the first medieval Hungarian chronicler, but his epoch-making work was modestly signed with the words that appear on the pedestal of the statue: GLORIOSISSIMI BELAE REGIS NOTARIUS. ('The notary of the most glorious King Béla.') This would be sufficent had not four kings been called Béla in the 12th and 13th century. His identity is still disputed by scholars. The sculptor has given him a hood so that his face cannot be seen (Miklós Ligeti, 1903).

A rest: Restaurant Anonymus — in the Castle

PETŐFI HALL 31B *XIV. Zichy Mihály út 14.* This youth centre hall, in a converted exhibition hall, was opened in 1985. It is now the stronghold of Hungarian rock and pop music. But it also has a fleamarket, theatrical performances for children, a Rollerskate Club and on Saturday evenings the Csillagfény Disco. In summer there is an open-air cinema, and they have also organized a new-wave fashion show, an underground theatrical performance, a disco-dancing competition, a 'hairshow'. In brief, it caters for and has caught the imagination of the young who flock to it.

Their 142-4327 telephone number is an important one for you if you want information on what's happening in Budapest and they can usually help you in English or in German. Or you can do what the young do: just turn up and see what's happening.

STATUE OF GEORGE WASHINGTON 31F *XIV. Városliget.* According to official American statistics three and a half million immigrants from Austria–Hungary arrived in the United States between 1871 and 1913. Half of them were Hungarian, but many others came from Bohemia — hence 'Bohunk' in old American slang. The funds to erect this statue were collected by the Bohunks (Gyula Bezerédi, 1906).

EXHIBITION HALL (MŰCSARNOK) 32B *XIV. Hősök tere.* The largest exhibition hall in the country was opened in 1896, at the time of the Millennary celebrations. It was designed by the same architects as the Museum of Fine Arts opposite. The ground plan shows the influence of the late Renaissance, as does the fine ornamentation of the façade. The latter was made from 'frost-resistant pyrogranite', a contemporary Hungarian invention. Funds ran short when it came to decorating the pediment, the mosaic of *St Stephen, Patron of the Arts* only being put in place in 1941. During World War I the hall housed a military hospital.

The Exhibition Hall began as a stronghold of conservatism and remained so until the early 1980's, when the era of opening to the world took place, still with more or less adequate funds.

Then came a total facelift. Műcsarnok reopened in January 1995, with a leadership crisis. Its much criticized lady director became the victim of a sort of political tug of war. She was demoted, obviously not at the best moment.

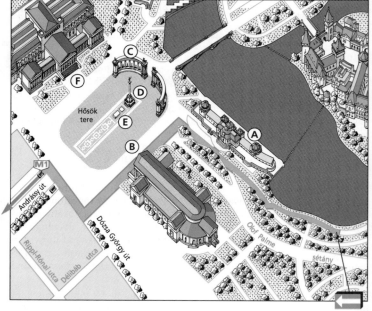

32 **A** Ice Rink Building **B** Exhibition Hall **C-D** Millennary Monument **E** Tomb of the Unknown Soldier **F** Museum of Fine Arts.

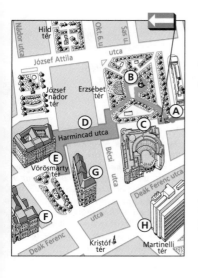

33 **A** Coach station, the most recent of Hungary's listed architectural monuments (1949), building site of the new National Theatre **B** Danubius Fountain **C** Grand Hotel Corvinus Kempinski **D** British Embassy **E** Gerbeaud **F** Vigadó **G** Luxus **H** Office block

The present director is also the subject of criticism, this time for his bias towards international trends, which is said to entail serious neglect of Hungarian offerings. I don't agree. He has made this a major European venue.

A rest: Café Műcsarnok
& Bookshop

Along the side of Városliget there is a wide concrete pavement which is called Felvonulási tér (Procession Square). It is here that celebrations involving huge crowds of people, such as those on the 4th of April or 1st of May, were held, and it was also the scene of the military parade, which took place only every five years. On such occasions there was a fly-past of fighter planes. In 1990, the 4th of April ceased to be a holiday — it celebrated the liberation of Hungary by the Red Army — to the sorrow of many small boys, henceforth deprived of military parades.

Opposite Városligeti fasor used to stand a huge statue of Stalin; it was pulled down in the Revolution of '56. It was from the pediment of this statue that the Communist leaders waved to the crowds that marched past in their tens of thousands. It was pulled down, just like the statue of Lenin which was taken away to be repaired because of 'metal fatigue', just when the ancien régime was collapsing. It never returned, of course. (It used to stand near the Exhibition Hall.)

This is the end of our walk in Városliget. As I have promised, we shall return to Vörösmarty tér by the Millennary underground. You should get off at Deák tér.

DANUBIUS FOUNTAIN 33B *V. Erzsébet tér.* A fountain with three basins, with a male figure symbolizing the Danube on the top (Miklós Ybl and Leó Feszler, 1893). The women sitting on the rim of the lower basin stand for three of the Danube tributaries: the Tisza, Dráva and Száva. The lower basin was carved out of a single piece of rock weighing almost 100 tonnes. Transporting a rock of this size presented quite a problem at the beginning of the 1890's. This is a copy of the original, which was destroyed in the war.

This walk took me five hours and I did not even look into the Museum of Fine Arts or the Exhibition Hall.

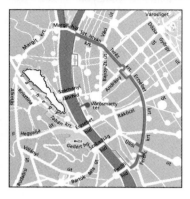

Along and behind Nagykörút

This walk takes us all the way down Nagykörút (or Grand Boulevard) from the Danube to the Danube. We shall look into some side-streets and peer behind the plastic cover of the Corvin department store. We shall pay our respects to the site where the National Theatre used to be, visit the Royal Waiting Room, a handsome railway station, see something of Új-Lipótváros and return.

Time: Six hours plus. From Vigadó tér, we board a 2 or 2/A Tram coming from the right. This will take us to the south end of the Nagykörút. While waiting you will probably notice how expansive the river panorama is. The two parts of Budapest are equally important, but totally different in character.

Directly opposite us is the large building of the Bazaar at the foot of Castle Hill. The ground floor was intended for small shops and it now houses sculptors' workshops. Legendary rock concerts took place on the top floor during the 1960's. These concerts affected the foundations of the building, which is now awaiting restoration.

We get off at the fourth stop, that is, at the third bridge down from where we boarded the tram. Let's walk to the southern end of the bridge. On the opposite side of the river is Lágymányos, a part of the XIth district, which was once a marsh. Over there on the riverbank stands the campus of the Technical University, to the left is the railway bridge (1873–76, designer unknown). The bridge was so far away from the city itself that the designer presumably felt no obligation to respect any aesthetic principles.

Behind the railway bridge you can see the tip of Csepel Island — the proposed site for some ambitious development. Some planners dream of a miniature Manhattan, or La Défense there. There is a lot of talk about an express train to Vienna that would

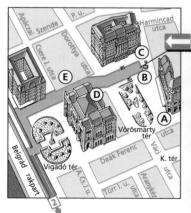

34

A Luxus Department Store **B** Fountain with lions **C** Gerbeaud **D** Vigadó **E** Shipping company headquarters, with sirens

only take 53 minutes. Also of incoming Hong Kong businessmen, who are on the way by the thousand to Hun Kong. The centre of the island can be reached in 13 minutes, if you use the commuter train (HÉV). Its terminus is next to the bridge.

Walking through the subways we come to the beginning of our Fifth Walk.

LÁGYMÁNYOS BRIDGE AND UNIVERSITY TOWN
The bridge was long overdue, and was built in an obvious location, completing the Outer Boulevard in Pest. Existing pillars were used — those of the Southern Railway Bridge. Every single route proposed for the approach roads on the Buda side was contested by locals; in the end the worst possible solution was chosen and there was an almighty scandal.

Anyway, most Budapest people like the bridge, especially the big mirrors that throw an even light on the road.

Meanwhile University Town is taking on an increasingly definite shape on the site once earmarked for the 1996 Expo. (That idea was dropped in 1994, when it was clear that the state should have provided all the funding.)

The Science Faculty of Eötvös University has moved here, establishing a long-awaited symbiosis with Budapest Institute of Technology, less than a kilometre away.

NAGYKÖRÚT (GRAND BOULEVARD)
This is the longest thoroughfare of the city, measuring exactly 4,114 metres. At this point the site was once a backwater of the Danube. By the end of the last century, the narrow streets of an unplanned suburb had developed here. Construction began in 1872, at the same time as on Sugárút, and lasted 35 years. A total of 251 buildings were pulled down and 253 much larger ones built. Nagykörút, which has a sewage system running underneath, is 45 metres wide for all its length, and crosses through five districts: hence its sections have different names — Ferenc, József, Erzsébet, Teréz (named after Habsburg kings and queens) and Szent István körút.

Nagykörút helped connect parts of the city that before its existence had been separate and socially very distinct. The boulevard started from the suburb of Boráros tér, through better-off districts, to the ill-famed slums of the Margit híd area, which became a fashionable, well-off district as a consequence of the shift in balance of the city towards the Parliament buildings. So when the boulevard officially opened in 1906, it led from a poor suburb towards better and better-off districts — just as it does today.

The blocks of flats along Nagykörút are all very similar. Their façades are all eclectic, showing elements of all sorts of architectural styles and usually have rendered walls decorated with plaster ornaments. The designs of the buildings imitate those of the townhouses along Andrássy út. On the street side, there were light and spacious flats with at least two bedrooms (and a bathroom). The kitchens are large and have a small annexe that was once the maid's room. The flats at the rear of the buildings are reached from balconies in the inner courtyard.

After World War II, when flats were nationalized, the larger front-facing flats were broken up into smaller units, often without any kind of logic. However, many flats at the rear acquired a bathroom. In the early 1980's the façades all along Nagykörút were restored and the interiors of some buildings, such as that at Ferenc körút 5., were renovated. Rents are low compared to the cost of maintenance. If you go into any building, you will see that they have two separate staircases: the main staircase leads to the front-facing flats and the one at the rear was originally for tradesmen and servants. The main staircase is usually much more ornate, though sometimes, as at Ferenc körút 5., it looks just the same as the one at the rear. Today everyone uses the main staircase or the lift if one has been installed, and the rear stairs are often left uncleaned. The courtyards were once the scene of animated social life. A reminder of those times is the wooden frame on which carpets were beaten, called the 'poroló'. Maids and later housewives used to take their carpets down to the courtyard and beat them there with a cane carpet beater (the 'prakker' which was also what children were threatened with for misbehaviour). Everyone had to have an agreed upon time for beating their carpets and this gave rise to many arguments. When the ladies made peace, they used to gather in the yard to chat. Sadly, the vacuum-cleaner, already in general use by the mid 1960's, brought this busy social life to an end.

Ferenc körút *divides Ferencváros, the IXth district. It was named after Emperor Franz I in 1792 when he came to the throne. It remained an agricultural area until the end of the last century, by which time large mills and meat plants had been established. The local population grew very quickly and became working class and artisan in character. The modernization of the district was interrupted by the Great Depression before the war.*

This history can be seen on a detour into Angyal utca, a street which could symbolize Ferencváros as a whole. Some buildings try to imitate those in Nagykörút, but on a smaller scale, others are single-storey buildings occupied by one family and a third type are single-storey buildings arranged around a courtyard and housing several families. And finally there is the only modern block built the way the city authorities had planned.

SECOND HAND FURNITURE STORE 35G *IX. Tűzoltó utca 14-16.* If you follow Angyal utca, it will lead you straight to this building which, with a slight exaggeration, could be called the museum of forgotten furniture. The ground floor is packed with wardrobes, the upper level with chairs and beds. Usually the furniture comes from older and poorer people without a family to leave it to. Many of the local households are furnished in this way. People who like home carpentry, slumming intellectuals or quite simply the poor come here to buy. If someone comes often enough, they are bound to find something they want in amongst the heaps of trash — on the cheap. I once paid 30 Ft here for an armchair — having it re-covered cost me 700 Ft.

MUSEUM OF APPLIED ARTS (IPARMŰVÉSZETI MÚZEUM) 35I

IX. Üllői út 33-37. In contrast to where we have just been, this place contains a collection of objects well worth preserving (Ödön Lechner and Gyula Pártos, 1896). There is an immediate clash between the exterior and the ceiling of the main entrance with the white interior; the aula is covered with a steel-framed glass ceiling. Some years ago a pendulum was hung from here to show the rotation of the Earth as part of the exhibition on the history of measuring time.

director's choice • director's choice • director's choice

DR. ZSUZSA LOVAG, DIRECTOR GENERAL 1. The colourful ceramic walls outside the main entrance (made using the so-called Zsolnay technique). **2.** The fancy hole that breaks through all the levels of the building, and through which we can look upwards at the small coloured glass dome. (We call it by a local nickname: 'The Well'.) **3.** Lady's Dress: dark red and striped velvet, dark and satin and tulle embroidered with pearls. Braided with lace fringes. Paris, circa 1875. (Ground Floor, right corner.) **4.** Silver dish, repoussé and chased work, by Paul Grill, Augsburg, 1680-85. Together with the silver model by Péter Varga, a member of our staff, which shows how the dish was made, phase by phase. (1st Floor, Arts and Crafts permanent exhibition.) **5.** A 13-piece silver toilet set, with copper inlaid ornaments, imitating fish, birds and insects. Louis Comfort Tiffany, New York, 1902-1907 (1st Floor, left corner). **6.** Peacocks on Halas-style lace, made of linen. Design by Árpád Dékány, realized by the Halas Lace Workshop, led by Mária Markovits, Kiskunhalas, circa 1906.

FORMER ARMY BARRACKS 35H *IX. Üllői út 49-51.* This large yellow building is the only one that was already here when Nagykörút was being laid out (József Hild, 1845–46). At the moment it contains offices, warehouses and temporary housing for people whose home is under reconstruction.

A DETOUR: HUNGARIAN NATURAL HISTORY MUSEUM — MAGYAR TERMÉSZETTUDOMÁNYI MÚZEUM *VIII. Ludovika tér 3.* The newcomer on the museum scene, a sort of new sensation in Budapest, specially for kids, is well worth a detour, possibly one stop by underground, from Ferenc körút to Klinikák station, and a five minute-walk, most of it through a park.

Like many of the other major museums, this one seceded from the National Museum in 1934. It was, however, another 63 years before it was assigned a building of its own: the former riding school of the Ludoviceum, the Hungarian military college, which after World War II was converted into a cinema called 'Alfa'. Inside the museum there is a history of the site, with a photograph of the cinema burning down. It could not be saved, and it stood there deserted for over a decade.

The elegant neo-Classical monument (Mihály Pollack, 1834) was fully reconstructed from the outside, while at the same time being given an ingeniously designed high-tech/postmodern interior (István Mányi, 1996).

In front of the musem there are two dozen big lumps of stone presented to the museum by the quarry industry; they are arranged chronologically (note the small plaques on the rocks). The entrance is from the side (they did not want to spoil the original, protected façade). There is little to see on the entrance level other than, under the stairs, the skeleton of an elephant recently deceased in the Budapest Zoo. The first floor is used for temporary

director's choice • director's choice • director's choice

DR. ISTVÁN MATSKÁSI, DIRECTOR GENERAL, HUNGARIAN NATURAL HISTORY MUSEUM *The marble mangers in the Lecture room, recalling the building's original use (Hall, Lecture room). • A mummy dissected by an 18th-century pathologist, discovered in the crypt of the Dominican church in Vác. (Ground floor, left side). • The cave of the Neanderthal woman with 'kitchen' utensils and spoils of the hunt (Gallery, left side). • The majestic diorama displaying the legendary richness of Hungary's game (Gallery, far end). • The modern kitchen with its undesirable animals, in contrast to the Neanderthal cave (Gallery, right side opposite the cave). • Noah's Ark, symbolising the efforts to preserve the threatened species of the Earth (Gallery).*

BUDAPEST BESTS : : BUDAPEST BESTS : : BUDAPEST BESTS

Péter Lengyel, Novelist, Short Story Writer, a Reclusive Cult Figure

My city is such a city. (She is always to be found among the men and women in my books.) Her visitors had better walk and walk and walk. We natives have no better way of getting close to her, intimately close, if that's what we want to do.

Sacrifice your entire day. Avoid Tárnok utca and Szentháromság tér up in the Castle, the place to meet the other visitors and pseudo-peasants — possibly computer technicians at night. Avoid everything that was created just to impress you — they are unreal things, never genuine. If you crave bustle, travel along the metropolitan underground to Eastern Station, and tread the streets around Garay tér. Visit Mátyás tér in District Eight, and have a look at the city that is never boasted about to foreigners. Slip into her subways, and feast on the bazaars of seven nations.

Nyugati tér, Astoria, Batthyányi tér. Put your money in the most secure of your secure pockets; if you do not happen to have any, madam, sew one somewhere inside, right away. The pickpockets' favourite hunting grounds are Váci utca and Petőfi Sándor utca, and the tramway line on Nagykörút (the Grand Boulevard to you). Beware of those who offer their services, whether their bodies or their bank rates — you'll find fault with them all in the end.

Take a 17 tram from the Buda side of Margit híd all the way to Old Buda. Get off at Szépvölgyi út. Have a look at the enclosure of the small car park, and try to imagine that on that couple of inches of concrete there used to be a market, complete with vegetables, fruit, food, with some rows of stalls, a well, with a street, a narrow alleyway, a sort of chaotic urban Eden, steaming with perspiration and heavy secrets. From Lajos utca cross Evező utca, turn into Uszály utca and stroll among the Bauhaus-style buildings, amid the three-storey high trees. From Dereglye utca go up to the banks of the Danube. Sit quietly on a

exhibitions, and has a discovery room where exhibits can be touched – a welcome addition to the somewhat backward Hungarian museum scene, still more or less dominated by professors interested in scholarly publications, rather than community outreach or education, let alone entertaining the public. This museum has a flavour of the latest developments in America – in places it even feels to me like Chicago's Field Museum. (Not as far as the exhibits and signs go, however. My all-out favourite is a reconstruction of one of the tens of thousands of miserably nondescript small kitchens from the prefabricated, ten-storey tower blocks, complete with all its 'undesirable denizens' magnified a bit, so they can be better seen.)

There are exciting plans to expand the museum into the former military college main block next door (through an underground tunnel); and Orczy park, beyond the museum, will sooner or later be incorporated into the institution as a sort of ecological park. (For the Botanical Gardens, 200 metres from here, see 'For Serious Addicts', in 'Twelve Impressions'.)

---

bench in Small Park under the tallest of the hollow willow trees and try to see the Uszály utca of the 1950's. The trees are not yet taller than a man. Street kids like me play foot tennis at the top of the street. '*Autó!*' they shout no more than three times a day altogether, and the game stops until the car has passed. Three cars a day. Not a bad life, to be a street kid, in that time, in that place.

At the northern side of the park turn back towards the city. To the right there is, within a couple of steps, the Military Amphitheatre of ancient Roman times. We are on the eastern frontier-rim *(limes)* of the Roman Empire, just as at other times we were on the western limes of other empires (Ottoman, Soviet). Old Buda alone has two amphitheatres: the other one, farther away, is the one for civilians. It was this one we went to in the breaks between classes from nearby Árpád Grammar School; that's where our gym classes were held by Master Iglóy, the trainer of the national athletic team, whose disciples then held *every single* world record for middle and long distance events.

Then, following the heavy work of imagination, you can have a rest in a street parallel with Duna river, bumpy, cobblestone-covered Bokor utca, in tiny Café Kiskorona. Order a soft drink. The lady owner knows everything you should ever know about popular medicine. From your table you can have an unobstructed view of the site where a small block was recently pulled down. That was the house where a hero in one of the books by the author of the present lines, a certain Rókus Láncz, the eminent fence of stolen goods, committed and re-committed his crimes. And lo, now life has hurried to imitate fiction. The company that operates in the new building on the same site bears the name of the heroine of the same novel*: 'Bóra BT'. Remember: Hungarians do read books — every now and then.

---

* His celebrated book, *Macskakő* ('Cobblestone') is now available in English, from Readers International, London.

35 **A** Petőfi Bridge **B** Memorial Column **C-D-E** Blocks of flats
F Ferencváros Parish Church **G** Furniture Hall **H** Former Army
Barracks **I** Museum of Applied Arts **J** Corvin cinema

CORVIN BUDAPEST FILM PALACE 35J *VIII. Corvin köz.*

The first cinemas in Budapest were usually installed on the ground floor of residential blocks; this is a rare exception (Emil Bauer, 1923). It used to have a lobby just about as large as its

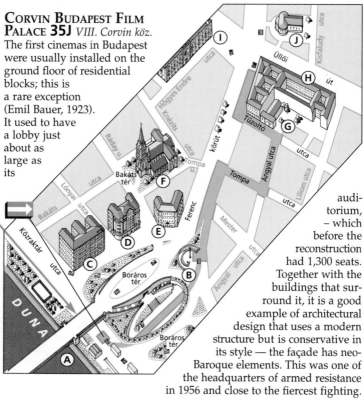

auditorium, – which before the reconstruction had 1,300 seats. Together with the buildings that surround it, it is a good example of architectural design that uses a modern structure but is conservative in its style — the façade has neo-Baroque elements. This was one of the headquarters of armed resistance in 1956 and close to the fiercest fighting.

In 1996 it was converted into a multiplex cinema with six screens (designed by Balázs Töreky, Dezső Töreky and László Rajk). Each of these is named after a legendary film director, and the interiors are decorated with old posters. On one side there is a pleasant café, called Casablanca, on the other an art video rental shop called Odeon.

Quite a good place to be in — only the entrance is too narrow. But that was one of the few constraints of the original design that was impossible to change.

József körút. The next section of Nagykörút is thus called because it crosses the VIIIth district, Józsefváros, named in 1777 after the future Emperor Joseph II. Behind the row of buildings towards Kálvin tér, the area becomes more and more elegant (the aristocrats had their town houses, 'palota' in Hungarian, built around the National Museum); to the right, however, it is rather less grand, with many single-storey houses. A lot of cloak and dagger films have been shot around here and there are whole streets where nothing has changed since the beginning of the century (Futó utca, Nagytemplom utca or another one, blasphemously called Leonardo da Vinci utca). Standing on the corner of Nap utca you can see a stately old hospital building to the left, at the end of the small street on the other side of Nagykörút, and to the right there is a new housing estate. A drastic method of inner-city renewal was adapted here: some ten high-rise blocks were built on the site of the old single-storey houses.

The area along Nagykörút on the city side and as far as Baross utca was called 'Cérnakorzó' (Thread-promenade) before the war. It was here that seamstresses used to walk after work to become acquainted with the craftsmen in the area. The ladies promenading here now are looking for less long-lasting relationships.

JÓZSEFVÁROS PARISH CHURCH

VIII. Horváth Mihály tér 7. This Baroque church, several times re-built, has a fine location as the gateway to Józsefváros (József Thalherr, 1798). In front of the church there is a statue of Péter Pázmány, the scholarly priest who began the Counter-Reformation in Hungary (Béla Radnai, 1914).

Further down József körút the number of small shops increases: a watchmaker's, a pipe shop, a souvenir shop disguised as a tobacconist's and the like. Souvenir shops have been flooded with things like quartz watches from the Far East or key cases which bleep when you whistle to them — it is difficult to find something typically Hungarian. Perhaps the plastic donkey which produces a cigarette from its backside when you pull its tail. That I have never seen anywhere else.

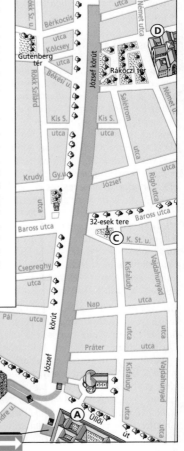

36 **A** Former Barracks **B** Museum of Applied Arts **C** War Memorial **D** Market Hall

Rákóczi tér is known not only for its market hall and the secondary school that trains dressmakers. It is also the centre of low prostitution. Since 1947 any form of 'selling a woman's body for money' has been illegal in Hungary. After years of desperate and vain struggle to end prostitution, the aim now just seems to be to keep it under control. As everywhere in the world, prostitution is interwoven with crime. Women satisfying the needs of fastidious customers can be found only in expensive nightclubs or luxury hotels.

The buildings here look the same as anywhere else. The value of flats, however, because of the notoriety of the location, is much lower around here. The area beyond Nagykörút is, if possible, an even more pathetic sight than other sections. If you peep into the ground floor flats in the dark, narrow streets, although it is not a nice thing to do even here, you can see that the lights have to be on in broad daylight and that some lightbulbs in the chandeliers are gone. A lot of lonely, hopeless, old people live here.

When I lived in this area for some years, I had the impression that alongside the old there lived a lot of young gypsies settling there from the country — gypsy musicians with a number of kids, or second-hand dealers. The courtyard my flat shared was in a five-storey high cauldron and it would have been impossible to keep any secrets there. You reached your flat by walking down the long access balcony and in so doing had to walk past the other flats that shared in. In summer, when people left windows open, you could hear the baker's alarm clock go off at three in the morning and then one by one, at 15 minute intervals, every other alarm in the building. Every district has a couple of pubs or restaurants where you can sense the atmosphere and all the distress of the area. In Józsefváros, it is the Góbé restaurant (József körút 28., on the corner of Bérkocsis utca). The regulars here are some of the girls working at Rákóczi tér, family men, often in tracksuits, as they pop in after (or before or even instead of) work and women of unidentifiable age. The furnishings are quite worn and you have a feeling that if anything new were put in here, it would soon take on the look of the miserable surroundings. I have never tried any of the food, though the lamb dishes have a certain reputation. On the other side of Nagykörút there are computer shops, on this side small shops of various kinds: a ballet-shoe maker, an old-fashioned hairdresser, a fountain-pen shop with a long tradition. And there is a Totó-Lottó betting office as well. **Lottó** is a form of lottery, you buy a ticket and you tick off 5 numbers out of the 90; **totó** is the Hungarian football pools where you have to guess the results of 13+1 matches.

Blaha Lujza tér is one of the central squares in the city. It bisects Nagykörút, which crosses Rákóczi út at this point. At one end of Rákóczi út there is Erzsébet híd, on the other you can see the great yellow mass of Keleti Railway Station. On the square was the old Nemzeti (National) Theatre and the famous clock standing in front of it, the standard rendezvous spot for ages. 'I'll meet you at seven at the Nemzeti, where the number six tram stops,' went the old song. The older generation still refer to the spot as the 'Nemzeti'. It would have been a nice gesture to call this stop of the Metro 'Nemzeti' since it was partly due to the construction of the Metro that the old theatre building had to be demolished in 1966. Architects did not consider rebuilding it as at that time the eclectic style that dominates Nagykörút was then considered worthless. Instead we got the kind of modernization that favoured angular and zig-zag lines.

The editorial offices of the once dreaded Communist party paper *Népszabadság* used to be here in the corner block (37A). Now it's by far the most

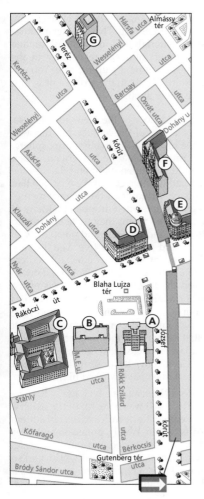

37 **A** The former *Népsza-badság* House **B** Corvin Department Store **C** Rókus Hospital **D** Block of flats **E** Block of flats, with a supermarket on the ground floor **F** New York Palace and the Café **G** Madách Theatre

successful and readable daily independent even of the left wing Socialist Party. It now has a very democratic setup — and German capital.

The 'new' façade of the Corvin department store (Ferenc Battka, 1966) is the memorial to this wild rage of modernism. If you want to know what the original façade looked like, turn to the left side of the building, the one which did not get its share of plastic facing. This store can no longer use its not wildly original slogan, which went 'The largest store — the largest choice' for there is now a larger department store.

Its customers are mainly people from the suburbs. I can hardly wait for the plastic façade to be taken off and the old wall underneath to be given some post-modern paint-job. It would be a perfect wall for that (37B).

In the subway you can buy newspapers day and night and in the early 1960's the first automatic food dispensers were placed here. If you were tall enough, you inserted the coin — but often nothing happened. You then had to bang on the machine, whereupon the person who filled it with food from behind unwillingly came up and gave you your chosen cake with his own hand or gave your money back. Now the said person sits behind a window. At New Year's Eve at midnight the carnival-like procession reaches its climax in streets around here; days before vendors invade the Körút selling the props: parking restrictions are set aside on this day and even the flowerboxes are taken away from the corners, where their purpose is partly to stop pedestrians from crossing.

The buildings of Nagykörút are not of much aesthetic value individually but there is an exception:

THE NEW YORK PALACE 37F *VII. Erzsébet körút 9-11* can be seen from afar as it is situated on the bend in the road. It faces three streets. Built as the headquarters of the New York Insurance Company (Alajos Hauszmann, 1891–95), it used to house Budapest's Fleet Street. The neo-Renaissance building was built of fine, long-lasting materials and in a tasteful, unique mixture of styles, already with hints of art nouveau (especially in the tower). The building is a little worn inside. Now it's up for sale. You can ask in the café if it has already been sold. Mr. Bitai, the scourge of young waiters, a retired manager, will surely know about it.

CAFÉ NEW YORK **37F** On the ground floor of the New York House. Budapest had more than 400 cafés at the turn of the century, but this was the most beautiful, the busiest and the one with the liveliest atmosphere. When it was opened, the playwright Ferenc Molnár and his friends threw its key into the Danube so that it should stay open night and day. As the saying goes, at that time every writer had his own café and every café had its own writer. The New York had many: virtually all the literary men of the era, since those who were not regulars here often dropped in. Many of them came to work here from dark, unheated rooms they rented nearby to fill themselves on the 'writers' plate' (cold meat, cheese and bread — with a discount for writers) and because ink and paper were free. The 'literary headwaiters' knew everybody's habits and latest works; better still, writers could dine on credit. A lot of them wrote here but some also sold their books or looked for a job and everyone read the latest papers. The titles of the papers the café subscribed to were set on a huge noticeboard: 'all the dailies and arts journals of the world'. Of course, it was not only writers and journalists who came here but people of all kinds, depending on the time of day. Actors, journalists and cinema staff early in the morning, retired actors later, elegant groups at dinner, card players, circus artists and waiters from other places enjoying the nights. The clock above the door to the basement restaurant called 'Mélyvíz' (Deep water) must have worked in those days.

The café had its golden age in the early 1910's, and a silver age in the second half of the 1920's and in the early 1930's. It was here, up in the gallery, that the most influential journals were edited. Caricatures of the old editors are still to be seen on the walls. After World War II, potatoes, and later shoes, were sold through the windows of the shelled and burnt out café. Still later, the café was seen as the symbol of the old, useless world, and so a sports shop was opened within these walls. The café reopened in 1954. Writers came here again for a while but eventually disappeared for good. The New York is listed in all the guidebooks and has become a tourist pilgrimage site. Nowadays you find just a few newspapers here, but although the Venetian chandeliers were replaced by inappropriate modern ones during a renovation, the interior still retains its splendour. Now it is only open between 9 a.m. and 10 p.m. and the 'Mélyvíz' restaurant from 11.30 a.m. to 3 p.m. and 6.30 p.m. to midnight.

There are some relentless customers, though. A pensive soft drinks magnate, in his late forties (?), always in a grey suit, seems to be here every afternoon standing at or leaning on the counter of the beer bar, the nearer the blonde barmaid, the better.

Some writers and men of letters have returned. I used to spend my Thursday afternoons here from 2 to 4 p.m., in the gallery. We did not have a proper editorial office back in the spring of 1989 when we established

2000, the influential egghead literary and social journal, a sort of a cross between the *New Yorker* and the *New Republic*. It still flourishes, and my friends — those who were not lured into government service — are happy and are here on Thursday afternoons. And though the waiters apparently don't read the highbrow literary and social monthly my friends own and publish, they have a 'literary toilet-attendant', a senior lady who does read our paper, and refuses to let us pay if we use her facility.

HORIZONT CINEMA *VII. Erzsébet körút 13.* Most cinemas in Budapest were built in the inter-war period and were quite modern for the time. This cinema opened in 1938 and looks exactly as it used to; only the films have changed. It no longer has a one-hour continuous programme, starting with a newsreel; but it does still have the two reliefs depicting the history of mankind on either side of the screen.

The Horizont is situated on the next section of the Körút, called **Erzsébet körút.** *It runs through the VIIth district, Erzsébetváros, named, like the bridge, after Francis Joseph's wife. It is the most densely populated part of the city; 55,000 people per square kilometre. You can find a number of single-storey buildings too. Along Nagykörút itself, there are innumerable small new shops, especially in the entrances of the buildings and some even on the upper levels. Anyone can get a licence to open such a shop (providing there are no sanitary or professional objections) and the hope is that*

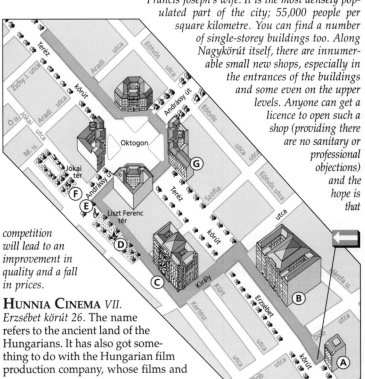

competition will lead to an improvement in quality and a fall in prices.

HUNNIA CINEMA *VII. Erzsébet körút 26.* The name refers to the ancient land of the Hungarians. It has also got something to do with the Hungarian film production company, whose films and

38 **A** Madách Theatre **B** Grand Hotel Royal **C** Academy of Music **D** Statue of Ferenc Liszt **E** Statue of Endre Ady, poet **F** Statue of Mór Jókai, novelist **G** Copy of Palazzo Strozzi, Florence

other Hungarian movies and art movies are shown here. It has also got something to do with the Hungarian Film Club Association. There is a pleasant café inside. A trendy place, full of intellectuals.

MADÁCH THEATRE 37G *VII. Erzsébet körút 31-33.* Madách Theatre was completed in 1961, on the site of an old cabaret (or 'orpheum'), designed by Oszkár Kaufmann, and soon became a flagship of new trends, a stronghold of innovation and fun. That was long ago. When the original innovators retired, a new generation began to resort to musical comedies to keep up audience levels. (*Cats* was the phenomenal first success, some 15 years ago.) Budapest has over 15 repertory theatres now, all, but one, subsidised by the city and the Ministry of Interior. Spectators pay roughly one tenth of the ticket prices. The theatres do not care to be reminded of each other's existence, and never coordinate their programmes.

The director/mastermind behind the Madách Theatre, Imre Kerényi, arrives in the mornings through the block to the left, and toils up to a tiny office on the top. He is passionate, persuasive and often seen on TV in debates about the theatre. Since he got rid of his long hair, it has been difficult to spot him. Look for a pair of glowing eyes, dark or black clothes, wide-flung gestures. The building is soon to undergo a thorough facelift, long overdue. I hope they will retain most of the inner design of the foyer: a rare, good example of Central European fifties and early sixties style.

HOTEL ROYAL 38B *VII. Erzsébet körút 49.* When it was opened, this hotel was one of the largest in the whole Austro-Hungarian Empire (Rezső Ray, 1896). The four cast iron statues on the façade (the Four Seasons) were brought from Paris. In 1915 its luxurious ballroom was converted into a cinema, which is still going strong, the Apollo (for 40 years called the 'Vöröscsillag', i.e. Red Star). Originally the building had a ground plan in the shape of an E but the two courtyards were closed in the early sixties. The modernized portal has recently been rebuilt in its original form.

LISZT ACADEMY OF MUSIC 38C *VI. Liszt Ferenc tér 8.* The official name of the institution, 'Liszt Ferenc Zeneművészeti Főiskola', is to be found between the two geniuses at the top of the building. Music teachers and performing musicians are trained here — about 300 students in all. The building, to the plans of Flóris Korb and Kálmán Giergl, took three years to build and was completed in 1907. Above the main entrance the bronze statue of Ferenc Liszt can be seen (by Alajos Stróbl). The Main Hall ('Nagyterem' in Hungarian) is 25 by 17 metres and has 1,200 seats, the best of which must be the first from the left in the eighth row — a former director of Hungaroton, the national record company, used to get his complimentary ticket for this seat. The 'best' just means that you have the best view of the stage from here, since the acoustics in the hall are extraordinarily good: you can hear everything even from the back row of the second gallery. These seats are usually taken by music students, who fill the gallery with loudly expressed opinions on the concerts.

If more than twelve hundred people are interested in a concert, the seats behind the stage are sold. If even more, then some chairs are placed on stage as well, as happened when Maurizio Pollini last played here.

On both sides of the Walcker organ there are two inscriptions in Latin. To the left: *Sursum Corda*: Raise Your Hearts; the other is *Favete Lingui'*: Hold Your Tongue, or, Be Quiet. There are hundreds of other details to notice on the walls and ceiling. At the bottom right-hand corner of the organ there is a cavity the size of a full-grown man. The radio commentators hole themselves up here to introduce the concerts, though they may be forced out on special occasions, like the recent performance of Monteverdi's Vespers, when the 'Echo' tenor solo was sung from here.

The Small Hall ('Kisterem' in Hungarian), which you can reach from the first floor, seats 400 people. It too has good acoustics, but sometimes you can hear what is going on in the Main Hall as well. This is the venue for the

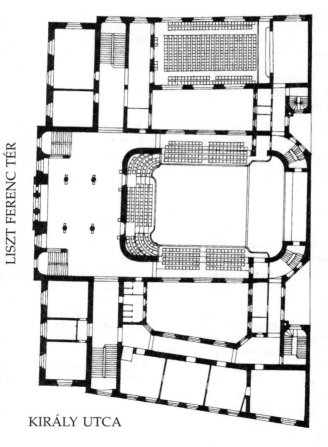

DOHNÁNYI ERNŐ UTCA

LISZT FERENC TÉR

KIRÁLY UTCA

Liszt Academy of Music — the first floor

examination concerts for music students. Here I threw a reasonably large bouquet of roses to my alto girlfriend after her graduation performance, not realizing that the contemporary pieces she sang towards the end were less than perfect, and were rewarded by a grade Three (more than she deserved, the music analysts commented). Everywhere in the building you can see the signs of an exceptionally careful and loving shaping of surfaces. This is generally true of most art nouveau buildings, but here there is also a special tranquillity: as if this art nouveau building had grown straight out of eclecticism — fire out of water. This reminds me: you should be careful with the marble basin between the ground floor doors — it is always full of water, it is just too clean to be noticed. During term-time you can always walk into the building through the side entrance in Király utca. It is worth buying a ticket for a concert that may not be first class just for the sake of the Main Hall.

CHILDREN'S LIBRARY *VI. Liszt Ferenc tér 6.* This is the library I joined at the age of 10 although it was a long way off from both my school and our home. The library was exactly like that of the adults, only everything was smaller, including the chairs and the tables. It has a reading room facing the square and many catalogue cases. There used to be a big lady with red hair, who helped us find what we wanted. Above one shelf there used to be the notice: 'A selection of adult literature'. The red-haired lady has now retired.

THE NEW LISZT STATUE *VI. Liszt Ferenc tér.* The statue was erected to commemorate the 100th anniversary of the composer's death, although there were already two full-length Liszt statues within a few hundred metres (László Marton, 1986). The statue aroused considerable resistance in musical circles. Critics denounced it as 'lukewarm-modern'. Passers-by ask each other who might the bald man on Liszt's lapel be. (It is the sculptor.)

A rest: Café Incognito — Liszt Ferenc tér 2.

'PALAZZO STROZZI' 38G *VI. Teréz körút 67.* Another work by Alajos Hauszmann, the architect of the New York Palace; this one dates from 1884.

The original in Florence is larger and better. Ours houses offices and on the ground floor there is a richly decorated wedding-hall, perhaps the most fashionable in the whole city. Marriage services are conducted at district councils and at central offices such as this. The bride usually wears a white dress and the bridegroom a dark suit. The young couple are taken to the ceremony in cars decorated with flowers. There is a small photographic gallery in the basement, with occasional exhibitions of historic pictures.

In the next section of Teréz körút you will have to forget my promise that we would walk through better and better-off areas, although the boutiques are of higher quality than those in Király utca.

Since the parking revolution of 1995, the Grand Boulevard is coming back to life. You can now park there for as long as you want. (Sensible, isn't it?) Here you can find the art movie-house Művész, a sort of small proto-multiplex. (See Bests of Budapest by Pál Schiffer, film director, p. 232) A recent newcomer on the scene is Café Underground, entrance to the left of the cinema. Don't be misled by the fact

39 **A** Hotel Béke Radisson **B** Post Office **C** Western Railway Station
D Skála Department Store **E-F** Blocks of flats

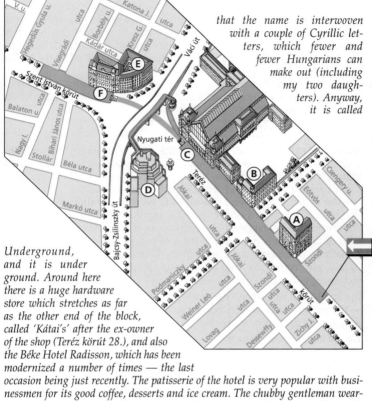

*that the name is interwoven
with a couple of Cyrillic letters, which fewer and
fewer Hungarians can
make out (including
my two daugh-
ters). Anyway,
it is called*

*Underground,
and it is under
ground. Around here
there is a huge hardware
store which stretches as far
as the other end of the block,
called 'Kátai's' after the ex-owner
of the shop (Teréz körút 28.), and also
the Béke Hotel Radisson, which has been
modernized a number of times — the last*
occasion being just recently. The patisserie of the hotel is very popular with businessmen for its good coffee, desserts and ice cream. The chubby gentleman wearing a suit deals with the orders as if everything there were his own. On the façade
two sitting lions hold a torch in their paws. Opposite the hotel there is Játékszín,
a small theatre which does not have its own company (VII. Teréz körút 48.). Rather
unusually for Hungary, each production has a specially assembled cast.

WESTERN RAILWAY STATION (NYUGATI PÁLYAUDVAR) 39C *VI. Teréz
körút 55.* Trains set out for the north and the east from this finely restored railway station, so the name (Western Railway Station) is misleading. A long
time ago the Vienna train had to make a long detour to the north on its journey since there was no railway bridge across the Danube. The building was
constructed by the Eiffel Company of Paris (August de Serres, 1874-77) in
such a way that the old railway terminal was able to function undisturbed
underneath. Over the next 100 years the 25,000-square-metre hall deterio-
rated and plans were made for a new building. Fortunately the conservationists won and most of the old iron structure has been re-cast; only the
paintwork has been changed to light blue, the favourite colour of post-mod-

ernism. Towards the end of the hall on the left there is a large closed door; above the lintel is carved in marble: VIRIBUS UNITIS (With Unity Strength). This used to be the door to the Royal Waiting Room. Although pretty from the outside it is not in use. The new wing has been occupied by a row of 26 shops, the Westend Bevásárló Udvar, where you can have a good idea of what sort of things people put their money into. The elegant glass screen of the station's main façade lets trains become part of the city's traffic. Once, about twenty years ago, a train did actually came through, when the brakes failed, but it came to rest at the tram stop.

The giant restaurant room to the right of the main entrance has been turned into a McDonald's. The interior is quite a success. Note the elegant, unobtrusive post-modern tower at the corner.

A rest: big Mac's biggest — Teréz körút 55.

SKÁLA METRO DEPARTMENT STORE 39D *VI. Nyugati tér 1-2.* In the 1970's and the 1980's the Skála Shopping Chain was perhaps the most dramatically developing company in the country. So said TIME magazine in a full page they devoted to this company with the headline 'Marks and Spencer of the East'. Their store in Buda wrested the title of 'the largest store' from Corvin. This store in Pest (György Kővári, 1984) is much smaller, occupying only the first and second floors of the building. The one-time CEO of this chain is now part of the international jet-set; he is to be seen sometimes in Canada, sometimes in the Ukraine. He has just built Bank Center (see Walk Two), and a very large Shopping Center along the M3 motorway, called the Pólus Center.

But apart from that, there is a real shopping mall craze now in Hungary — the retail trade is being transformed. People simply love the new malls, even if they find them expensive.

The old and the new character of the square is reflected in the two clocks. On the façade of the railway station, just below the copy of the crown, a traditional clock shows the time; in front of the department store, however, there is a digital clock. The time of the two clocks rarely coincide.

Vígszínház — a cross section

40 **A** Vígszínház **B** The block 'with the electric switches' **C** Block of flats **D** Margaret Bridge **E** 'White House'

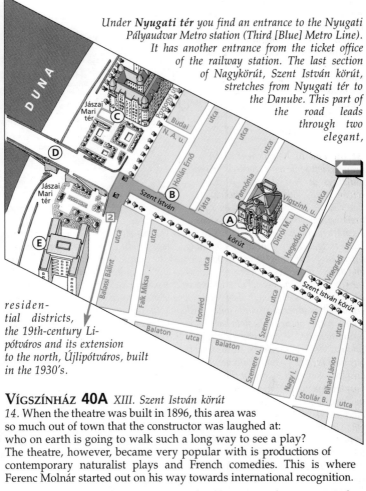

Under **Nyugati tér** you find an entrance to the Nyugati Pályaudvar Metro station (Third [Blue] Metro Line). It has another entrance from the ticket office of the railway station. The last section of Nagykörút, Szent István körút, stretches from Nyugati tér to the Danube. This part of the road leads through two elegant,

residential districts, the 19th-century Lipótváros and its extension to the north, Újlipótváros, built in the 1930's.

VÍGSZÍNHÁZ **40A** *XIII. Szent István körút*

14. When the theatre was built in 1896, this area was so much out of town that the constructor was laughed at: who on earth is going to walk such a long way to see a play? The theatre, however, became very popular with is productions of contemporary naturalist plays and French comedies. This is where Ferenc Molnár started out on his way towards international recognition.

In hardly any other theatre company do actors enjoy the star status they have here. The present management is trying to establish a balance between popular plays and cautious experimentation. They have also produced several musicals. At the time the building was constructed by the Viennese Fellner and Helmer Company, scenery was much simpler and smaller. Nowadays it has to be stored behind the building in a large container or in the open air, as can be seen from the window of the Művész restaurant behind the theatre building. Totally reconstructed for its centenary, Vígszínház was reopened in 1994, with a no-text play entitled 'Dance for Everyone' (*Össztánc*), written by Pál Békés, a Hungarian playwright, taking the general idea of a famous Italian film, and arranging twentieth-century Hungarian history in a witty, professional, very entertaining show, that can give you an insight into both this land's history and the superb quality of our acting and dancing. Highly recommended for people who speak no Hungarian.

A rest: Pampalino Salad Bar – XIII. Hollán Ernő utca 7.

41 A Thonet House
B Vigadó C Gerbeaud
D Luxus Department Store

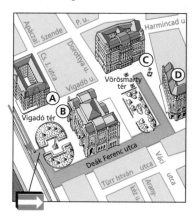

At the end of Nagykörút art nouveau has left some more traces, as in the buildings at Nos. 12 and 10 Szent István körút. The latter is nicknamed the 'electric switch building' by children because its white, square stone

decoration brings modern switches to mind. The bus-stop for Bus 26, which serves Margitsziget, is in front of this building. These buildings may look pleasant and interesting, but from the inside they are just the typical Nagykörút blocks: narrow and dark. The part of Újlipótváros near the river has quite different buildings. On the site of an old industrial district dozens of modern blocks of flats were constructed in the 1930's. Although they seem to be massive, closed structures, these blocks enclose large inner courtyards onto which only the windows of the kitchens and the maids' rooms opened. The flats had modern, practical features built in and were all centrally heated. Almost every room has a balcony and the flats receive a lot of light through the large windows. At the time these were strange and unusual buildings, but they became popular with young, progressive sections of the middle class. The area was described by one of the residents, Antal Szerb, the writer, in his book, A Guidebook to Budapest for Martians *(1935): 'Nowadays you find the flattest modern palaces here. Inside the palaces young psychoanalysts are laying out each other's souls on the sofas, splendid bridge-party amazons are daydreaming in snow-white bathrooms, extraordinarily intelligent clerks tune their radios to the broadcast from Moscow… Everything is modern, simple, objective and uniform here. The whole district is made up of two-room flats with a small sitting room, and its residents are stubbornly, youthfully and energetically trying to conceal the only reality in their lives: that none of them has any money at all.'* The main street of Újlipótváros is Pozsonyi út, which has as its centre the elegant Szent István park. The residents who once were modern, young people, cling to the area they live in, as is clear from the advertisements for changing flats. The value of these flats is almost as high as of those in Buda. Vígszínház draws its audiences from this area. In the auditorium, just as in the shops of the district, there are many elderly people: energetic, talkative, widowed ladies wearing quantities of jewellery, and neatly dressed gentlemen.

Their children often live somewhere around here, at least no further than the housing estate built further north on the riverbank. There are a lot of new cars and pretty small shops around. The whole district apparently enjoys a sparkling life. If you decide not to finish your walk in Újlipótváros or in Margitsziget, just board the Tram 2 at the bridge; the fifth stop is Vigadó tér.

This was the longest walk, leading us a long way away from the fine marble tables of the Gerbeaud café. Not that you cannot discover anything new just by sitting around in the café. Only after completing this route

---

BUDAPEST BESTS : : BUDAPEST BESTS : : BUDAPEST BESTS
István Rév, Historian, Maverick Political Scientist, True Son of Buda

Take Bus 91 from the Vígszínház and, after it winds its way up *Rózsadomb*, get off in the quietness of Áfonya utca to a stroll up to the József-hegy look-out point on the very top of Rózsadomb, for a truly charming view. In clear weather, looking north, not only can all the Danube bridges and the hills lying beyond the city be seen but also the contours of the Carpathians themselves. A clear view all round is blocked only to the south-east by two boorish houses that obscure the hill known as Svábhegy. In the house that ruins one of the city's finest views, on József-hegy, lives A -J-, who at the time he moved in was responsible for the city's development and planning.

At the beginning of the century, Rózsadomb was essentially a place of parks, vineyards, gardens and kitchen gardens; building only started here between the wars, when the comfortably-off classes started to escape the noise of the city into all kinds of detached houses and rented villas. After World War II, Rózsadomb became the quarter for the déclassé: wives of arms manufacturers who painted scarves, wives of business magnates who became daily helps, widows of distillery proprietors who survived by giving German lessons, barons reduced to smuggling antiquarian books, chairmen of foundations, retraining as carpenters. Here they all lived in the seized and expropriated houses that used to be their own.

During the 1950's Communist functionaries began moving into the vacant expropriated villas. Pre-war Chevrolets and the Soviet cars that arrived immediately after the war, the Zims, the Zils, the Pobyedas, could be seen all over the hill. After 1956 János Kádár the dictator himself came to live at Nos. 19-23 Cserje utca at the foot of the József-hegy look-out tower. For 32 years he stood at the helm of the country and the Party... It is because of him that it is still difficult to reach the vantage point by car, the streets being one-way and filled with 'no stopping' signs.

From the mid-1960's, as constraints on the real estate market if not on the country began to be relaxed, the *nouveau riche* who had made their fortunes in the 'second economy' began to appear on the hill. Their dull apartment houses gradually gave way to suburban villas copied from West German magazines, and to Disneyland dreamhouses.

To a Central European Beverly Hills.

myself and collapsing onto a chair there, did I first notice that the surfaces of the tables fall into two groups: some are homogeneous and some seem to have several layers — like the Gerbeaud cakes. Surely you have noticed already that the legs of the tables are of three different kinds: bronze, copper and curved… If you wish to make even more profound observations and have some more time to spend in Budapest, go on to the chapter called *For the Second Time*. You can find some distressingly non-touristy tips there — even less touristy ones than in Walk Five. To those leaving the city, may I say 'Jó utat' — Bon voyage. I hope you come back sometime.

BUDAPEST BESTS : : BUDAPEST BESTS : : BUDAPEST BESTS
Richard Baltimore III, former Deputy Chief of Mission, US Embassy

Budapest: if you want to get to know this town well, plan on hoofing it. While downtown, look up: you may discover a seldom noticed recessed statue, elegant turret or an original turn-of-the-century roof design. Meandering into apartment courtyards may reveal anything from an elaborate iron gate to an antique elevator.

Hungarians are a very friendly people; dogs or small children often help break the ice quickly. Athough I have travelled in 78 countries, this is the only city in which a kind smiling restaurant hatcheck *néni* ('aunt') returned my overcoat and commented nonchalantly that she decided to sew up its loose button while I was eating. On an entirely subjective basis, here are a few of my personal choices.

Architectural eclecticism at its best: the upper portion of the former stock exchange, now the headquarters of Hungarian TV, on Szabadság tér which has been described as 'Angkor Wat meets the Greek Temple'. **Best soup in town:** venison with tarragon at Kispipa restaurant, in Akácfa utca. **Finest turkey dishes:** Szindbád restaurant, in Markó utca. **Most unusual brew:** 'fig coffee' at the Museum restaurant in the National Museum. **Choice local throat drop:** 'Negro, a torok kéményseprője': the chimney sweeper of the throat. **Waiters with the best memory:** Hotel Intercontinental Grill where following a forty months absence my favourite dish was served as casually as if I had been away for a weekend. **A hidden first class restaurant in Óbuda:** Garvics at Ürömi köz 2. **Most misleadingly labelled statue:** Raul Wallenberg in Buda, commissioned by then US ambassador Nicholas Salgo. Plaque gives credit to local city council.

This chapter is for those who are already past the beginner's stage in Budapest. It recommends various things to see off the traditional tourist routes.

TWELVE BUILDINGS

ENTRANCE TO THE ROYAL GARDENS *I. Groza Péter rakpart.* Built in 1872, at the foot of the gardens of the Royal Palace, and guarded by two elegant lions, it was originally planned to house shops, and is now used by sculptors as workshops. The separate 'kiosk' building was built to hide the chimney of the boiler-house that heated the Palace. Both buildings were designed by Miklós Ybl, whose statue is nearby.

THE MUNICIPAL LIBRARY (KÖZPONTI SZABÓ ERVIN KÖNYV-TÁR) *VIII. Szabó Ervin tér 1.* The neo-Baroque palace (1889) of a baronial family. Except for Wednesdays, it is open daily between 9.00 a.m. and 1.00 p.m. In the cloakroom on the ground floor to the right hang some lines from a poem by János Arany: 'Oh, what a burdensome life / dressing and undressing every morning and night!'.

THE CHURCH IN REZSŐ TÉR *VIII. Rezső tér.* This Catholic church, which has a central arrangement with a dome, is situated on the main square of an eighty-odd-year-old housing estate. It was built after a competition for which only neo-Classical plans were accepted. The church was finished in 1928; the ornamentation recalls the time of the Hungarian settlement (towards the end of the 9th century). The huge bulk of the building can be seen far off from Üllői út, the main road leading south-east (and to the airport), though only few people try to get any closer.

MONUMENT TO THE MARTYRS OF 1956 — PLOT 301 *X. Új Köztemető (New Public Cemetery).* This is the monument erected by public subscription after a competition won by the sculptor György Jovánovics. The site is in the remotest part of the cemetery and was covered by weeds until 1989; it was here that the martyrs of the revolution, among them Prime Minister Imre Nagy, were buried, far away from visitors, in unmarked graves, and face down — a deliberate disgrace.

The monument is a very complex work of art, relying in its symbolism on the will of one of the executed revolutionaries, István Angyal, who mentioned a 'big white piece of stone'. In the centre of the monument there is a column exactly 1956 mm high.

'NEW' CITY HALL IN VÁCI UTCA *V. Váci utca 62-64.* The southern, less elegant part of Váci utca has just been pedestrianised. The new City Hall, where the 66-member City Council holds its sessions (usually on the last Thursday of the month), stands here, rather hidden away in the narrow street. It is open to the public. Sometimes sessions are noisy and disorderly, but I don't agree with an old friend, who works here, and once said to me, describing the Council: 'A Flea Circus, isn't it?'

GOZSDU UDVAR *Between VII. Dob utca 16. and VII. Király utca 11., near Deák tér.* A long row of buildings with a passageway through them

urtyards, between Dob utca and Király utca, with small
hops. There is a bend in the middle of the passageway so
here you started out from if you look back. The area was
e former Jewish quarter, and has preserved something of

THE FORMER HOUSE OF REPRESENTATIVES *VIII. Bródy Sándor utca 8.*
The palace, overlooking Museum Gardens, was commissioned by Emperor
Francis Joseph on 5 August 1865; the representatives had their first meeting here as little as five months later. During this time the site was chosen,
plans drawn and the work done. This kept 800 workers busy day and
night. Today it houses the Italian Cultural Institute.

KELETI RAILWAY STATION *VIII. Baross tér.* This main rail terminal of
the city was at first planned to be built in line with the Nagykörút-like
Nyugati Railway Station, which was still Austrian property at that time. In
spite of its name (Eastern Railway Station) this is the terminus for the major
express trains going westward. It was commissioned by Hungarian Rail-
ways (MÁV) and planned by Hungarian architects (Gyula Rochlitz, János
Feketeházy, 1884). On each side of the glass main entrance there are the
statues of George Stephenson and James Watt.

THE NAPOLEON COURTYARD *VI. Hajós utca 25.* This art nouveau
block, with three façades, should really be seen from a distance, but it is
built in a very narrow street. Notice the fine glass windows and the interesting small details of the building. High above, in the middle of the
façade, the figure of Napoleon looks down in contempt at the traffic crawl-
ing far below. No one walking there would ever guess that the Emperor
was watching them.

VIII. NÉPSZÍNHÁZ UTCA 16. A typical block in the Józsefváros district,
with two inner courtyards, in which I had the pleasure of living for two years.
The structure has had to be shored up with enough timber to make a forest.
The tenants in the rear court are especially dependent on each other. The
moving spirit of the building is Mr. Laci, who accepts all sorts of duties, even
delivering packages in his old Volkswagen. Naturally he also brings soda-
water bottles up for the tenants and lets repairmen into the flats.

THE MOST SCAFFOLDED BLOCK IN CENTRAL EUROPE *VIII. Pollack
Mihály tér 1.* Inside the scaffolding stands the Institute of Sociology, part of
Eötvös University. Behind that: Hungarian Radio, now a Corporation. To
the right: a beautiful gate that does not lead anywhere. To the back: the
National Museum, with the Crown Jewels.

THE WATER-LEVEL TOWER *Opposite I. Bem rakpart 3.* An ornamented iron
tower as tall as a man which keeps a diagram record of the water-level of
the Danube. Now it works by electricity. At the Buda end of Lánchíd.

TWELVE STREETS AND SQUARES

VII. BARÁT UTCA The short street has only a few houses and looks as if
it has been left behind from the 1930's. Uniform buildings with trees in
front of them and mostly with their original signboards. It was rumoured
that factory owners bought small flats here for their girlfriends, hence the
name 'Friend Street'.

VIII. BAROSS UTCA This is the main street of the Józsefváros district, leading from elegant Kálvin tér through increasingly poorer parts to the suburbs. Many joiners and upholsterers opened workshops here and their typical products are often mocked by the name 'Baross utca style'. This nickname refers to richly ornamented, old-fashioned furniture which has not changed for years and years and is bought almost exclusively by the tradespeople living in the area. From Horváth Mihály tér on, the street looks like the main street of a provincial town.

VII. DOB UTCA This street leads through the whole Erzsébetváros district from Károly körút to Rottenbiller utca. The rows of buildings are nowhere in line with each other, and they vary widely, from ramshackle single storey houses to large four storey buildings. The area between Kazinczy utca and Klauzál tér is 'block 16', which is where a complex experiment in rehabilitation was carried out. Soon after the successful reconstruction, a number of fashionable shops opened here and a post-modern building went up, in perfect harmony with its surroundings. It would seem that the deterioration of the area was successfully stopped here.

II. ENDRŐDI SÁNDOR UTCA Symbol of the new Rózsadomb. In the early 1980's large villas, breaking with the tradition of being laid out at a right angle to the road, mushroomed on this part of the hill. Large vacant sites bordered by this street, Törökvész út, Fullánk utca and Kapy utca, seem to have received building permission at the same time, giving the whole the character of a German suburb.

See Rómer Flóris utca for an example of the old Rózsadomb.

II. GARAS UTCA One of the most pleasant streets in Buda, between a park called Városmajor and Fillér utca. This is where the fashionable Rózsadomb area begins. There are some carefully built apartment blocks in the street, taller than the villas from the beginning of the century, and there are many tall trees. It looks somewhat like the XVIIth arrondissement of Paris.

VI. VÁROSLIGETI FASOR (FORMER 'GORKY' LANE) One of the most attractive streets in Pest, which leads from Lövölde tér to Városliget; that is, it runs parallel to Andrássy út — though it is much quieter. The rows of horse-chestnuts grow unmolested too. There are old and modern villas, embassies, schools and even a factory in the street. And on the corner of Bajza utca there is the legendary Grammar School of the Lutheran Church where a dozen Nobel-prize-winning émigré scientists were educated. (The school was reopened in 1989 but is still struggling to regain its reputation.)

II. GÜL BABA UTCA A steeply rising, picturesque, cobbled street, near the Buda end of Margit híd. This street leads to the tomb of the 16th century Turkish holy man Gül Baba. The 'Father of Flowers' died in Buda in 1541. His memorial is the northernmost Islamic holy place to be kept up with subsidies from the Turkish government. Next to the tomb there is a small look-out tower.

XV. DRÉGELYVÁR UTCA The main street of a housing estate called Újpalota, all ten-storey blocks, now with a good confectioner's and even a second-hand bookshop. Unfortunately the trees are growing slowly and may never reach as high as the tenth floor. Recently hundreds of small shops opened on the ground floors, changing hands and characters all too often in this Budapest of a million small entrepreneurs.

VIII. MÁTYÁS TÉR A square with a unique atmosphere in the heart of the Józsefváros district, a sort of Budapest Harlem. It is surrounded by single-storey and six-storey buildings, workshops and pubs. The atmosphere perhaps comes from the fact that the traditional Jewish middle-class share the area with gypsies originally from Koszorú utca and Tavaszmező utca; there is a touching statue of a tin-plate Christ.

II. NAPRAFORGÓ UTCA Called the 'experimental housing estate' and of real interest to those who like architecture. It was built in 1931, with the support of the city, by a building entrepreneur. The twenty-two small buildings are on a small site but very cleverly arranged. On one side, the back of the buildings overlook a small stream called Ördögárok. The names of the architects can be seen on a memorial column in the middle of the plot.

XIV. ABONYI UTCA This is an elegant, expensive short street between City Park and the busy Thököly út. Almost totally free of noise and dirt. Blocks built in the 1920's, for diplomats and generals. Halfway along there is a landmark red brick school building, the former Jewish Secondary School (Béla Lajta, 1934). Now it bears the name of Miklós Radnóti, the poet. (Jewish by birth, killed by Fascists in a forced labour camp in 1944.) This is a rare school for kids from 6 to 18. It has an atmosphere that is both inspiring and funny. My daughters attend it, having sweated through the hellish four and a half hour entrance exams, both of them.

Between 7.20 and 7.45 you can spot some of the best cars and some of the most concerned Jewish mothers, plus a couple of ministers, driving their official Volkswagen Passats. Also, some adolescents looking down on fellow-students being brought by cars. (Corner of Cházár András utca.)

XIX. KÓS KÁROLY TÉR Construction work on this working-class housing estate started in 1909, and was named after the Prime Minister who initiated the work, hence the name: Wekerle-telep. Over 900 houses were built here in very varied formats. The centre of the estate, Kós Károly tér, can be approached through four ornamental gates built in a style common in Transylvania. Altogether the impression is of a large village that has been swallowed up by the city. This square can be visited on the way to Ecseri Market.

TWELVE OLD SHOPS AND WORKSHOPS

A BUTCHER'S IN THE LEHEL MARKET *XIII. Lehel tér.* This shop, entirely built of wood, is at the southern edge of the market, near Váci út. The walls are blue and from the ceiling hangs a huge metal fan which I have never seen in operation. The butchers, just as their predecessors must have done a hundred years ago, produce pencil stubs from behind their ears to write the price of the meat on the wrapping paper. The diploma hanging above the door certifies that it is an 'Excellent shop'. The better-looking a lady-customer is, the better the meat she gets — in Budapest as in every other city, butchers are great admirers of the gentle sex.

CSIZMADIA CAR ELECTRICS *VI. Podmaniczky utca 75.* A tall, bespecta-cled, good-humoured man, Master Csizmadia is always surrounded by four or five busy assistants. He is the guardian angel of taxi drivers and will always help immediately if he can. He also gives an immediate and accurate diagnosis, free of charge. The workshop is partly equipped with fifty- or sixty-year-old tools and, at the back, he also has a classic American rolltop desk, always full of piles of paper.

FLEISHER SHIRTS *The corner of VI. Paulay Ede utca and VI. Nagymező utca.* There are very few people who still buy their shirts bespoke. This shop has remained here, almost unchanged, from the 1920's. Between the shopwindow and the shop itself the partition is made from the traditional, vertically striped engraved glass.

GLASS SCULPTURE (ÜVEGSZOBRÁSZAT) *V. Váci utca 68.* A very clumsy, awkward shop that produces useful objects and kitsch ornaments in equal measure. Like the overweight adolescent who set off for a wed-ding in the next village, but found herself instead at a ball in the royal palace. Funny and moving, a bit ridiculous.

LÁSZLÓ KLEM, FURRIER *XIII. Tátra utca 18.* The small shop was modern-ized in the early 1960's and it still has the curved plastic letters. The sign advertising 'Latest Models' must have been there since that time. At the entrance to the right a puppet dressed in a tailcoat offers notepaper and the card of the shop.

LAJOS LIBÁL, OPTICIAN *V. Veres Pálné utca 7.* Some of the shopfittings might well be a hundred years old — the small drawers for example. Contact lenses are now increasingly common. Several new shops have computers to examine their customers' eyes. They also have lengthy queues.

SÁNDOR PUSKÁS, SIGN-PAINTER *VI. Podmaniczky utca 18.* A tradi-tional sign-painter's workshop very near Nyugati Railway Station. Everything is done by hand here, the brushes are put against a mahl-stick to measure the spacing. Behind the shopwindow, to the left of the entrance, one or two ageing assistants are hard at work. In the shopwindow a dis-play of samples can be seen, not much influenced by changes in fashion.

A TOBACCONIST *XII. Márvány utca 24/b.* The usual, run-down tobac-conist with everything under the sun in the shop from shoelaces through fresh wafers to magnifying glasses fastened on pens.

But there are hardly any souvenirs, which makes it different from the tobac-conists in the city area, which have been flooded out by bits and bobs of kitsch, electronic games and expensive perfumes.

DÉNES VÁNDORFFY, WOMEN'S BUTTONS *V. Váci utca 75.* This shop is in the southern end of Váci utca, the section towards Szabadság híd. The bespectacled gentleman in a white coat hardly looks his age as he moves briskly about his small shop. There are some quite extraordinary buttons here. If he needs some special material, he goes and gets it even 'from under the earth', as the saying goes. If you stay long enough, and buy enough, he tells you about his youth. Together with a group of boy scouts he visited an infamous German totalitarian leader with a moustache. He specializes exclusively in women's buttons.

THE VELVÁRT BICYCLE REPAIR WORKSHOP *VII. Wesselényi utca 56.* Nándor Velvárt was a champion cyclist in the 1920's, and won several big international races. There are old photos, drawings and newspaper clippings in the shopwindow. Everybody thinks that the repairman is the famous one-time cyclist. Every year the word goes around that he is retiring but then he changes his mind. He simply cannot stop working. His workshop is a fine example of poetic disorder.

LAJOS ZSUREK, CABINET MAKERS *V. Irányi utca 9.* You can peep into the workshop through the door and the window. 'Contemporary' furniture is made here. There are torsos, unfinished pieces in the gallery. The light is always on until late at night.

ÁGI GYÜMÖLCS GREENGROCERS *XIII. Tátra utca 20. (Corner of Raoul Wallenberg utca).* A family greengrocer, offering the freshest and best quality produce in the area. It is a small corner shop, with an entrance on each street. Inside, there is stern-looking Ági in her sixties (careful! do not call her Aunt Ági!), who does not pamper her customers. A lot of family pictures on the wall, children and grandchildren — most of them have been known to work in the shop. And there are motorcycle ads, too. But the hallmark of the shop is beyond doubt a poster, one bought in Western Europe in the late 1960's. It shows a very small boy, who is lifting the very short skirt of a very tall young lady, and peeping upwards. The outside of the shop is witness to the same shameful visual pollution that is spreading all around Budapest: the two biggest soft drinks producers in the world want to win the decisive battle here in New Leopold Town. Both are here, on the façade, and bigger than the original, clumsy sign.

TWELVE IMPRESSIONS

THE 'ECSERI' SECOND-HAND MARKET *XIX. Nagykőrösi út 156.* The market, which has been driven step by step further and further out of town, is more interesting and varied than fleamarkets in many Western cities. It is rather like an antique shop crossed with a junk store, having all sorts of tit-bits some Western treasure hunters are looking for. There are silver pocket watches, Thonet chairs, re-cast copper lamps; there are also trendy Italian jeans, the latest pop records and plastic carrier bags just for the price of a few litres of milk. There are folk costumes, art nouveau blankets, 'Everything-for-20-Forints' piles of clothes and all sorts of goods which may not be available in town. Although foreigners are usually overcharged, they can usually find something that is in fashion again at home but is still rubbish here. Bauhaus furniture is now becoming fashionable here, but 1950's pieces still count as trash. As it is quite difficult to get good quality modern furniture in Budapest, some young people furnish their homes from here, fighting over a piece with props men from the theatres or with dealers over from Austria. The market is a museum of man-made shapes, where there is a mixture of old and new, poor and rich, fine and chaotic. Nobody likes being photographed here but you can get old pictures and postcards.

The Ecseri Market can be found at the start of the E5 motorway, coming from the city, next to the first footbridge over the road. Accessible by Bus 54. (See also Best of Budapest by András Váradi, p. 231.)

THE WALLED-IN LADY, AWAITING HER HUSBAND *XIV. Thököly út 61*. On the side-wall of a yellow apartment block a strange, life-size statue watches the street. According to the legend, this woman with her hair in a bun spent many a day on this balcony, waiting for her husband's return from the Great War. She died of the Spanish flu, two days before he arrived home. The husband had the statue erected in honour of his wife's fidelity.

THE 'FUIT' STONE *XIV. Városliget, between Olof Palme sétány and Hermina út*. A simple tomb stone with the one Latin word carved into it: FUIT ('was'). A lawyer in Pest, who wished to remain unknown, left a large amount of money to the city and asked in return to be buried here and in this manner. On All Souls Day, November 1st, many people light candles at his stone, remembering their own loved ones. Near the Museum of Transport, in the direction of Dózsa György út.

BOTANICAL GARDENS (HORTUS BOTANICUS) *VIII. Illés utca 25. T: 133-4333*. A pathetically neglected garden, full of the scents of the six thousand types of plants. The octagonal, glass-covered palm-houses in the middle (József Drescher, 1867), are in an awful state; there are whole families of squatters in some of them. Buying tickets is not taken seriously, nor is closing time. The huge, old, white dog hardly moves. Plants are arranged by their taxonomical classification, and can be seen between 9 a.m. and 4 p.m. on weekdays and between 9 a.m. to 1 p.m. at the weekend. The city has not protected this treasure. A large high-rise block now stands right next to it.

THE SECOND-HAND SHOP IN HERNÁD UTCA *VII. Hernád utca 7*. The shop offers things like bronze chandeliers, used prams and cheap chinaware. They have probably the widest range anywhere of products of the East-European souvenir industry: glass fish, tapestries, plates to hang on the wall. There is no danger of being accused of smuggling art treasures on leaving the country if you buy anything here.

THE LUKÁCS'S GARDEN AND THE THANKSGIVING TABLETS *II. Frankel Leó út 25-29*. There has been a spa on the site of this 100-year-old building since the 16th century. It is also since then that those cured have placed tablets here to express their gratitude. The tablets on the wall praise the medicinal power of the spa itself. The old-fashioned swimming-pool called Lukács (St Luke's Bath), on the same site, used to be THE place to be for an aspiring young intellectual and writer. It was an informal literary salon, latterly with a dissident flavour, from the 1950's to the mid-1980's and beyond. It badly needs a complete modernisation, anyway.

THE TOTALITARIAN STATUE THEME PARK *XXII. Balatoni út, corner of Szabadkai utca. T: 227-7446*. The debate over what to do with the Lenins, Marxes and local versions in marble and bronze (to let them stay where they were or to destroy them) ended in a wise compromise: they were relocated to the outskirts of Budapest. Most of them are bad art, but not all. The park is hardly visited; the derelict, neglected atmosphere is an unintended bonus. A must for the serious addict of Budapest, and a very pleasant outing, which takes about 30 minutes by car from the centre. On the way home it is stylish to have lunch or dinner in the theme restaurant called Marxim's (II. Kisrókus utca 23. T: 115-5036. Open 11 a.m. to 1 a.m. Mon-Sat, 6 p.m. to 1 a.m. Sun). This place became famous when they were taken to court for violating the law that bans the display of totalitarian symbols. The lady judge in the case visited the place and dismissed the charges, declaring that 'the danger posed to society is negligible'.

THE MAIN HALL OF THE POLYCLINIC IN PÉTERFY SÁNDOR UTCA

VII. Péterfy Sándor utca 8. The hospital was built by the Insurance Company for Civil Servants in 1934. Seeing the gaunt outside of the building, you would not guess how elegant the double height hall is inside; the fine glass roof can be opened up. In the hospital wing there used to be sitting rooms and kitchenettes on every floor. There was even a roof garden for sunbathing and the wards had only three to five patients. That was no longer the case even when the author of this book was born here.

XIV. ÖRS VEZÉR TÉR — THE EASTERN GATE OF THE CITY

The Örs vezér tér terminal of the Second (Red) Metro Line decants people by the thousand into the subway. Some are hurrying towards the housing estates, some are travelling on to neighbouring villages by suburban train. 300,000 people use this subway every morning. This is where one of the funniest newsvendors in the city can be found. His most famous cry is: 'Ma még van még' (Some more left, just today). Real or made-up headlines make up the rest of his advertising; and this popular, bearded man collects some 60-70 kilogrammes of coins every single day. One of his famous 'headlines' is: 'The wandering knife-grinder drank himself to death.'

DUNA CLUB OF THE MINISTRY OF THE INTERIOR

V. Zrínyi utca 5. This place used to be one of the three 'casinos' in Budapest, which were actually more like clubs in the English sense. The 'Lipótváros Casino' was built in 1895 by the Jewish upper-middle-class industrialists and financiers, who were not admitted to the two more elegant clubs.

The interior is somewhat over-the-top, wherever one looks. By the way, one couldn't look wherever one wanted here... from 1945 to 1990, this was the service club of the Ministry of the Interior. Entry was strictly prohibited to non-members. Now there is a worse- and cheaper-than-average restaurant with maddeningly slow and incompetent service. While waiting, you will have surely enough time to examine the successive strata of decoration: the furniture the comrades liked in 1965, 75 and 85. Also the recent, desperate attempt at modernisation.

By the way, Mark Twain delivered a lecture here, on 29 March 1899, during the six days he spent in Budapest. (As few people here spoke English then, the organisers commissioned a Hungarian-American to give his moustache a good tug whenever a laugh was required... or so the papers of the day said.)

This is the kind of social safari you were promised in the Preface of this book. Worth every penny.

XV. PÓLUS CENTRE SHOPPING MALL

XV. Nyírpalota utca, corner of Szentmihályi út, off Motorway 3. The biggest of the recently built shopping malls, with an interior in the style of a Wild West town — very appealing to visitors. Several hundred small shops, an ice-rink, a multiplex cinema. Occasionally you might come across a business with an imaginative name. I liked a bonds and shares vendor called 'Góg' there, a name originates in a poem by the great early 20th-century poet Endre Ady. Budapest's Chief

Architect, István Schneller, is convinced and convincing that shopping malls will soon erode the traditional shop network of the inner city. He has attempted a crusade against new malls, but the twenty-three districts of Budapest are independent fiefdoms, and Budapest is really a loose Commonwealth.

TWELVE STYLES
The most typical buildings of the city are listed here. Some of them have already been mentioned in our Walks. No pre-18th-century styles are mentioned, only those which play a major role in the city's present appearance.

BAROQUE *(especially its Austrian version)* St Anna's Church (I. Batthyány tér), Egyetemi templom (The University Church — V. Eötvös Loránd utca 5.), Orthodox Serbian Church (V. Szerb utca 4.), Franciscan Monastery and Church in Buda (II. Mártírok útja 23.), the Town Hall in Buda (I. Szentháromság utca 2.), Endrődy palace (I. Táncsics Mihály utca 3.), the Semmelweis-house (I. Apród utca 1-3.), the Central City Hall, formerly the 'Invalidusház', a hospital for disabled soldiers, (V. Városház utca 9-11.), the Castle in Nagytétény (XXII. Csókási Pál utca 9-11.).

NEO-CLASSICISM The National Museum (VIII. Múzeum körút 14-16.), the former Valero Silk Factory (V. Honvéd utca 26-30.), the synagogue in Óbuda (III. Lajos utca 163.), the County Hall (V. Városház utca 7.), the former Ludovika Academy of Military Sciences (VIII. Ludovika tér), the Trattner-House (V. Petőfi Sándor utca 2.), Károlyi Palace (V. Károlyi Mihály utca 16.), the former István Főherceg szálló (Archduke Stephen Hotel — V. Akadémia utca 16.).

ROMANTIC The Vigadó in Pest (V. Vigadó tér), the synagogue (VII. Dohány utca 2-8.), the Unger-house (Múzeum körút 7.), the Pekáry-house (VII. Király utca 47.), the Kauser-house (VIII. Gyulai Pál utca 5.), Toldy Grammar School (I. Toldy Ferenc utca 9.), Nyugati Railway Station (VI. Nyugati tér), the former House of Representatives (VIII. Bródy Sándor utca 8.).

ECLECTIC *(We have seen so many examples of this style during the Walks that here I am listing only some fine but lesser known buildings)* The new Town Hall (V. Váci utca 62-64.), the Palace of Alajos Károlyi (VIII. Pollack Mihály tér), the Parish Churches in Ferencváros (IX. Bakáts tér) and Erzsébetváros (VII. Rózsák tere), the Ádám-house (VIII. Bródy Sándor utca 4.).

ART NOUVEAU The Museum of Applied Arts (IX. Üllői út 33-37.), the Parish Church in Kőbánya (X. Szent László tér), a block of flats (V. Honvéd utca 3.), Gresham Palace (V. Roosevelt tér 5.), the Geological Institute (XIV. Stefánia út 14.), the Academy of Music (VI. Liszt Ferenc tér 8.), the Post Office Savings Bank (V. Hold utca 4.), the Gellért Hotel and Baths (XI. Szent Gellért tér).

FOLKLORISTIC-MODERN ('NATIONAL ROMANTICISM') Elementary School (XII. Városmajor utca 59.), two residential blocks (VIII. Népszínház utca 19. and XIII. Váci út 36.), the Nerve Surgery Institute (XIV. Amerikai út 57.), the Calvinist Church in Városligeti fasor (VI. Városligeti fasor 4.), the Palatinus-houses (XIII. Pozsonyi út 2.).

NEO-NEO-BAROQUE ('CORVIN-CINEMA STYLE') The Corvin Cinema (VIII. Kisfaludy köz), Kaffka Margit Grammar School (XI. Villányi út 5-7.), the former Cistercian Grammar School (XI. Villányi út 27.), the block of flats built for a mining company (V. Kossuth Lajos tér 13-15.), the former Cyclops Garage (VII. Kertész utca 24.), the new part of the Széchenyi Baths (XIV. Állatkerti körút), the original façade of the Corvin Department Store (VIII. Blaha Lujza tér).

BAUHAUS The row of apartment blocks lining XIII. Szent István park, the Atrium-houses and the cinema (II. Mártírok útja 55.), an apartment block (V. Régiposta utca 13.), the airport in Budaörs, the bell tower of the Catholic Church in Városmajor (XII. Csaba utca 7.), an apartment block (VII. Rákóczi út 4.), the Post Office headquarters (VII. Hársfa utca 47.), the Calvinist Church and office buildings (V. Szabadság tér 2.), the housing estate in Napraforgó utca (IInd district).

THE STYLE OF THE 1950's The Council House of the IInd District (II. Mechwart tér), the Dubbing Film Studio (II. Vöröshadsereg útja 68.), the College of Applied Arts (II. Zugligeti út 9-25.), a building complex (XIV. Pákozdi tér area), the Party Headquarters in Óbuda (III. Flórián tér), a student hostel (XI. Bercsényi utca 28-30.), the MOM Cultural Centre (XII. Csörsz utca 18.).

THE STYLE OF THE 1960's An office building (V. Bécsi utca 3.), a transmission station (IX. Csarnok tér 3.), Trade Union Centre (XIII. Váci út 73.), Kőbánya Cinema (X. Szent László tér), an apartment block (V. József nádor tér 8.), the Budapest Hotel (II. Szilágyi Erzsébet fasor 47.), the headquarters of the Hungarian Automobile Association (II. Rómer Flóris utca 4.), the staircase block (I. Gellérthegy utca 35.), the temporary National Theatre (VII. Hevesi Sándor tér 4.), the false front of the Corvin Department Store (VIII. Blaha Lujza tér), the Aluminium Industry Trust Building (XIII. Pozsonyi út 56.).

THE STYLE OF THE 1970's The Skála Budapest Department Store and the market (XI. Körösy József utca 6-10.), office building and car-park (V. Szervita tér), Marriott Hotel, University of Horticulture, the lecture-hall wing (XI. Villányi út 35.), Conference Centre (XI. Villányi út 35.), the central buildings of the Medical University (IX. Nagyvárad tér 1.), Athenaeum Printing House (X. Kozma utca 2.), the Domus Furniture Store (XIII. Róbert Károly körút 67.), the Hilton Hotel (I. Hess András tér).

THE END OF MODERNISM The Novotel, Penta, Intercontinental and Hyatt Hotels, the Institute of Haematology (XI. Daróczi út 24.), the Recreation Centre in Almássy tér (VII. Almássy tér 6.), the Krisztina Telephone Exchange (XII. Városmajor utca 35-37.), the Skála Metro Department Store and office building (VI. Nyugati tér 1-2.), the new section of the Museum of Transport (XIV. Városligeti körút 11.), the Waste Recycling Works (XV. Szántóföld utca 119-121.).

POST-MODERN The Taverna Hotel and Trade Centre (V. Váci utca 20. and 19.), a block of flats (VII. Klauzál tér 12.), the villa district in Endrődi Sándor utca (IInd district), the Bartók memorial building (II. Csalán utca 29.), the Ady Endre Cultural Centre (IV. Tavasz utca 4.), the Hotel Kempinski Corvinus (V. Bécsi utca), the International Trade Centre (V. Bajcsy-Zsilinszky út 12.), Hotel Liget (VI. Dózsa György út 106.), an office block (I. Hegyalja út 21.), the National Police Headquarters (XIII. Teve utca 1.).

PERIODS OF HUNGARIAN HISTORY

895–896	THE SETTLEMENT (Hungarian tribes reach the Carpathian Basin)
955	Raids and incursions into Western Europe
1000	ST STEPHEN CONVERTS HUNGARY TO CHRISTIANITY
1000–1541	INDEPENDENT HUNGARIAN KINGDOM
	1241-42 Mongolian Invasion
	1458-1490 King Mátyás (Matthias Corvinus)
	1526 Utter defeat of the Hungarian army by the Turks
1541–1686	TURKISH OCCUPATION
1686–1867	THE HABSBURG DYNASTY
	1703-1711 War of Independence led by Ferenc Rákóczi II
	1848-49 Revolution and War of Independence
	1867 The Austro/Hungarian Compromise
1867–1918	AUSTRO/HUNGARIAN COMPROMISE
1918–19	HUNGARIAN REPUBLIC
	1918 Revolution
	1919 Hungarian Soviet Republic (Béla Kun)
1919–46	KINGDOM WITHOUT A KING
	Admiral Miklós Horthy as Regent
	The Versailles Treaty of 1920 assigned three-fifths of the country to successor states
1941	Entry into the war as an ally of Germany
1944	Attempts to negotiate an armistice
1944	GERMAN INVASION
1944–48	HUNGARIAN REPUBLIC (Multi-party parliamentary democracy)
1948	'Year of the Turnover': Communist coup d'état
1956 23 Oct	REVOLUTION
1956 4 Nov	János Kádár returns in Russian tanks
1956–58	The Revenge. Over 400 executions, including Imre Nagy and his circle
1963	Amnesty for most political prisoners
1968	New Economic Management
1972–73	Reform refrozen
1979	Stagnation starts
1984–86	Debts doubled — but policies to boost economy fail
1988 May	Kádár, ailing and outmanoeuvred, is deposed after 32 years in power
1990 25 March	First democratic elections

NAMES ON STREET SIGNS AND STATUES

This is a selective list of people whose names we have met on street signs. There is a law to prevent streets being named after people who have died less than five years previously.

ADY, ENDRE (1877-1919) Poet, journalist, founder of modern Hungarian lyric poetry; central figure of intellectual life at the beginning of the century.

ANONYMUS (late 11th century – early 12th century?) Chronicler, author of the earliest Hungarian historical work, the *Gesta Hungarorum*. See Walk Four, Vajdahunyad Castle, about him and his statue.

APÁCZAI CSERE, JÁNOS (1625-1659) Hungarian theologian in Transylvania, writer, teacher. Author of the Hungarian Encyclopedia.

ARANY, JÁNOS (1817-1882) The greatest Hungarian epic poet. His statue is in front of the National Museum.

ÁRPÁD, PRINCE (?-907?) Leader of the alliance of tribes which conquered the territory of present-day Hungary, chieftain of the tribe known as the Magyars. Ancestor of the Hungarian kings.

AULICH, LAJOS (1792-1849) General, Minister of Defence during the 1848 War of Independence. One of the 13 generals executed after the defeat.

BABITS, MIHÁLY (1883-1941) Poet, literary translator and novelist. Major figure in literary life.

BAJCSY-ZSILINSZKY, ENDRE (1886-1944) Political writer and politician, a leader of the Resistance during World War II. Executed Christmas 1944.

BALASSI, BÁLINT (1554-1594) The great poet and womanizer of the Hungarian Renaissance. One of the first to write poetry in Hungarian, rather than Latin. His statue is in Kodály körönd.

BAROSS, GÁBOR (1848-1892) Politician known as the Iron Minister. Initiator of the nationalization of the railway system and the organization of cheap transport. His statue is in the square named after him.

BARTÓK, BÉLA (1881-1945) Composer, pianist, musicologist and teacher. A major figure in 20th-century European music. Died in New York. He declared in his will that no street could bear his name until there were a Hitler Square and a Mussolini Square in Budapest.

BÁTHORI, ISTVÁN (1533-1586) Prince of Transylvania, King of Poland from 1576.

BATTHYÁNY, LAJOS (1806-1849) Landowner and politician. The first Prime Minister in 1848. Executed after the defeat.

BEM, JÓZSEF (1794-1850) Polish army officer, Hungarian general, leading figure in the 1848-49 War of Independence.

BLAHA, LUJZA (1850-1926) Leading actress and prima donna, the 'Nightingale of the Nation'.

BORÁROS, JÁNOS (1755-1834) Chief Justice, later Mayor of Pest. He opened Városliget to the public.

BRÓDY, SÁNDOR (1863-1924) Writer, dramatist and muckraking journalist. Persuaded Hungarian public to appreciate naturalism.

CLARK, ÁDÁM (1811-1866) Scots architect settled in Hungary. Directed the construction of Lánchíd and designed the Tunnel.

CSOKONAI VITÉZ, MIHÁLY (1773-1805) Poet, dramatist, teacher. The major figure of the Hungarian Enlightenment.

DEÁK, FERENC (1803-1876) Politician, lawyer, the 'Sage of the Nation'. Played a decisive role in the Compromise with the Habsburgs (1867). His statue is in Roosevelt tér.

DÜRER, ALBRECHT 'Ajtósi' (1471-1528) German painter and graphic artist. His father emigrated to Nüremberg from a Hungarian village called Ajtós. The name Dürer – 'doorkeeper' – is a literal translation of the name of the Hungarian village.

EÖTVÖS, JÓZSEF (1813-1871) Writer, poet and politician. Introduced Public Education Law. His statue is outside the Marriott Hotel.

EÖTVÖS, LORÁND (1848-1919) University professor of physics, minister, son of József Eötvös, inventor of an important instrument named after him and still used in geological research.

ERKEL, FERENC (1810-1893) Composer, conductor and pianist. Founded the national opera and composed the music for the national anthem.

ERZSÉBET (Elizabeth, 'Sisi'), Queen (1837-1898) Wife of Francis Joseph Austrian Emperor and King of Hungary. She learned the Hungarian language and spent a great deal of time in Hungary.

GÁRDONYI, GÉZA (1863-1922) Writer, poet and teacher. Still one of the most widely read writers in Hungary.

HUNYADI, JÁNOS (?1407-1456) Regent and army leader. His victories over the Turkish army temporarily held up the Turkish onslaught. Father of King Matthias. His statue is on Halászbástya.

INNOCENT XI (1611-1689) Pope, born Benedetto Odescalchi; called for the liberation of Hungary from Turkish rule. His statue is in the Castle District in Hess András tér.

JÁSZAI, MARI (1850-1926) Great Hungarian tragic actress. Played many leading Shakespearian roles in the National Theatre.

JÓKAI, MÓR (1825-1904) Prolific novelist, the greatest figure of Hungarian romantic prose. A hero of the 1848 Revolution, he kept its spirit alive. Sometime Member of Parliament.

JÓZSEF, ATTILA (1905-1937) Poet, the greatest figure in 20th century Hungarian poetry. His statue is near Parliament, on the banks of the Danube.

JÓZSEF, Palatine of Hungary (1776-1847) Austrian regent who promoted the development of Pest. His statue is in József Nádor tér, the square named after him.

JULIANUS THE MONK (?-?1289) Hungarian monk and traveller who, on his journey in Asia, found the original home of the Hungarians and warned of the Mongolian invasion. His statue is behind the Hilton Hotel.

KAPISZTRÁN (Capistrano), (St) János (1386-1456) Monk, inquisitor and army leader. Played a major role in the victory over the Turks in 1456.

KARINTHY, FRIGYES (1887-1938) Writer, poet, classic Hungarian humourist, legendary jester.

KÁROLYI, MIHÁLY (1875-1955) Landowner, politician, the first President of the Hungarian Republic (1918). His ashes were ceremonially brought back to Hungary in 1962. His statue is to the right of Parliament.

KODÁLY, ZOLTÁN (1882-1967) Composer, musicologist, teacher of music. Colleague and friend of Bartók.

KOSSUTH, LAJOS (1802-1894) Lawyer, journalist, politician. Outstanding figure in the Reform Age just before the 1848 War of Independence, and Hungarian leader (as Regent) during the War. Died in exile in Turin.

KOSZTOLÁNYI, DEZSŐ (1885-1936) Poet, novelist, literary translator, journalist. One of the first to use urban life in large cities as a subject for novels. See 'Reading'.

LECHNER, ÖDÖN (1845-1914) Architect, philosopher of architecture, master of the Hungarian art nouveau.

BUDAPEST BESTS : : BUDAPEST BESTS : : BUDAPEST BESTS
Peter Doherty, Translator, Teacher, Virtuoso of English

The riverscape, the finest in Europe. The Danube scurries through Vienna, avoiding eye-contact, like an elderly aunt who lives with relatives who are ashamed of her. But she parades through the heart of Budapest in grace and beauty, boldly returning the admiring looks she draws. There are many vantage points to admire her from. In autumn one of the best is from the Pest side of the Margaret Bridge: Parliament rises from the curve of the river, the Castle lies aslant opposite and Gellért Hill looms over all the grey stillness.

The Budapest markets, better than any calendar. Budapest people, so many still with their roots in the country, have the countryman's appreciation of fresh produce, and follow the progress of the year through their tables.

Fő utca, stories in stone. The history of the city is encompassed in this one street, every building a talkative witness of what is past, passing and to come.

Jókai bean soup. A Hungarian variation on a Central European theme. A supper for a winter evening, to dispel the cold outside, to warm the heart. Like almost all the delights of home cooking, ignored by the luxury restaurants — but can be savoured in those scruffy, over-heated, cheerful places that the locals know and treasure.

Hungarian folk music. An atavistic experience, especially when the solo voice is that of a woman.

The Holocaust Memorial by Imre Varga, the poetry of pity. Varga is the creator of some of Budapest's finest modern public sculptures. When near any of them, there are many who steer themselves so as to pass by. This, in the courtyard of the Great Synagogue, thunders in quiet remembrance of Hungarian Jews murdered by Nazism.

BUDAPEST BESTS : : BUDAPEST BESTS : : BUDAPEST BESTS

Iván András Bojár, Art Historian, Professional Passer-By, A Castle District Kid

What I especially like in my native city is its transitional character. These days I prefer those corners, quarters and buildings that have been reshaped by economic and social change in the strangest ways. The former 'Stalin Baroque' style workers' hostel in Fehérvári út, for instance, was converted into a cheap hotel by some smart guys (now it's called the Hotel Ventura). The stern Classicism of the one-time dictatorship was diluted into some tacky postmodern shapes.

Another building I like is subject of an attempt to turn the clock back. Architectural progress (or 'progress') reawakened the ideals of an earlier epoch. In Váci út (No. 202/a) there was a featureless, seventies style building: ten stories of modernistic, flavourless boredom. When the former Main Street of the Dictatorship of the Proletariat was being radically revamped by multinational developers, a native real estate businessman decided to make his own mark among the other new trade centers. He bought this block, detested by others, and had it redecorated inside. Outside, he commissioned half-columns (so-called pilasters) on the hitherto bare façade, which had perfectly matched the older (mostly 1950's) buildings around. He managed to have it painted in the most vulgar of pinks, and let Coca-Cola paint its biggest ad in Central Europe on the side of the building.

A third of my 'favourites' is the Trade Center on the corner of József Attila utca and Bajcsy-Zsilinszky út, designed by József Finta, who is the defining architect of present-day Budapest. This dusty, greying building was one of the first trade centers built for foreigners. Its perplexing hodgepodge of forms is a most charming visual expression of the identity crisis of an age of transition.

These buildings, no doubt, will be hard to interpret in thirty years' time. Appreciate, please, the added value. Now, and in thirty years' time.

LISZT, FERENC (1811-1886) Romantic composer, pianist, founder of the Academy of Music.

MADÁCH, IMRE (1823-1864) Dramatist who lived in isolation in the country. Author of *The Tragedy of Man*, the classic Hungarian drama. His statue is on Margitsziget.

MIKSZÁTH, KÁLMÁN (1847-1910) Novelist, polemicist on social issues. A prolific literary figure who revived popular prose.

MUNKÁCSY, MIHÁLY (1844-1900) Realist painter, well known in Europe. His paintings are in the National Gallery.

NAGY, IMRE (1896-1958) Communist politician turned revolutionary. See more of him in Walk Two, in the commentary on his statue.

PÁZMÁNY, PÉTER (1570-1637) Cardinal-Archbishop of Esztergom, writer. Leading figure of the Counter-Reformation in Hungary. Budapest University used to bear his name.

PETERMANN, JUDGE (late 13th century-early 14th century) Hungarian judge in Buda from 1302 to 1309, when the citizens of Buda excommunicated the Pope.

PETŐFI, SÁNDOR (1823-1849) Prolific romantic poet and revolutionary politician. His statue is on the banks of the Danube.

RÁKÓCZI, FERENC II (1616-1735) Hungarian prince who became the Regent and led the War of Independence between 1703 and 1711. Died in exile in Turkey.

SAVOY, EUGENE OF (1663-1736) Franco-Austrian prince, general, liberator of Hungary. His statue is in front of the Royal Palace.

SEMMELWEIS, IGNÁC (1818-1865) Professor of Medicine, the 'Saviour of Mothers'. The first surgeon to realize the importance of antisepsis.

SZÉCHENYI, ISTVÁN (1791-1860) Hungarian count, politician and writer, called 'the greatest of Hungarians'. The prime mover behind innumerable Hungarian public institutions and enterprises. His statue is in Roosevelt tér.

SZENT ISTVÁN, St. Stephen (?977-1038) King, founder of the Hungarian state, converted to Christianity in 1000. His statue is on Halászbástya.

SZONDI, GYÖRGY (?-1552) Soldier, commander of a castle which he defended with a garrison of 150 Hungarians against 10,000 Turks. He fell there with all his soldiers. His statue is in Kodály körönd.

TÁNCSICS, MIHÁLY (1799-1884) Politician, journalist. Several times imprisoned for his ideas in the street which now bears his name. His portrait is on the wall of his former prison.

VAK BOTTYÁN, JÁNOS (?1643-1709) Legendary military leader of the Rákóczi War of Independence, a talented strategist. He lost one eye in battle, hence his nickname of 'vak' (blind). His statue is in Kodály körönd.

VÖRÖSMARTY, MIHÁLY (1800-1855) Romantic poet, author of one of the most influential patriotic poems of the last century. His statue is in the square named after him in the City.

WESSELÉNYI, MIKLÓS (1796–1850) Political writer, reformer, the 'Hero of the Flood' of 1838. One of the leaders of the anti-Austrian opposition before the Revolution.

YBL, MIKLÓS (1814-1891) Leading Hungarian architect, designer of the Opera House, the Basilica and many other public buildings, master of the neo-Renaissance style. His statue is on the banks of the Danube, at the foot of Castle Hill.

ZICHY, MIHÁLY (1827-1906) Painter, graphic artist, welcomed in several European royal courts. He died in St Petersburg.

ZRÍNYI, MIKLÓS (?1508-1566) Hungarian nobleman, who was killed at the siege of Szigetvár, defending the castle. His statue is in Kodály körönd.

ZRÍNYI, MIKLÓS (1620-1664) Army commander, poet, the 'Hero of the Sword and the Lute'. Wrote a famous epic on the heroic deeds of his great-grandfather (above). His statue is in front of the Vígszínház.

A CITY TO ENJOY

EATING WELL AND NOT TOO MUCH

Those with long memories speak nostalgically of the Budapest restaurants of the inter-war years. In what was 'the most peaceful, easygoing and least expensive city in Europe', an enormous number of restaurants competed for the discerning customer. Then came the war and the lean years that followed. In a dictionary of mine, published in the fifties, the entry for 'banana' is an illustration with minimal attempt at explanation of a phenomenon so outside ordinary experience. Like many other children of the sixties I felt that things were getting better, improving all the time. The exception, however, was eating out. My childhood memories are of rows of waiters and of food left barely touched on the plates. I later came to understand that all restaurants had the dead rigid hand of large catering companies on them. The new hotels that went up in the seventies brought new standards with them and they attracted the talented and ambitious. Eventually in the early eighties a system of contract leasing whereby restaurants were let out on three to five year leases to the highest (sealed) bid, came into being. This has led to a proliferation of privately run restaurants — often in impossible locations, for example in a street famous only for its courts of justice and rows of ambulances parked on standby alert. Over the past five years, establishments ranging from those serving hamburgers to those using silverware have joined together to provide good home cooking for their delighted neighbours.

Who remembers that now, just after the restaurant revolution?

HUNGARIAN COOKING
The predominant influence on Hungarian cooking has long been Austrian and thus, indirectly, French. Interestingly enough it was French chefs, mainly employed at the great houses, who 'liberated' Hungarian cooking from the Austrian yoke. Just as French cuisine had turned to peasant and traditional dishes for inspiration, so too did these chefs look to Hungarian peasant cooking and brought it into the mainstream of European taste.

The basis of Hungarian peasant cooking is a heavy 'rántás', a thick roux of flour and pork lard. This naturally requires rich spicing and gets it from red paprika. Ground paprika is a genuine Hungarian innovation, but although paprika is now thought of as a defining feature of Hungarian cooking, its use in fact only dates from the latter half of the eighteenth century. The eating of the fiery pepper slowly became a Hungarian virtue and as the saying goes, 'a real Magyar can handle his strong paprika well'. Another feature of Hungarian cooking is the use of sour cream. Soups and pasta also figure strongly — the latter because of the excellence of our hard flour. Our traditional cooking was only 'Europeanized' about a hundred years ago, and this conjoining is Hungarian cooking today.

The heyday of hospitality and eating out was that commonly-evoked European golden age — the two decades before the outbreak of World War I. In Hungary it has its own chronicler: the novelist and short story writer, Gyula Krúdy (1878-1933; his statue is in III. Szentlélek tér). His work, still as popular as ever, abounds in sensuous evocations and celebrations of food and its eating. His name has been bequeathed to more than a hundred dishes, all of which are worth trying. It would be only a slight exaggeration to say that the Hungarian cooking of today is his interpretation of the peasant cooking already referred to.

For many of us Krúdy's name evokes a marrowbone. Let me explain. Zoltán Huszárik's film *Szindbád* (1971) was based on Krúdy's stories of the same name. (The film deservedly features high in a recent critics' poll of the twelve best Hungarian films ever, see 'Entertainment'.) It contains a scene in which the eponymous hero — and the camera — gaze lovingly at a golden bowl of soup. Szindbád expertly cracks the marrowbone and the camera closes in on the marrow as it shimmers on the surface of a crispy slice of toast. Audiences involuntarily and inevitably gasped with pleasure. The scene has passed into the subjective consciousness of the nation and may well have contributed to the revival and rejuvenation of traditional dishes.

This process has gone far, even though Budapest can still not bear comparison with a French or an Italian city for the range and quality of its cooking. (Hungarian cooking has not encompassed the wide use of herbs or vegetables and the recent revolution in French taste is still in the offing.) Nevertheless I doubt that anyone will be seriously disappointed in any of the establishments I list below. They have all been checked personally and in consultation with two restaurateurs. This selection from more than 5,000 eating establishments should provide sustenance and more to the visitor.

For good cookery books see 'Reading'.

ELEGANT RESTAURANTS *Listed below are those which do not cater for block-booked tourist groups — hence the omission of one or two well-known names. This is not to say the latter produce bad food, but I feel that the individual customer may have difficulty in getting reasonable attention from a staff busy with and harassed by these groups. Nor are restaurants of the major hotels included since what they serve is, in general, standard international hotel fare. I am told that the restaurants of the Gellért, the Marriott and the Intercontinental enjoy a high reputation within the profession.*

AMADEUS *V. Apáczai Csere János utca 13. T: 118-4677.* Open noon to midnight, weekdays; 6 p.m. to midnight weekends. No credit cards. Capacity: 50. A recently enlarged chic place with designer decor. No printed menu, just the blackboard over the counter. Everything, except for the superb salads, is cooked on charcoal — which is why it takes ages. They overcharge shamefully for bottled mineral water. A favourite of Hungarian intellectuals in the fast lane.

BAROKK *VI. Mozsár utca 12. T: 131-8942.* Open noon to midnight. Capacity: 45. A theme restaurant, a good one. Waiters wear a costume and serve the period dishes very attentively. They really mean the style, but the décor does not stand up in the light of day.

BELCANTO *VI. Dalszínház utca 8. T: 111-8471.* Open 6 p.m. to 2 a.m. Capacity: 100. Another theme place, a curious one, 50 metres from the Opera House. The waiters stop and sing an occasional quartet or quintet, with the aid of some opera singers. Understandably overpriced. Always tourist-

and celebrity-packed. It seems doomed to naffness, but somehow isn't naff for reasons I don't understand. (Maybe because the waiters really love the opera? Or the propinquity of the most beautiful opera house in the world?) A welcome addition to the restaurant scene.

CYRANO *V. Kristóf tér 7-8. T: 266-3096.* Open 11 a.m. to midnight. Capacity: 40. A favourite of the trendy Budapest business community: a place to linger. The idiosyncratic décor includes a big chandelier that was the stage prop during the shooting of the Cyrano film (the Dépardieu version), hence the name. Considering all that, reasonably priced. The small balcony has pleasant tables. The picture of the horse on the wall (the one that looks like a Fellini Roma discovery), is of course a fake; it's by the restaurateur, an amateur designer, who conceived the whole place.

FAUSTO'S *VII. Dohány utca 5. T: 122-7806.* Open noon to 3 p.m., 7 p.m. to 11 p.m. Mon-Sat. Capacity: 60. An outstanding, unpretentious place, where it is pretty impossible to park. Come by taxi or in your chauffeur-driven company car. The Venetian kitsch décor is two grades lower than the food. Booking is of course essential. Reputed to have the best Italian food in Central Europe — no small feat, considering the supplies available.

GARVICS *III. Ürömi köz 2. T: 168-3254.* Open 5 p.m. to midnight. Closed on Sundays. Capacity: 45. A sort of éminence grise of the Budapest culinary scene: hardly advertised, and not every nouveau riche robber baron knows about it. In the III. district, in a quickly gentrifying neighbourhood called 'Újlak', in a building by a contemporary star architect of the 'National Heritage School'.

GUNDEL *XIV. Állatkerti körút 2. T: 321-3550.* Open noon to 4 p.m., 7 p.m. to 12 p.m. daily. The crowned king of the scene, with prices to match. See Walk Four for more details, p. 140.

LÉGRÁDI *V. Magyar utca 23. T: 118-6804.* Open 7 p.m. to 1 a.m. Capacity: 35. An almost secretive luxury restaurant, never advertised. Incredibly elegant — it could be the stately home of an eccentric baron from the beginning of the last century. Look for it in a cellar in a winding street in the non-touristy part of Inner City, just opposite what was once 'Maison Frida', a house of ill-repute. There are oil paintings on the white walls and the furniture is all antique. Herend china, silver cutlery, tailcoated waiters and the white-tied Légrádi brothers, whose name the establishment bears, keeping an eye on the quiet, unhurried service: it has everything of an age-old established place. Booking essential. Quiet live music. Ladies get menus without prices.

LE LÉGRÁDI ANTIQUE *V. Bárczy István utca 3-5. T 266-4993.* Open noon to 3 p.m., 7 p.m. to midnight, Mon-Fri. On the outer wall of the side of City Hall, camouflaged by a luxury antique shop downstairs, which you actually have to go through when entering the elegant-but-not-posh place which is known only to the initiated, or those invited by Mayor Demszky or one of the deputy mayors with style. Really attentive, smooth, impeccable service: you might be in a French small town aristocrat's mansion at least 150 years ago. Hardly known to the Budapest nouveau riche community, maybe because they want to be seen.

MÚZEUM *VIII. Múzeum krt. 12. T: 138-4221.* Open 10 a.m. to 2 a.m. Capacity: 150. As the name suggests, it is just round the corner from the National Museum. It's been there since 1885, one of the oldest places in town. With high ceilings, exquisite tiles high up and some original menu items — all in all, the menu is a good balance between modern cooking and traditional Hungarian killer dishes. The wine list is equally broad-minded. Prices OK.

ROBINSON *XIV. Városliget, Állatkerti körút, on a small island on the lake, overlooking the righthand side of the Museum of Fine Arts and Restaurant Gundel. T: 142-3776.* Open noon to 3 p.m. and 6 p.m. to midnight. A very elegant place in a singular setting. Views over to a fountain in a lake. Several rooms, all kinds of tables. Very smooth service, even on the somewhat less elegant open-air terrace. International menu, not very extensive. You shouldn't miss Robinson palacsinta, a sort of crépe stuffed with vanilla cream and fresh fruit salad.

SZINDBÁD *V. Markó utca 33. T: 132-2966.* Open noon to midnight weekdays, 6 p.m. to midnight weekends. Takes its name from Krúdy's hero (see introduction to this section) and not from the Arabian Nights, which gives a hint as to its culinary ambitions. A sensibly restricted menu á la carte, fully detailed, is a true delight. Excellent desserts and a good wine and liqueur list. The picturesque ceiling arches permit interference-free eaves-dropping on every conversation in the room.

VADRÓZSA *II. Pentelei Molnár utca 15. T: 135-1118.* Open 6 p.m. to midnight. Closed on Mondays. Capacity: 100. The restaurant is housed in a little, elegant villa in the most fashionable 'old money' neighbourhood in Buda: eggheads generally find the whole place a little too formal. The polyglot headwaiter likes to go over the limited, but fine menu and show you the raw ingredients. There is also a menu without prices, to prevent you from going into petty calculations.

'SHIRTSLEEVE' GOURMET RESTAURANTS *To my mind it is these restaurants that are rejuvenating Hungarian cooking. Their menus generally list many dishes cooked in the manner of the last century and they make an effort to make use of fresh and seasonal ingredients. 'Shirtsleeve' indicates that they have no desire to overwhelm their guests by their ambience. Service is straightforward and friendly. Cordon Bleu is not (usually) mis-spelled on their menus — a mark of their culinary ambitions. The early nineties saw the arrival of a different kind of shirtsleeve place, where the environment is glitzier, carefully designed by the best in town, and the menu combines the traditional Hungarian menu with international items, with an occasional effort to offer something for vegetarians.*

REMÍZ *II. Budakeszi út 5. T: 275-1396.* Open 9 a.m. to midnight every day. The old-fashioned, evocative name stands for Tram Depot; there is a big one two hundred metres away. There is a very visible landmark: the front of a yellow tramway from the interwar period, made of brick. A place where you can meet pretty much everybody from the inner-Buda new middle-class to artists, business people and junior diplomats fom nearby embassies. Not a very touristy place. It has a nice garden, with a fountain, one that presents the 'self-portrait of the artist as an acrobat' (the same one mentioned in the Budapest Bests of András Váradi, see pp. 231). The extensive menu offers Hungarian and international items. An informal place, I mean with regard to the dress code and behaviour expected. Parking is very difficult, and booking is essential.

KÉHLI VENDÉGLŐ (Mrs Kéhli's Place) *III. Mókus utca 22. T: 188-6938.* Perhaps the only more or less genuine place left of the many that used to be patronized by the immortal gourmet writer, Gyula Krúdy. You can still see a plaque commemorating his table. His spirit is everywhere — in the menu, in the decor, in the witty inscriptions on the wall. The recent facelift fortunately hasn't spoil the atmosphere (it used to be much smaller and dirtier, and much cheaper). To incorporate the cobblestoned gate area was a good idea, to flaunt the Gösser beer signs was not. The menu, in several languages, is a delight in itself. If you want to try the famous scene in the film *Szindbád*, you should order 'Forró fazék velőscsonttal' (hot-pot with marrowbone), which is served in the cosy red pot used by impoverished old ladies. Other favourites (there is a full explanation in the menu): 'Szindbád margitszigeti étke' (What Szindbád liked to eat on Margaret Island), and 'Fidó Apó magyarkúti medvetalpa' (The Magyarkút Bear Sole of Uncle Fidó). Live accordion music. Miscellaneous music from a very cheap stereo — a less than perfect sight here.

BAGOLYVÁR (Owl Castle) *XIV. Állatkerti körút 3. T: 321-3550.* Part of the Gundel complex. Open noon to midnight every day. After Gundel opened, the adjacent Owl Castle building was left empty for a year. In the end it was turned into a theme restaurant: 'Grandma's Home Cooking'. It is an all-female operation, with a limited menu that changes daily. A variety of tables and chairs, today's specials on a plain blackboard. And ah! Some of the most beautiful waitresses in town, with some of the nicest, nonsexy smiles. As if the waitresses flaunted the proverbial dignity of the Hungarian peasant girls. A very nice place for a business dinner or a Sunday lunch with the kids. In summer, families with kids usually gravitate afterwards to the zoo. Guests of all castes are invited to a free tour. Maybe they give their leftovers to the lions in return; roaring can often be heard in the restaurant. Reservation advisable, especially if you are not a friend of the owner.

KISKAKUKK (Little Cuckoo) *XIII. Pozsonyi út 12. T: 132-1732.* Open noon to 11 p.m.; noon to 4 p.m. on Sunday. Closed on Sunday in summer. On the Pest side of Margit híd, near the bridge. (See Fifth Walk.) Has kept up its reputation for a good ten years. Game specialities, with an Italian bias. Service can be fitful. But they have done something about their carpet and chairs — if not yet enough. The redhaired proprietress, from a village near Pest, is said to be complaining that it is hardly worth keeping the lease, prices being what they are. That would be a great pity.

KISPIPA (Small Pipe) *VII. Akácfa utca 38. T: 142-2587.* Open noon to midnight, daily. Hidden away in a street running parallel with Nagykörút. Fish swimming in a tank, forty-year-old posters on the wall, the charm hasn't disappeared, despite the several facelifts that have added more and more brass to the once shabby decor. The restaurant has its devoted regulars. Mr. Aubel, its proud proprietor, supervises his waiters, serves regulars personally, copes with accidents. He will cook anything to order which is not on the extensive menu. Booking is advisable for lunch, essential for an evening meal. There are four-course 'full dinners', which are worth a try.

KISBUDAGYÖNGYE (Small Pearl of Buda) *III. Kenyeres utca 34., T: 168-6402.* Open 4 p.m. to midnight every day. Booking essential... Reborn out of a well-known, shabby but charming place. The décor is a cross between post-modern and fin-de-siècle. The designer ransacked all the low quality antique shops and the Ecseri fleamarket. All the walls are panelled with sides and doors of cupboards, pieces of drawers: hardwood of all kinds, tints and patterns. It adds up to a very elegant and intimate atmosphere. Hungarian and international dishes. A nice, three-language menu, with very few misprints. The last time I was there, I enjoyed listening to a pianist and a violinist. The latter looks like a 19th-century anarchist just back from Siberia. The place seems to be thirty years old — a real compliment in Budapest.

NÁNCSI NÉNI *II. Ördögárok út 80. T: 176-5809.* Open noon to 9 p.m. In Hungarian you do not tell it to the marines, you tell it to Auntie Náncsi. The lady in question was a simple, credulous countrywoman. The restaurant is in a charming district, quite far from the centre, called Hűvösvölgy — around 20 minutes by car. It has a pleasant garden and a formidable menu and it has a regular clientèle who swear by it. Busy at all times so be prepared for a wait. Live music, menu in English and German.

SMALL RESTAURANTS *'Kisvendéglő' in Hungarian means a small dining area with room for up to 40-45 people, where the food is relatively cheap and which most often has a village feel to it (checked table-cloths, candles, wine jugs). Although they may not pay too much attention to their furnishings and fittings, they usually have a family atmosphere about them. In some places you are even expected to share your table if the place is full. With the advent of total privatization this is an endangered species. Everyone is tempted to turn his/her newly acquired place into a luxury establishment.*

BOHÉMTANYA (Bohemian Den) *VI. Paulay Ede utca 6. T: 122-1453.* Open noon to p.m. daily. The sign above the door simply says 'Söröző' — beerhouse. At the bar in the back there are always half a dozen customers having a beer while they wait. Only seats 52. Has large, well-cooked dishes and real beer-hall atmosphere. Deserves the loyalty of its regulars.

BOSZORKÁNYTANYA (Witch's Den) *III. Pacsirtamező utca 36. T: 168-9413.* Open noon to midnight, daily. Near the Buda end of Árpád híd, one of the friendliest small restaurants, run by the Bátkis. Air-conditioned, semi-elegant, with a TV-set and a huge white contraption for heating with a notice: 'Do Not Touch'. Printed menu in German and Hungarian. The staff are very easy-going, but still swift and attentive. With a small bar; the cocktail-sticks have witches riding on them. Specialities: Treasure of Belzebub and the like.

CSARNOK (Market-Hall) *V. Hold utca 11. T: 112-2016.* Open 9 a.m. to 10 p.m., Saturdays and Sundays closed. Close to the market (csarnok), this contains a few snugs in which you can eat and where you drink 'real' (cheap and rough) draught Kőbányai beer. Market stall-holders come here as well as a famous faculty member of the Department of Philosophy with her students. There is a rather uncomfortable terrace open in the summer. Specialities are lamb, mutton and marrowbone dishes.

CSENDES (The Quiet) *V. Múzeum körút 13., entrance from side-street.* T: 117-3704. Open 12 p.m. to 10 pm, closed Sundays. Quartier Latin atmosphere, for this is a favoured meeting place of university students and alumni. Rather uncomfortable seats contribute to the 'rustic' feel. Transylvanian and Slovak dishes usually on the menu — try them.

GÖRÖG TAVERNA (Greek Tavern) *VII. Csengery utca 24.* T: 141-0772. Open noon to 11 p.m. daily. Five minutes from Nagykörút, a neat, white, air-conditioned cellar. Two rooms, seven tables, for a maximum of 40 people. Oil paintings (Greek peasants). Huge, silk Greek flag. Tender Greek moussaka. Live music on Wednesday and Saturday. Bilingual menu.

HORGÁSZTANYA (Angler's Hut) *I. Fő utca 27.* T: 201-0683. Open noon to midnight daily. On the corner of a street parallel to the Buda bank, not far from Clark Ádám tér. The awkward combination of the fittings creates the ambience: a whisky advertisement, a fishing net hanging from the ceiling and a boat at the rear. The food has a country taste to it, the service can be a bit fitful and the foliage is rich.

KISBOJTÁR (Small Shepherd Boy) *XIII. Dagály utca 17.* T: 129-5657. Open 12 a.m. to 11 p.m. Closed on Sundays. A museum piece of a restaurant that preserves the genuine coziness of the late fifties and early sixties. The small shepherd boy can be seen on an incredibly kitsch oil painting and the iron railings on the windows. Several rooms, each with unforgettable design subtleties. A camp experience proper, to use the term as it was elaborted by Susan Sontag.

Food is delicious — all dishes represent Hungarian home cooking traditions. The head waitress is exceptionally warm and unobtrusive, and speaks with a slight accent in Hungarian. She is of Slovak origin. She also speaks German.

KIS ITÁLIA (Little Italy) *V. Szemere utca 22.* T: 111-4646. Open 11 a.m. to 9 p.m. Closed on Sundays. A very simple, reliable place just off Nagykörút, with about eight tables. Quick and attentive service. Very few mistakes in the Italian menu. A small drinks counter. Their slogan: If you've been satisfied, come again, and recommend us to friends; if not, send your enemies. Moderate prices.

MAKKHETES (Seven of Clubs) *XII. Németvölgyi út 56.* T: 155-7330. Open 11 a.m. to 8 p.m. daily. Named after a playing card — we call them 'magyar', but they are of Swiss origin. One of the more neglected of this type of restaurant. Nice, intimate atmosphere and packed with local families for Sunday lunch. Service is cheerful and very fast — even when crowded. Good country cooking.

SPORT *XVI.(Rákosszentmihály), Csömöri út 198.* T: 183-3364. Open 10 a.m. to 10 p.m. Closed on Mondays and Tuesdays. Anyone willing to make the pilgrimage out to this end of town is in for a pleasant surprise. One of Pest's best restaurants is located in what appears to be a shambly, tumble-down barn. Inside however it is an entirely different story, for the food has no connection with the place's exterior: well worth the 25 minute drive from the centre of town. Uncommonly rich selection of beer and wine. Specialities: Frogleg stew with gnocchi, Roast Duck with crepes filled with marrow, Beefsteak Nivernaise.

TÜKÖRY SÖRÖZŐ (Tüköry Beerbar) *V. Hold utca 15. T: 131-1931.* Open 10 a.m. to midnight, closed Saturdays and Sundays and on all public holidays except August 20th. In the centre of Lipótváros and our Second Walk. It can get almost unbearably hot in summer, even in the closed-in terrace. Inside there are snugs and a long central table. Serves Dreher (Hungarian) draught beer. At noon it is full of clerks from the banks nearby. It can be full in the afternoon as well. One has the feeling that the customers always talk business here. The décor is unbelievably shabby. On the walls you will find paper reproductions of a modern Hungarian painter just glued to the wall. The pony-tailed waitress has the nicest smile in all Budapest. The food is plain Hungarian village cooking at its best.

PROBABLY THE BEST SALAD BAR is to be found in a side street off the shorter end of a not very large Pest street, ridiculously called the 'Pest Broadway': a salad bar specializing in raw 'nuclear' salads and 'falafel' (Middle Eastern chick-pea balls). You help yourself and pay downstairs and then go upstairs and sit down. The whole place is small-scale, family-run and efficient. You can even wash your hands before or after eating.

The place is very near the Music Conservatory, so is always full of nice, musical teenagers. The other day I saw a familiar adult face at the salad bar. He moved very slowly, as if he was listening to some inward voices. He had a cap on, that's why it was difficult to recognize him. If you are fortunate, you can have a salad in the company of Miklós Perényi, the cello wizard. Have you heard his rendering of Tchaikovsky's *Rococo Variations*? If not yet, there is something substantially great ahead in your life. (VI. Paulay Ede utca, at Nagymező.)

THE KIFŐZDE: A GENRE OF ITS OWN *Called 'kifőzde' in Hungarian, this is the sort of place where there are rarely more than ten dishes available and where you would expect to find a stew made with heart or tripe or even tongue – all cooked in peasant style. Where there are tables, they are automatically shared. The kitchen is thinly partitioned off, but every comment can be heard. They get less busy at around two o'clock. Most of them close around four o'clock (unless stated otherwise). They tend to have a two-three week holiday in August. Below there are two examples, the only two that are here to stay – two Budapest institutions.*

OBVIOUSLY THE BEST KIFŐZDE: KÁDÁR ÉTKEZDE *VII. Klauzál tér 9.* Open weekdays 11.30 a.m. to 3.30 p.m.. A charming, legendary establishment in a once predominantly Jewish neighbourhood. With two soda water bottles on each table and celebrity photos on the wall (Mastroianni included). Jewish dishes on Fridays.

AN APPENDIX: EXPENSIVE PLACES WITH GYPSY MUSIC FOR TOURISTS *The following places are not among my favourite ones. However, I can't avoid mentioning them in a book for tourists and travellers. Gypsy music is a highly problematic genre. My generation, which was brought up with genuine folk music from an early age, unanimously sneers at this music, which is often confused with Hungarian folk music all over Europe (Ferenc Liszt was no exception here). The bands play pieces called 'magyar nóta' ('Hungarian song') — sugary, quasi-folkloristic songs, originally written for the hundreds of thou-*

sands who migrated to Budapest. Later magyar nóta was adopted by the upper classes as well. Nowadays it is rapidly losing its audience, even in the country. Twenty years ago there were about twenty thousand professional gypsy musicians in Hungary, as opposed to two thousand today — and they live largely off the tourists. The classic gypsy band originally consisted of no fewer than eight musicians: the 'primás' (violin), the 'kontrás' (second violin), the bass, the cymbalo-player, the clarinettist, the second 'kontrás', the cellist and the second 'prímás'. Now they are rarely seen in bands of more than four or five. Interestingly enough, a number of outstanding figures of Hungarian jazz come from gypsy musician families (from the Lakatos dynasty, among others). If you are interested in genuine gypsy (folk) music, you might buy two brilliant recordings of a band called 'Kalyi Jag' (Black Flame). Also on CD.

ALABÁRDOS *I. Országház utca 2.* *T: 156-0851.* Open 6 to 12 p.m. (from 1 May to 15 September: 10 a.m. to midnight.) Closed on Sunday.

APOSTOLOK *V. Kígyó utca 4-6.* *T: 118-3704.* Open 10 a.m. to midnight daily.

ARANYHORDÓ *I. Tárnok utca 16.* *T: 156-6765.* Open noon to midnight daily.

MARGITKERT *II. Margit utca 15.* *T: 135-4791.* Open noon to midnight daily.

MÁRVÁNYMENYASSZONY *I. Márvány utca 6. T: 175-3156.* Open 11 a.m. to midnight.

MÁTYÁS PINCE *V. Március 15. tér 7. T: 118-1693.* Open 11 a.m. to 1 a.m.

MÉNES CSÁRDA *V. Apáczai Csere János utca 15. T: 117-0803.* Open noon to midnight daily.

NEW YORK *VII. Erzsébet körút 9-11. T: 122-3849.* Open 11.30 a.m. to midnight.

PEST-BUDA *I. Fortuna utca 3. T: 156-9849.* Open 5 p.m. to 1 a.m., on Sunday: noon to midnight.

POSTAKOCSI *III. Fő tér 2. T: 168-7801.* Open 11 a.m. to midnight daily.

RÉGI ORSZÁGHÁZ *I. Országház utca 17. T: 175-0650.* Open 11 a.m. to midnight daily.

VASMACSKA *III. Laktanya utca 3-5. T: 188-7123.* Open noon to midnight. Closed on Sunday.

DRINKING WINE

or Anything Else, if you Have to*

In a beautiful essay entitled 'The Philosophy of Wine', one of the most original Hungarian thinkers of this century, Béla Hamvas, set up a classification of cultures according to their drinking customs. Hungary, of course, falls into the category of wine-drinking countries. When in Hungary, do as... well, no, to be more honest than patriotic, I cannot simply advise you to do as most Hungarians do. Fourty years of Really Existing Feudalism (1949–1989) topped with unexpected and ill-advised fits of modernization did so much harm to the well over a thousand years of the Pannonian tradition** of vine growing, wine production and wine drinking that you had better be armed with some background information before buying or ordering your first bottle in Hungary. We will start by doing away with some widespread misconceptions about Hungarian wines.

FIVE UNTRUE STATEMENTS ABOUT HUNGARIAN WINES:

1. Hungarian wine, at its best, is a cheaper, and accordingly lower quality substitute for Australian, New Zealand, South African, etc. wines. This view is generally held by foreigners and is unfortunately reiterated in many wine guides, encyclopaedias, etc. It can be explained by the disastrous marketing indulged in by Hungarian wine producers and the Hungarian state, who failed to emphasize that the traditions of Hungarian winemaking are in the same league as those of France, Italy, Germany, Spain or Portugal, and that very promising efforts have been made by many small winemakers and a few larger-scale wineries since 1991.

2. Hungarian wine is the best in the world. Full stop. The intimate conviction of most of my compatriots. This, along with some similar statements concerning various other domains of life, is the logical counterpart of Hungarian defeatism.

3. Egri Bikavér (Bull's Blood) is the best Hungarian wine. Thanks to its captivating name, this red blend from the Eger region (there is also Szekszárdi Bikavér, often of superior quality: try Vesztergombi's) acquired a certain reputation (especially in the US and Canada) as a cheap table wine, sold on the bottom shelves of supermarkets. At the same time, one of the most important grapes of the traditional blend, a variety called Kadarka, practically disappeared from the Eger wine region. Some wine

---

* This chapter has been fully rewritten by a friend of the author, András Egyedi, who currently lives and works in the Tokaj region. For more information see Rohály's Wine Guide, an annual to be found in most wine shops, as well as the excellent book by S. Kirkland, The Wines and Vines of Hungary, New World Publ. Inc., Budapest-Warsaw-Prague 1996, sold in the wine shop of the Budapest Wine Society (I. Batthyány u. 59.).

**The first significant vine plantations in the Roman province of Pannonia date back to the reign of the Emperor Probus (A.D. 276-282), a 'martyr of wine' killed by his soldiers for making them work in vineyards along the Danube and the Rhine.

makers are now considering replanting it to give back to their Bikavér the spicy aroma that once distinguished it. At the moment there are some attractive Bikavérs in the Eger region (Thummerer, G.I.A.), but for the time being wine makers (including those two) tend to make other wines their top of the range product: typically single-variety Cabernet Sauvignon.

4. There is so little real Tokaji wine produced in the Tokaj region that it is no use buying it: you are doomed to buy a fake bottle. An old myth that has caused a lot of harm to this unique (and not so small!) wine region producing over almost 5,000 ha (12,350 acres) of what Louis XIV of France called 'the wine of kings, the king of wines': Tokaji Aszú. It is for its extraordinary quality and for its legendary reputation that the name Tokaji has in fact been borrowed by different wines around the world. The most famous among these are probably Tokay d'Alsace (actually a Pinot Gris, a French variety widely cultivated also in Hungary and giving some very pleasant wines north of Lake Balaton under the name of Szürkebarát) and the Italian white varietal Tocai — neither wine has anything to do with Hungarian Tokaji and their confusing names will soon disappear from wine labels, but they are not fake Tokaji: they are different wines made from different varieties with different vinification methods.

5. Tokaji wines are 'for women' because they are 'too sweet'. No comment.

WHERE SHOULD I BUY WINE IN BUDAPEST?

Avoid buying wine in supermarkets or in the grocery shop round the corner. This general precept that might be corroborated by painful experiences from your own country, applies even more to Hungary where the first (very auspicious!) steps have just been made towards restoring our wine culture to its pre-war glory. Stick to the best wine shops that only sell wines from reliable producers and where the staff can give you the necessary information on the wines they have in stock or even advice on matching wine with occasions, individual tastes or food. Here is a list of selected wine shops in Budapest.

1. THE BEST WINE SHOP IN TOWN:

Wine shop of the Budapest Bortársaság (Budapest Wine Society) *I. Batthyány utca 59., 5 minutes' walk from Moszkva tér on the way up to Castle Hill, Tel./Fax: 212-2569, (06) 20 322 400.* Open Mon-Fri 10 a.m.-8 p.m.; Sat 10 a.m.-6 p.m. — if you go there, don't miss the 'habos mákos', a delicious cake with poppy seeds and meringue to be found at 'Bécsi Kapu' a confectioner's just around the corner in Ostrom utca. A functionally and tastefully furnished cellar wine shop (mind the steps on leaving though) where Attila Tálos and his colleagues will guide you in fluent English around the stunning complexity of Hungarian wine regions, grape varieties and the growing number of quality-conscious wine producers. Good choice of Hungarian wines from all the interesting wine regions. Very reasonable prices. Free tastings on Saturdays between 2 and 5 p.m..

2. RUNNER UP

La Boutique des Vins *V. József Attila utca 12., 2 minutes walk from Vörösmarty tér. Tel: 117-5919.* Open

Mon-Fri 10 a.m.-8 p.m.; Sat 10 a.m.-3 p.m. The owner, Malatinszky Csaba, an ex-Gundel sommelier is an outstanding expert on Hungarian wines; if you find him in the shop, he will be glad to share his knowledge. His staff are competent too. Good choice of Hungarian wines from all interesting wine regions but it is difficult to see what is actually on the shelves.

3. OTHER EXCELLENT WINE SHOPS:

Borház *VI. Jókai tér 7., off Andrássy út, near Oktogon. Tel. 153-4849.* Open Mon-Fri 10 a.m.-8 p.m.; Sat 10 a.m.-6 p.m.. A very pleasant shop, though you may find neither the range nor the degree of professionalism of the two listed above. But Borház still offers a remarkable choice at reasonable prices.

Demijohn *Cukor utca 4., 2 minutes' walk from Ferenciek tere. Tel. 118-4467; Fax 118-6509.* Open Mon-Fri 11.30 a.m.-7.30 p.m.; Sat 10 a.m.-4 p.m.. (Also a branch on the way up to Rózsadomb, at *Margit utca 27. Tel. 325-0714.*) One of the first quality wine shops in Budapest, this belongs to Interconsult Winery Neszmély. The choice is for the most part restricted to their own wines which, however, span various wine regions. (They also sell a number of French, Spanish, Italian, and New World wines, not necessarily the best though, because of Hungarian import duties.) In 1996 Interconsult's wine maker Ákos Kamocsay was elected East-European wine maker of the year by the UK trade.

Wine City *V. Párisi utca 1., off Váci utca. Tel.: 118-2683.* Open: Mon-Fri; Sat. Don't let the tourist trap atmosphere deceive you: the choice of wines is excellent. They also sell cheese.

Le Sommelier *V. Régiposta utca 14., off Váci utca. Tel.: 266-1314.* Open: Mon-Fri 9 a.m.-8 p.m.; Sat 9 a.m.-2 p.m.; Sun 11 a.m.-5 p.m.. (And a branch in the Budagyöngye Centre, *Szilágyi Erzsébet fasor 121. Tel.: 275-2194.*) Reasonable choice.

4. MORE WINE SHOPS IN ALPHABETICAL ORDER:

Bacchus Wine Shop *V. Váci u 30.*
Bor-Tár *XII, Böszörményi út 34/a.*
Corvinum-Gasztrovin *XII. Ugocsa u 5.*
Ex-Veritas *VI. Káldy Gy. u 4.*
Exkluzív Palackozott Italok *V. Régiposta u 7-9.*
Goldvinter *III. Kolosy tér 5-6.*
Rea Wines and Antiquities *II. Lukács u 1.*
Tálentum *V. Bajcsy-Zs. út 66.*
Venyige Borház *IV. Szentimre u. 1.*
Vinarium *XXII. Dézsmaház u. 19/a.*

HUNGARIAN WINE REGIONS

The North-west
1. Sopron
2. Pannonhalma-Sokoró Foothills
3. Ászár-Neszmély
4. Mór **5.** Etyek **6.** Somló

Lake Balaton
7. Balatonmellék **8.** Badacsony
9. Balatonfüred-Csopak
10. South-Balaton

The South-west
11. Villány-Siklós
12. Mecsek Foothills
13. Szekszárd

Great Plains
14. Hajós-Vaskút **15.** Kiskunság
16. Csongrád

The North-east
17. Mátra Foothills **18.** Eger
19. Bükk Foothills **20.** Tokaj

THE CLIMATE AND THE LAND The whole of
Hungary is within the vine-growing zone. This fact along with the special soil and climatic qualities of various regions explains how such a small country can boast twenty strictly delimited quality wine districts. Indeed, one of the most amazing facts about Hungarian wines is their great variety: Hungary belongs to the few vine-growing countries in the world to produce the entire range of classic wine styles including whites, rosés, reds and natural sweet wines (botrytis whites). These different wines are made from an impressive range of grape varieties characterized by a certain equilibrium between international* and local** varieties. Hungary is often considered a white wine country — this opinion, though to some extent well-grounded, is at the very least complicated by a few wine districts (especially Villány, but also Szekszárd, Eger, Sopron, and Hajós-Vaskút) producing mostly red wines of constantly improving quality. Lack of space precludes discussion of all twenty, so the following is an introduction to fewer than half of our quality wine districts, arranged alphabetically.

LAKE BALATON There are four completely distinct wine districts around Lake Balaton: Balatonfüred-Csopak, Badacsony, Balatonmellék on the north side, and Dél-Balaton on the south side. The three wine districts on the north produce almost exclusively white wines from Pinot Gris (Szürkebarát), Olaszrizling (Welschriesling), Kéknyelű (a local variety from Badacsony which gives wines of amazing quality and elegance, but which did not escape the fate of low-yielding varieties in a planned economy and so has almost completely disappeared), Chardonnay, and Sauvignon. These wines are usually marked by high acidity (especially in Badacsony) beautifully counterbalanced by a rich, full-bodied texture. Viticulture in the North Balaton districts suffered a lot from lakeside tourism during the Communist era and recovery has been hindered by extremely high land prices and by complicated real estate conditions caused by the steady advance of week-end cottages up hills where vines had been cultivated since Roman times.

South Balaton, though historically less important, has evolved into one of the most prominent wine districts in Hungary, producing mostly whites (including sparkling wines) but also some remarkable reds.

BEST PRODUCERS
Balatonfüred-Csopak: Figula Mihály, Csopakvin. *Badacsony:* Szent Orbán Pince. *Balatonmellék:* Kál-Vin Pincészet, Scheller Szőlőbirtok. *Dél-Balaton:* Eifert és Légli, Légli Ottó, Szt. Donatus, Öregbaglas, BB Chapel Hill.

EGER It may be surprising that this wine region in the northern hills of Hungary produces more reds than whites. However, the reds, though something less than full-bodied, are often distinguished by an elegance

---

* *I.e. Cabernet Sauvignon, Cabernet Franc, Merlot, and Pinot Noir for reds; Chardonnay, Sauvignon blanc and Rhine Riesling for whites.*

** *By local, I do not only mean exclusively or originally Hungarian varieties, but also the typical varieties of Central Eastern Europe: Kadarka, Kékfrankos, Kékportó, and Zweigelt for reds; Furmint, Hárslevelű, Welschriesling, Kéknyelű, Ezerjó, Juhfark, Leányka, Királyleányka, etc. for whites.*

and refined complexity that is hard to find in wines with higher alcohol and tannin. Major varieties include Kékfrankos (Blaufränkisch), the Cabernets, Merlot, and Oportó (Blauer Portugieser) for reds (Kadarka might come back in a few years and experiments with Pinot Noir are worth watching); Leányka, Királyleányka, Chardonnay, Pinot Gris (Szürkebarát) and Hárslevelű (esp. in Debrő) for whites.

Meanwhile, thriving in the shadow of the gigantic Egervin Winery (which has some interesting vintages of old Bull's Blood, proof that this wine saw better times before the 'Bull's Blood project' started in 1979), are a few small producers who have gone a long way in reviving quality-conscious viticulture and wine making.

BEST PRODUCERS Gál Tibor (G.I.A.), Pók Tamás, Thummerer Vilmos, Vincze Béla as well as Egervin for old vintages.

SOMLÓ The smallest and perhaps the most beautiful wine district in Hungary. Five hundred hectares of vines extend over the hillside beneath the basaltic 'organ pipes' that form the top of the hat-shaped volcanic hill. Somló produces some of the best traditional Hungarian dry whites to accompany the more solid glories of Hungarian cuisine. A good Somló is a very acidic, 'masculine' wine (legend has it that royal couples drank it on their wedding night to have a baby boy), and utterly unmistakable: once you have tasted a Somló, you will always recognize wines from this region even if you don't bother much about regularly brushing up your olfactory memory. Somló is not the place to produce fashionable light whites distinguished by a pleasing varietal character: whether you drink a Furmint, a Hárslevelű, a Juhfark (a local variety, virtually restricted to this region), or an Olaszrizling (Welschriesling) it will first and foremost be a Somló. During the Communist years Somló wines were practically unobtainable and they are still relatively rare because of the contrast between the reputation and the size of the region. But don't leave Hungary without tasting one.

BEST PRODUCERS Fekete Béla, Györgykovács Imre, Inhauser István.

SZEKSZÁRD along with Villány, is one of the most dynamically developing Hungarian wine regions. A growing number of quality-conscious wine makers are trying to combine modern vinification methods and traditions to produce some of the best reds in Hungary and also some delicious white wines. Szekszárd red wines are somewhere between the finesse of the Eger, and the richness of the Villány reds. Kadarka, a classic Hungarian variety, survived somewhat better quantity-oriented viticulture here than in Eger, but Szekszárdi Kadarka remains a rarity that you should taste to have an idea of traditional Hungarian red wines that go well with paprika-based dishes. Major varieties include Cabernet Sauvignon, Cabernet Franc, Merlot, Kékfrankos, Kékoportó, used either for varietals or for the Szekszárdi Bikavér blend, more ancient than its Eger counterpart, even if for some reason the Hungarian state gave Eger exclusive rights to use the name in 1977. This is why until recently these wines were bottled under the Szekszárdi Óvörös label.

Even if Szekszárd is mostly associated with red wine, slightly more white is actually made, and Szekszárd now produces some delightful single-variety Chardonnays, Zöld Veltlinis (i.e. Austria's major variety, there called Grüner Veltliner), and Királyleánykas.

BEST PRODUCERS
Aliscavin, Bátaapáti Kastélyborok, Dúzsi, Heimann, Sárosdi, Takler, Vesztergombi, Vida.

TOKAJ A quasi-mythic wine region with completely original vinification methods and the world's oldest system of classified growths. A mainly clay soil of volcanic origin; a micro-climate characterized by a hot summer and a long, sunny autumn with morning fogs to encourage the development of *botrytis cinerea*, or noble rot; labyrinthine cellars to provide a constant temperature of 10-12°C and a very high humidity; the survival of centuries-old traditions; and last but not least the large-scale investment that followed the renewal of interest in the international wine scene: all add up to produce one of the greatest wines of the world.

Only four varieties are authorized for the production of Tokaj wines*: Furmint, Hárslevelű, Yellow Muscat, and Oremus. The harvest begins late, traditionally on the feast of Simon, i.e. October 28. If there are enough good quality Aszú-berries, i.e. if botrytis and sunshine have sufficiently desiccated a considerable proportion of the grapes, they are harvested separately, grape by grape, or selected immediately after the picking on large tables. The non-botrytised grapes are used to make the dry varietals Tokaji Furmint, Tokaji Hárslevelű, etc., some of which are used as the base wines for the production of the sweet dessert wine called Tokaji Aszú. According to the traditional method first described in the 17th century, and which is still the basis of Aszú production, three to six (occasionally seven) times 25 kg (the content of a 'puttony', i.e. a hod originally used for the harvest) of raisin-like aszú-grapes, crushed to form what is called aszú-paste, are added to 136 litres of base wine or must. The aszú-paste and the base wine must re-ferment together to make a wine with approximately 12-13% by volume of alcohol and a very high degree of residual (non-fermented) sugar, ranging from 60 g/l to over 180 g/l. Obviously, it is first of all the number of hods of aszú-berries that determines the concentration of the final product; thus Tokaji Aszús range from 3 puttonyos through 4, 5, and 6 puttonyos up to Aszú Eszencia, which is the equivalent of a 7 puttonyos (a term which is never used). Tokaji Aszú Eszencia is not to be confused with Tokaji Eszencia, which is the free-run juice of the aszú-grapes, racked off without pressing and giving a nectar of unequalled, almost honey-like concentration.

When aszú-grapes are not picked separately, the entire grape clusters including botrytised parts are vinified as a standard white wine to give Tokaji Szamorodni,** which can be dry (száraz) or sweet (édes), according to the proportion of non-selected aszú-berries in the crop. Both Aszú and Szamorodni wines are matured in oak barrels.

---

* *Wines made here from other varieties are rare and are not entitled to use the Tokaj appellation: e.g. Zempléni Chardonnay.*

** *This word of Polish origin means 'as it grew'.*

Since 1991 a number of important foreign investors including the wine writer Hugh Johnson, the 'Bordeaux baron' Jean-Michel Cazes and the owners of the most famous Spanish bodega 'Vega Sicilia', have created new wineries in a bid to combine ancient traditions with state-of-the-art technology and restore Tokaj wines to the glory of their 18th-century heyday.

BEST PRODUCERS

Árvay J., Bodrog-Várhegy (Dereszla), Bodvin, Disznókő, Hétszőlő, Lauder-Láng, Megyer, Monyók J., Oremus, Pajzos, Royal Palatine, Royal Tokaji Wine Co., Szepsy István, Tokaj Kereskedőház (ex-state farm)., Úri Borok.

BEST ASZÚ VINTAGES 37(!!!), 40, 41, 56, 57, 59, 63, 68, 72(!!!), 75(!!!), 83, 88, 93(!!!), 95.

VILLÁNY-SIKLÓS This is a wine region with two faces: Villány produces perhaps the best red wines in Hungary, whereas Siklós is known for its whites. This is the region where small private vintners responded the most rapidly and effectively to the new situation created by the onset of the market economy and by the collapse of the Soviet market, which had favoured low-quality mass production. Villány has become the flagship of Hungarian quality wine since 1990. This is where stainless steel tanks and new oak barrels first became standard equipment in some wineries.

Villány reds are undoubtedly the most full-bodied in Hungary, usually characterised by high tannin, alcohol, and extract content. They are also the country's most suitable wines for maturation in new oak barrels. Top Villány vintners typically have a range of wines going from light reds and rosés made from the local varieties Kékoportó and Kékfrankos through blends of the latter with Cabernet or Merlot to more robust wines often based exclusively on the Bordeaux varieties.

BEST PRODUCERS

Bock József, Gere Attila, Gere Tamás, Polgár Zoltán, Tiffán Ede, Vylyan, different vintners under the 'Le Sommelier' label. The ex-state farm now called Villányi Borászati Rt. also has some fine wines including older vintages.

GOOD AVAILABLE VINTAGES 87, 91, 92, 93, 95.

WINE TOURISM This is a Budapest guide, but I cannot help suggesting a trip right to the source of oenological discovery. Tasting wine in a producer's cellar, seeing the vineyards, and talking to the people who make the wine adds a great deal to the pleasure of drinking the end product and leads to a much more profound understanding of wine. Ask one of the wine shops mentioned in this chapter for advice on how to organise such visits and for more addresses. Consulting Kirkland's book (see page 196) may also be useful. I can only give here a few telephone numbers of producers who are well organized for visitors:

Ászár-Neszmély: Interconsult Ltd. (Kamocsay Ákos) T: (34) 350-051

Balaton: Eifert és Légli (85) 350 600; Figula Mihály T: (87) 343-557

Eger: Thummerer Vilmos T: (60) 352-754

Somló: Inhauser István T: (30) 562-741

Tokaj: Disznókő T: (47) 361-371; Hétszőlő (47) 352-009; Megyer T: (47) 312-310. You can also contact the Tokaj Renaissance Association which represents the seventeen top wineries of the region: T: (47) 380-765.

Villány: Bock József T: (72) 492-388, (60) 362-380; Gere Attila T: (72) 492-839 You can also contact the Villány-Siklós Wine Route Association T: (72) 479-700.

TWELVE BUDAPEST RESTAURANTS WITH A GOOD WINE SELECTION

Bel Canto, Café Kör, Chez Daniel, Fausto's, Fortuna, Gundel, Kacsa, Kisbudagyöngye, Légrádi Antique, LouLou, Múzeum, Náncsi Néni. (See details in the chapter 'Eating Well'.)

FOR THE SOCIAL EXPERIENCE, *rather than for their oenological merit, I suggest that you try one of the occasional wine-bars called* **borozó,** *many of which are supplied by wine growers' co-operatives. (There is another type of place called* **talponálló,** *a wine counter, which is generally filthy and full of drunks.) However, the wine-bar here, unlike its counterpart in London or New York, is neither overpriced nor pretentious. Many a borozó has stand-up tables where customers take their wine at leisure, occasionally helping it down with slices of* **zsíros kenyér** *which they buy at the counter. (Try it: it is bread and pork dripping sprinkled with paprika, often topped with fresh onion slices.) In Hungary it is common to add soda to your wine. Our word for this is* **fröccs** *and there are five varieties of this spritzer.*

	wine	soda	meaning
kisfröccs	10cl	10cl	small spritzer
nagyfröccs	20cl	10cl	large spritzer
hosszúlépés	10cl	20cl	long step
házmester	30cl	20cl	janitor
viceházmester	20cl	30cl	under-janitor

The selection below takes into account general ambience as well as the quality of the wine served. They usually open at 9 a.m., but bear in mind that most of them close between 8 p.m. and 10 p.m.

SOME WINE BARS

Szarvas pince *I. Szarvas tér 2.* Expensive. Next to the restaurant of the same name.

Hattyú *I. Hattyú utca 1.* Near the bottom of Castle Hill. Cheap and cheerful.

Postakocsi borozó *III. Fő tér 2.* Expensive and favoured by tourists. Bar in form of coach, meals served.

Gresham borozó *V. Roosevelt tér 5.* See the Second Walk for information on the building. The entrance is on Mérleg utca. Marble tables but not pricey.

Grinzingi *V. Veres Pálné utca 10.* Table and counter service. Hard-boiled eggs, sandwiches and salads, wine from the barrel. Middle price range and off the tourist track.

Rondella borozó *V. Régiposta utca 4.* Touristy and the prices are San Francisco.

Villány-Siklósi borozó *V. Gerlóczy utca 13.* Close to Deák tér. A wine-counter but serves wine from two interesting areas.

Móri borozó *XIII. Pozsonyi út 39.*

Tortilla borbár *XIII. Budai Nagy Antal utca 3.* Hungarian drinks and Spanish tortilla. Tiny figurine of Bacchus on the wall.

IF YOU HAVE TO: BEER AND BEER DRINKING It is only in the last dozen years or so that Hungary has become a beer drinking country. Now the figure has come up to about 100 litres per head per year, around four times the figure for wine. We have a preference for 'világos', that is lager or light beers although 'barna' (dark) beer is also brewed. (This latter tends to be too sweet for the English palate.) The beer most popular in the shops is Kőbányai Világos, the cheapest type, brewed in the Kőbánya district of Pest. This brewery is an old established one. The Kőbányai Brewery runs two beer halls of its own, serving what a native of Budapest considers as the only real beer on draught: the Sörcsárda on the brewery premises themselves and the Aranyászok in the inner city.

Three Kőbányai beers are sold in the shops: the Világos (pale), the Korona and the Jubileum. Look out also for the excellent Czech bottled beers such as Pilsner Urquell and Budweiser. Tuborg and Holsten are brewed here under licence. Beer sold in small 33cl bottles or cans is rather more expensive than in half litre bottles. All these bottled beers are better chilled.

Over the last few years, several foreign companies — mainly Austrian and German — have sponsored beer-houses selling their products.

Also, bear in mind: a true Hungarian never clinks his beer-mug.

IF YOU ABSOLUTELY HAVE TO: HUNGARIAN SPIRITS The best known of Hungarian spirits is 'barackpálinka', apricot brandy, which is perversely drunk as an aperitif, thus well and truly numbing the tastebuds. A variation is 'óbarack', old apricot. The other fruit brandies are 'cseresznye', cherry, 'szilva', plum and 'körte', pear: a worthwhile brand of the last is called Vilmos Körte. The best cognac-type drink distilled here is Tokaji Borpárlat.

Tourists may often be offered a lethal concoction that was invented for their benefit a few decades back: 'puszta-koktél', which is three parts apricot brandy to two parts Mecseki liqueur and three parts Tokaji Szamorodni wine and all parts lethal.

All cafés and coffee-houses serve spirits in a measure of 5 cl called 'féldeci' or 'feles' (a half decilitre) and waiters tend to turn up their nose if asked for a 'kis' (small) measure of spirits, this being 'only' 3 cl. It is advisable to ask for a 'kis szóda' or 'kísérő', which will get you a glass of soda water. Mixers and ice are generally unknown. If you ask for a vodka and tonic you will get a glass of vodka and a glass of tonic.

Cocktails have made some penetration in the larger hotels and a few of the places calling themselves 'drinkbár', cocktail bars, are recognizably such.

Another drink worth noting is Unicum, a dark brown liqueur containing 23 herbs which has a passing resemblance to Underberg and Fernet Branca. (The old pre-war placards for Unicum are much sought after for decorating walls.) After decades of shortage, you can get it in practically every shop selling spirits. (Opt for the ones with a red, white and green top if there is a choice.) The expat authors of the *Time Out Guide to Budapest* call it 'The Hungarian National Accelerator'. They also say that 'it looks like an old style anarchist's bomb, and smells like a hospital corridor... It's vaguely sweet and minty, and bitter as a winter's night.' It made me wonder why I like it. But I do.

CAFÉS AND BARS TO TRY
HUNGARIAN SPIRITS

Angelica *I. Batthyány tér 7.* Open 10 a.m. to 8 p.m. daily. Entrance a few steps below street level. In an old house, neo-Baroque furnishings. An old-fashioned, though not old place, ideal for discussing the meaning of life.

Café Pierrot *I. Fortuna utca 14.* Open 5 p.m. to 1 a.m., Sundays 10 a.m. to 11 p.m. On the site of a six hundred-year-old baker's. Great lengths gone to in finding the Far Eastern fixtures. The pianist is eager to play your favourites. Music from 8 p.m. when the cover is peeled off the piano.

Ruszwurm *I. Szentháromság utca 3.* Open 10 a.m. to 8 p.m. Closed on Wednesdays. A Baroque coffeehouse dating from 1824, still with its ambiance intact. Its confectionery was so famous that couriers were sent from Vienna to buy it. Marvellous ice-creams too. It is swamped by tourists, although you may be able to get a table in its tiny salon between 2 and 3 on a winter afternoon. Its famous speciality is its Linzer, given the name by an owner who shared a prison-cell with a man of that name in the aftermath of the 1848–1849 War of Independence.

Miniatűr presszó *II. Rózsahegy utca 1.* Open 7 p.m. to 3 a.m. Closed Sundays. A genuine Pest place, despite being in Buda, with red silk décor, intact from the sixties. Not everybody is invited into the inner room. Full of aged burghers, bohemians, and couples wildly in love. Service is old-fashioned and very attentive. Music from 9 onwards, by a real classy Budapest pianist.

Csendes drink *V. Múzeum körút 13.* Open noon to 8 p.m., closed Sundays. Entrance on the side street.

Galéria drink bár *V. Vitkovics Mihály utca 6.* Open 11 a.m. to midnight daily. Pleasant fin de siècle bar. Pottery and pictures on display are for sale. Remarkably nice and friendly barmaids, not for sale but innovative mixers.

Café Gerbaud *V. Vörösmarty tér 7.* Open Main hall 9 a.m. to 9 p.m. daily. Side-room 7 a.m. to 9 p.m. Discussed in the 'Introduction to the Walks', the great monument to the old coffeehouse life. Owing to the huge number of foreign visitors, service can be fitful. If an elderly lady in a blue smock comes to the table and reaches for your coat, do not be alarmed — she is the cloakroom attendant.

John Bull *V. Apáczai Csere János utca 17.* An English pub — as genuine and expensive as its location suggests. In the middle of the tourist reservation, opposite the back of Intercontinental Hotel.

Mumm Champagne bár *V. Kristóf tér 8.* A beautiful tapestry shows the whereabouts of Otard county (adjacent to Cognac). Drinks of the same brand. Possibly the most expensive place in town.

Pertu drink *V. Váci utca 39.* American cocktails — has made the Manhattan stylish.

Café Művész *VI. Andrássy út 29.* Open 8 a.m. to 8 p.m., Saturdays 10 a.m. to 8 p.m., closed Sundays. Mirrors, statues and paintings surround the rather elderly regulars who sit over their papers. The terrace is pleasant though a little noisy. The chairs are chained up in the evening to stop them from being stolen. For more, see Walk Four.

Café Incognito *VI. Liszt Ferenc tér 3. T: 267-0239.* Open 10 a.m. to midnight Monday to Friday, noon to midnight Saturday and Sunday. Was obviously the trendiest café in Budapest in the spring of 1997. It brought Liszt Ferenc tér back to life. Students, expats, yuppies, also musicians from the nearby Music Academy. Overpriced draught Heineken, and tables of all shapes and kinds. I like the series of funny pictograms by the door: what not to bring in. Also the signs on the two toilet doors: 'Zsuzsi' and 'Rudi', respectively. Guess where you should go.

Paris, Texas *IX. Ráday utca 22. T: 218-0570.* Open 10 a.m. to 2 p.m. Monday to Friday, 4 p.m. to 2 p.m. Saturday and Sunday.

ART TO SEE, ART TO BUY

A FIRST SWALLOW IN THE GALLERY SCENE 'The only good artist is a dead artist — the age-old Budapest art dealers' witticism seemed to have lost some of its validity in the spring of 1995 when the first glitzy New York-style gallery opened in downtown Budapest, between the river and the touristy part of Váci utca. The openings at this new gallery are as popular with the more elderly of Hungarian yuppies as with egghead society — what little of it remains from the good old days.

The gallery's artists tend to paint huge, colourful, sensuous canvases. The couple who set the gallery up must know all too well that their investment was unlikely to show much of a return in the next hundred years. One of the owners, an exceptionally elegant lady in her mid (late?) thirties, actually runs the gallery — and it is her ancestral name, an Irish one, that it bears. Her husband, the other owner, is a successful real estate dealer — always present at the evening openings (perhaps they are always that late so he can make them) flaunting his unorthodox dress code. He somehow (some days) looks like a cross between a futures trader and a rock opera set designer.

With the opening of this gallery, contemporary Hungarian art inevitably began its long march towards one day becoming chic.

Dovin Gallery (V. Galamb utca 6. Open 10 a.m.–6 p.m., Sat 11 a.m.–2 p.m.)

AND THE SECOND About the same time Design Center Budapest (a small publicly owned agency that recommended designers and services to businesses, held exhibitions and operated a wonderful small library) had to close down, a new, three-level shop opened in a somewhat unlikely place: in Theresa Town, an impoverished area but, it is true, only 300 metres east from downtown.

In the shop and gallery there was everything from copies of Mackintosh and Rietveld through classic Breuer to recent Philip Starck chairs and tables. Over in the corner there is a spacious design studio, which is said to have frequent visitors from the Russian nouveau riche, who come to order furniture both for their homes and their new office buildings.

Then a second gallery was opened, at a more predictable address, in the southern section of Váci utca (just before it was converted into a pedestrian zone), in the basement of the New City Hall, which is a hundred-year-old fine Beaux Arts palace. This was cold-bloodedly designed to be a tool of owner Miklós Vincze's vision: to match the latest international design with recent Hungarian fine art — and lure his clients who buy modern furniture into buying some paintings, just to go with it.

The space is highly original, capitalizing on the brick vaults, and the random tubes — things that are impossible to hide anyway. The name of the gallery is coined from the names of the two owners: VAM = Vincze **Agnes** and Miklós. (**VAM Design 1.** VI. Király utca 20., corner Káldy Gyula, **VAM Design 2:** V. Váci utca 64.)

BY FAR THE BEST IN SZENTENDRE Szentendre is the classic out-of-Budapest destination for tourists, and also for travellers; the latter avoid the museum devoted to the potter Margit Kovács, who was an innovator in the thirties, and later an over-decorated Grand Dame of Kitsch. The serious traveller will find a great amount of great art, by artists hitherto unknown to him. Mr Erdész and his recently enlarged gallery, in one of the nicest inner courtyards of Szentendre, is a revelation both for those who have always admired, and those who haven't heard about early 20th-century painting. Sándor Bortnyik and Lajos Vajda are the two fortes of the gallery, amongst a dozen other names. Here you can have a close and intimate look at them, in an unusual atmosphere.

Erdész Galéria (Szentendre, Bercsényi utca 4. T: (0626) 317–925).

THE STATE AS SANTA CLAUS Just as in literature, the advent of liberty favoured the very good and the very bad artists in Hungary. The mass in the middle, the vast majority in fact, found themselves frustrated, poor and with their careers somewhat in question.

Beginning in the early eighties a new generation emerged — much more market-oriented, familiar with the modern museums of Europe (and some of them even with those of America), able to speak foreign languages, even if not brilliantly. A little later they capitalized on a somewhat artificial, politically oriented interest in Hungarian art, during a wonderful half decade, the second half of the eighties.

But thousands had to learn that they were on their way to becoming Sunday painters. Now they are art teachers, civil servants, paste-up artists at illustrated papers and graphic designers during the week.

The once all-powerful Fine Arts Fund, which used to buy pictures from hundreds of artists on a weekly basis, had in the meantime lost its monopolies and most of its marketable assets. But it was not relieved of its duty to pay pensions to old artists, and this it now had to do with insufficient income. It was turned into a quasi-independent foundation, a purse into which the state has to put money from year to year. It still has some of its galleries, selling a very mixed, commercial stock.

Magyar Alkotóművészeti Közalapítvány ('Public Foundation for Creative Artists'): VI. Báthori utca 10.

(One of the surviving **'Képcsarnok' Galleries**: VI. Teréz körút 11.)

A FORMERLY REALLY FAVOURED ARTIST Few contemporary Hungarian artists could hope to live to see a museum solely devoted to their work. Imre Varga, the maverick septuagenarian sculptor is one of the few. But the road was a long one for the artist, so much liked by the general public, and so much sneered at by quite a few fellow artists.

For a decade or so, in the fifties and early sixties, he was treated like a pariah: he came from a landowning family, and as a young man during the war was even a fighter pilot in the Hungarian air force.

Later on, during the first 'thaw' he let himself be lured into the role of 'conspicuously-non-party-member-favoured artist', hoping that fate and good luck would allow him to influence things for the better. In the end he was even 'elected' to be an MP, in that parody of a Parliament, which had four sessions a year, one per season and each a maximum of 3 days long.

There was a year when Varga was said to have used about 75 per cent of the capacity of the one and only bronze statue foundry in Hungary. He slowly fitted into the cookie-cutter-mould of a great Hungarian artist, known all over Europe, able to blend tradition and modernity, often on TV. He has had no fewer than 300 works accomplished and erected, a rare feat. His undoubted masterpiece is the Wallenberg monument. This is in a tucked-away part of Buda, because in 1986 it needed considerable bravery to commemorate the Swedish diplomat who saved tens of thousands of Jews before finally vanishing into the Soviet Gulag.

With the advent of democracy Mr Varga again became a sort of a pariah, accused of having been some kind of collaborator. He mainly works for Germany now, but recently a Bartók statue of his was erected in Brussels. He spends his time in the museum devoted to his works, a wise old man still with an imposing presence, over six foot tall, ultra-short silver hair, like a retired four-star general of the US Air Force. He speaks German and French well, though not as far as I know English.

Imre Varga Collection (III. Laktanya utca 7.)

ARTIST-WATCHING, BUDAPEST Artists live everywhere around the country. If you want to be sure to spot them, you can go to at least two places in Budapest where there are purpose-built artists' colonies. The bigger of the two is in outer Joseph Town, a hundred metres from Népstadion (People's Stadium) underground station. Built before World War I, it consists of about three dozen homes of varying sizes, each one with a studio — some of them very big. Around them all is a communal garden. There is one fence around the colony, with an iron gate that is never locked. The style is sometimes loosely called National Romanticism. It consists of a lot of woodwork, complicated latticed roofs, and undressed stone on the outside, especially near the bottom. The colony is a lovely place, even after some major alterations were made, not always with the necessary expertise, so to speak. The right to live here was theoretically granted to artists, not to their widows or their offspring. But few of the families ever left. There are unfinished statues all around the place, and even some finished works of totalitarian 'art', by the dreaded former dean of the Academy of Fine Arts. A famous Hungarian prose writer turned film director lives here with his sculptor wife, as does a brilliant illustrator with an interest in Oriental art. It is definitely worth the walk.

The other one is a nice art nouveau block of flats, with studios, built in 1903 only a hundred metres from the elegant Gellért Hotel, a little way up the hill. You saw it if you didn't skip Walk Three. Typical tenants here are a couple, both painters, who launched themselves into successful careers in graphic design. They work a lot, participating in the rat race. So they leave early, and get back home late. The husband gets away for three weeks once or twice a year, to a summer colony for artists in Kecskemét, about a hundred kilometres south of Budapest. During that time he does not want to hear about business. He even switches off his cellular phone. Or at least the bleeper.

Százados út Artists' Colony (VIII. Százados út 3–13.), **Block of Flats with Studios** (XI. Kelenhegyi út 12–14.)

ARTIST-WATCHING, NORTH-WEST HUNGARY

Lake Balaton, the 'Hungarian Sea', is a naff place on the whole. But not the relatively untouched villages north of it, roughly between Veszprém and Tapolca, one of the most attractive parts of Hungary, admired for its volcanic hills. The fashion for buying summer homes and studios here started some fifteen years ago, as more and more villagers abandoned their houses. The craze spread from a village called Kapolcs, where the composer István Márta and friends organize the annual 'Valley of Arts' festival with hundreds of smaller events (mid-June/mid-July) on the fringe. By now not only do several dozen of the better-known painters have studios here, but writers and actors are also crowding in. (György Konrád has a wonderful house in a village called Hegymagas.) The traditionalist painter/semi-professional hussar Győző Somogyi moved permanently to a village called Salföld and gathered quite a herd of different animals. His house is a frequent destination of pilgrimage for dewy-eyed egghead students, dreaming of the simple life.

The last outpost is a shore resort called Szigliget, where there is a Writers' 'Creative Center' (a relic of past times – even the name), a big, yellow, dilapidated complex on a big estate that once belonged to an aristocratic family. One of their scions, the cult figure/writer Péter Esterházy traditionally spends three weeks there (with some of his four kids) at the beginning of August, always with the same bunch of friends — writers, musicians and artists. It is no small privilege to be invited, even for the day.

Szigligeti Alkotóház — Szigliget Creative Center, Veszprém County.

CONTEMPORARY GALLERIES: PROBABLY THE TWELVE BEST

Artpool VI. Liszt Ferenc tér 10. T: 121–0883. e–mail: artpool@art-pool.hu

Bartók 32 XI. Bartók Béla út 32. T: 186–9038

Bolt Galéria VIII. Leonardo da Vinci utca 40. T: 324-7769

Dovin V. Galamb utca 6. T: 118–3673

Erdész Galéria Szentendre, Bercsényi utca 4. T: (0626) 317–925

Galéria 56 V. Falk Miksa utca 7. T: 269-2529

Körmendi Galéria II. Nagybányai út 25. T: 176-2110

Hans Knoll VI. Liszt Ferenc tér 10. First Floor. T: 121-1556

Pandora Galéria VIII. Népszínház utca 42. T: 113-4927

Stúdió 1900 XIII. Balzac utca 30. T: 129-5553

Várfok 14 I. Várfok utca 14. T: 115-2165

Vam Design 2 V. Váci utca 64. T: 118-1594

BUYING ARTWORK During the last two or three decades most art of any quality was sold straight by the artists, from their studios, to friends and collectors. If you are a collector, you should go to a gallery and look around, and ask them to organize a visit to an artist who catches your eye. It is worth paying the gallery's mark-up. You can leaf through catalogues and colour transparencies, and you are helped with formalities (you need a permit to take works of art out of the country) which might save embarrassing moments at the border.

The gallery world is still a small one in Hungary: friendliness, jealousy and pickiness are all features. It is worth visiting some artists, through their galleries, to see the rather old-world, unspoilt way of life they lead: artists, daydreamers, social critics, craftspeople at the same time. So different from the stars of the Western hemisphere.

A good prelude to any purchase of Hungarian art might be a visit to the recently opened Contemporary Museum of Art, (if you happened to have missed it during Walk One). Bear in mind that you can visit any of the artists exhibited there, through practically any of the galleries mentioned above.

NAME-DROPPING: ART TO LIVE WITH

Here is a list of my favourites, a highly subjective listing. I know many artists, and I will try to avoid offending them by emphasizing that the following list is not about their artistic greatness, but about their friendliness and decorative value. There are others, who are great for museums or for real collectors (who will hardly rely on my advanced amateur advice concerning what to buy).

In my home there are two paintings by **Gábor Karátson**, the writer, painter, eco-advocate, and Oriental thinker. He is a living legend, a man in his early sixties, with long silver hair, who practically never sells his art: he would rather face difficulties in paying his electricity bill. I especially like his oil paintings from the seventies with picturesque titles, like the one that hangs in my living room: 'Borg hits the ball during serving in the 1974 Monte Carlo Open Tournament', and his illustrations to Goethe's *Faust*. Obviously, he is not represented by any of the galleries, but any of them can contact him.

Károly Kelemen paints large, sensual canvases, full of bright colours, that since the mid-eighties always include some teddy-bears. He loves to paraphrase some classics of Picasso. He is a large, ever-smiling man, very easygoing, like a giant teddy-bear, who rarely says no to one more glass.

László Fehér is a rare case when the man in the street, Hungarian art critic gurus and the international gallery world can agree on and universally acclaim his importance as an artist. Fehér has intense, usually large canvases, often with a white, outlined little boy against a black backdrop. And his other favourite colour is yellow. I don't think you will have enough cash here with you to buy a picture. And only certain kinds of American Express card let you withdraw the amount in question.

Being his godfather, I have long been biased towards the art of **István Orosz**, at least since I suggested he take a Greek pseudonym ΟΥΤΙΣ ('oohtis') which means Nobody in Greek. Odysseus pretended to be called this when the Cyclops, the one-eyed giant asked him his name. (So when he had been blinded and was howling in agony and his fellow-giants asked who had hurt him, he thundered: 'Nobody hurt me! Nobody hurt me'.) István is a self-confessed disciple of M. C. Escher, the Dutch graphic artist, and much more. He resurrected the ancient medieval genre of 'anamorphosis'; he has been a cartoon film director, and also a highly successful poster-designer. In my flat there are some of the brilliant, illusionist etchings that express his constant homage to classical antiquity and to Piranesi. He isn't represented by galleries, as far as I know. (He lives in Budakeszi, a suburb of Budapest about 20 kilometres to the west.)

I mentioned **Győző Somogyi**, the Salföld hermit above. Until about ten years ago he only made bitter black-and-white prints that provided a sort of X-ray of an impoverished Hungary sinking into an intellectual mediocrity and torpor. Then he decided to switch to painting colourful, large canvases of historical scenes. He became obsessed with military heroism. He is also active as an illustrator of books on the history of Hussars. You might come across some of his original drawings made for these books.

I also own some work by my friend and co-author of this book, painter/illustrator **András Felvidéki**, who helped a lot in opening my eyes to the subtleties of Budapest's architecture and urban fabric. They are etchings of Budapest details and of imaginary, symbolic scenes that are unmistakably Budapest. Over the last couple of years he has begun to paint city scenes, trolley bus interiors, a lit-up telephone booth at night, a couple kissing on a bench in the old underground. He is a solitary figure, involved in teaching art students, who had a brief adventure contributing high-quality design for a computer game you might well be playing at home.

Another Six Names I Would Buy, If I Ever Sold An Unexpectedly High Number of Copies of The Present Book: Imre Bak, Ákos Birkás, István Mácsai (an old master, who has always loved the city), Károly Pollacsek, Tamás Soós, Erzsébet Vojnich.

GOING OUT

BUDAPEST AS A MUSEUM *Most of Budapest is still a big open-air museum. So going out for a walk, in whatever direction, can be most enjoyable, if you keep your eye out for adventure.*

There is a curious old-fashioned quality to most of the streets outside the tourist reservation but within the green belt and before the pre-fab 'suburbia'. You can walk into most blocks unhindered and watch people come and go on the staircases. People live in closely knit communities, sometimes terrorized by newcomers, who do not care about rules more or less respected by most of the tenants. Budapest remains a mostly unsegregated city: you still can't tell what kind of people live behind a certain façade. If you bought this book back home, in the Tattered Cover in Denver, or Powell's in Portland, or Kramerbooks in DC, or the Triangle Bookshop in London, or the Atheneum Boekhandel in Amsterdam, and read the Crash Course in your very own armchair at home, then you will have your pair of binoculars with you here. If not, you can still buy a cheap pair at one of the fleamarkets. Then you can start your fieldwork in 'applied people-watching'. You should have a close look at Budapest balconies. Most people storing stuff on balconies are oblivious of the fact that it is not hidden from the eyes of others. The balcony of a family is as telltale a sign of their values and tastes, as their rubbish. But easier to have a look at.

Of course the very rich have already left, but in the urban jungle of quickly gentrifying Pest there are tens of thousands of middle class people who like it there. Especially since, thanks to the parking revolution, locals can park for free.

That is the situation in Pest, the big open-air museum, where I have lived all my life. After all, 'nothing ever happens in Buda'.

THE SMALL MUSEUM EXPERIENCE In Budapest museums, big or small, we find old underpaid ladies as attendants. But in the small ones one often finds a peculiar, and very pleasant, small-town quality, a sort of personal pride on the part of the attendants, who go out of their way to show you the collection. A unique character for Budapest, though travellers might recognise it from other cities, London for instance, at the Sir John Soane Museum.

While the big museum means alienation for the attendant, and perhaps job insecurity, in the small one it means indispensability and family. And for the visitor it almost always gives something extra. A nice example is the

STAMP MUSEUM *(VII. Hársfa utca 47.)* This small museum is really a big one — one of the biggest of its kind in the world. It is housed in a classic modern building from the late twenties: a huge ministry block in a small, impoverished side street. As a matter of fact it is on the line of 'the least finished avenue' in Budapest. It was planned in the twenties, but it was never realized except for a big arch at the beginning and the first hundred metres. (VII. Madách Imre út, beginning at Madách square).

The permanent exhibition of about eleven million stamps is displayed in quite an ingenious way (something had to be done, otherwise it would have taken up the whole building) on 3200 pull-out metal frames, uniting the requirements of storage and exhibition. The stamps are shown by country and continent. There are also temporary exhibitions including shows of prize-winning designs and of counterfeit stamps.

Hungarian stamps are still painfully picturesque and painfully obsolete to look at. The state has always used a heavy hand in deciding what to put on the stamps, at least since the museum was founded in 1930. (As a matter of fact, since 1918.) In the Dark Fifties so many stamps were published that the collector's market was ruined. In the late fifties the Post Office had to make a ridiculous regulation: to prevent stamps from falling below face value, they declared that any Hungarian stamp issued since 1946, i.e. the forint era, could be used to pay the postage.

The Post Office has been given a facelift recently, with a corporate identity designed by the same British design company that redesigned the Royal Mail image. That should affect stamps soon. Perhaps the officials deciding about stamp designs should visit the Art Pool mail-art collection at VI. Liszt Ferenc tér 10.

AN OVERSIZE SMALL MUSEUM: THERMAE MAIORES — THE BIG BATH Most Budapest people do not know about the Big Bath, they simply drive over it on the flyover leading on M11 toward Szentendre and the Danube Bend. The Bath, a small piece of which was unearthed as early as 1778 (!) is, to of many of us Budapest freaks, nothing less than the symbol of a changed attitude towards the city.

During its heyday, in the first part of the 3rd century, the Roman settlement in North Buda, called Aquincum, had at least ten, perhaps twelve thousand inhabitants; it was a really sizeable town for those days. There has been a big museum here since 1892 to show the public the very extensive remains of the centre of the civilian town 'the municipium'. (III. Szentendrei út 139., open from spring to autumn.)

The area in the immediate neighbourhood of Óbuda or Old Buda was bulldozed in the mid and late seventies, and the most awful ten-storey pre-fab buildings were erected by the hundred. In 1981, when the pillars of the flyover were dug, they hit a part of the Big Bath, just in the place where some of the experts expected it. So it was now impossible to go on with the building, and bury the ruins forever, as some of the construction lobbyists quite possibly wanted to. Instead the pillars were redesigned almost overnight, the site was excavated, and a unique underground passageway built that criss-crosses all around the open-air museum.

The Bath was really huge, even by modern standards: 120x140 metres. There were all kinds of pools, hot, lukewarm and cold, the hot heated from underneath, by hot air conducted through a network of pipes. In the underground passage there are dozens of replica statues and tablets and big glass-covered panels that tell you about the history of the bath. The glass seems to be a problem with the younger generation. The more liberal society became in the early eighties, the more glass was broken here. The authorities should experiment with enameled, graffiti-resistant signs. Do they exist at all?

12 OTHER GREAT SMALL MUSEUMS

The Underground Museum
(in the Deák tér subway) the carriage in which Emperor Francis Joseph travelled when he opened the line in 1896.
György Ráth Museum, Chinese art downstairs, Japanese upstairs (VI. Városligeti fasor 12.)
Pál Molnár C. Collection the charming family establishment of an artist much influenced by Art Deco; many stylish prints from the thirties (XI. Ménesi út 65.)
Telefónia Museum the old, mechanical switchboard of the Castle District. (I. Úri utca 49.)
'Golden Eagle' Pharmacy Museum (I. Tárnok utca 18.)
Lutheran Museum a former school. Sándor Petőfi, the great poet, was a slightly problematic schoolkid here; now you are shown round by retired priests (V. Deák tér 4.)
Music History Museum
(I. Táncsics Mihály utca 7.)
Jewish Museum in the Great Synagogue (VII. Dohány utca 2.)
The Imre Varga Collection the representative sculptor of the seventies: he is often around (III. Laktanya utca 7.)
Vasarely Museum for those who fancy the op-art master (III. Szentlélek tér 1.)
Museum of Electrotechnology in a massive, elegant Art Deco building, in the heart of the former Jewish District (VII. Kazinczy utca 21.)
Gizi Bajor Actors' Museum great for émigré eggheads, who usually remember childhood performances better than anyone.
(XII. Stromfeld Aurél út 16.)

INFORMATION ON GOING OUT — NOT TO MUSEUMS You'll perhaps forgive me for not stressing the obvious. You can find information in the first place in the two competing English-speaking weeklies — both have excellent listings, and they are constantly improving their readability and reliability. This competition is especially strong in movie listings. *Budapest Sun*'s film guide is laid out with an excellent grid, showing the movie theatres across, and the days down. *Budapest Week* recently changed its format; it is called 'Now Playing — Pull Out Film Guide'. It gives ratings, relatively well written summaries (miles away, though, from their apparent role model, London's *Time Out*).

Of the booklets you are likely to be bombarded with, the Budapest volume produced by *Where Magazine* ('Where in Budapest') is quite low-key and reliable.

Below I have compiled 'Twelve Obvious Places to Go Out', and twelve more adventurous destinations. But I can't produce an invitation to a Hungarian home, I mean I can't invite everyone to my very own home. (There were times, when I attempted that. Especially, when we moved to Leopold Town, and quite incidentally, we found ourselves on the route of Walk Two, and I often met readers of mine, scrutinizing the rooftop ornaments of the immortal Post Office Savings Bank. I had to discontinue this practice, succumbing to more than symbolic pressure from my wife.)

GOING TO A HUNGARIAN HOME would beat most of my ideas below. As a matter of fact, it is relatively easy to be invited to a Hungarian home. As to how to elicit an invitation there is only one good piece of advice:

always forewarn the friends of the friends of the friends of your close friends, whose phone number was reluctantly given to you. Call them in advance that you'll come, even better write in advance. Most Budapest professional people (not only eggheads) tend to have at least one extra job, so it might not be easy to devote to you two evenings while you are in Budapest. They also have a busy social life.

If you want a guaranteed non-invitation, call them while you are in Budapest, give them very short notice.

On the day you arrive, offer to take them out to some luxury/moderately-priced chic restaurant (See 'Eating Well'). When you talk to them over the phone, give them five or six ideas, remarking that they were reported to be a well-known gourmet couple/person in town. (They will be flattered and your invitation to their home come an inch nearer.)

You might offer to expand the invitation to some of their friends for that first meeting. That might make it easier for them (they can include some people with whom a meeting was long overdue). Your local contacts will be grateful, and it is unlikely that they will let you pay the friends' bill. If the invitation finally materialises, you can mention again that you would be delighted to meet some other friends of theirs.

GOING IN Once you are invited, you can relax, and be as inquisitive as you wish. 'You don't mind if I look round, do you?' is considered an entirely natural question, but it is rarely heard, since the hosts will almost certainly show you around. You will probably see many more books in the homes of Hungarian professionals than in the homes of their European or American counterparts. And it can be embarrassing how in Hungary a high IQ and a fine wit are not necessarily accompanied by good taste. You can see incredibly low quality, naff furniture (especially lamps!), and neglected, broken parts in an intellectually exuberant, vibrant home.

The naffest part of a home (if you like that kind of inverted, camp enjoyment) is often the balcony. It is rarely shown, unless you ask, as I often do when I look round homes on my first (and sometimes it is my last) invitation: 'Can I enjoy the panorama for a moment?'

And I can't withhold a reluctant warning: in some élite intellectual homes you might be confronted with toilets you do not regularly meet, except on movie screens. If you know what I mean.

TWELVE OBVIOUS PLACES TO GO OUT IN BUDAPEST

The Music Academy: A major concert in the Great Hall.

The Music Academy: Graduation concert in the Small Hall (a bouquet of roses needed).

An opening in Műcsarnok (Exhibition Hall).

Gundel: Taking your time. Meeting friends at the bar at seven, sitting down to Table 8 at nine, finishing the evening in the cellar.

Watching a Hungarian Movie in the rented room of Odeon Art Video (8 seats).

The Opera House: *Cosí Fan Tutte*, then dinner at Bel Canto Restaurant.

Genuine folk dance evening at the National Theatre (as a spectator).

Genuine operetta in the Municipal Operetta Theatre (*The Csárdás Princess*).
Organ concert in the Matthias Church: Bach and Liszt, by the organist of Notre Dame, or a rising Hungarian star.
Friday evening in the Great Synagogue.
Shakespeare or Kleist in Katona József Színház.
Shakespeare or Kleist in Új Színház.

TWELVE ADVENTUROUS EVENINGS OUT

People-watching in Picasso Point Corner of Hajós and Ó utca.
Alternative Theatre Event: Watching the audience.
Dance House Event in the Almássy tér Community Center (spectator – or participatory).
Reading *Paul Street Boys* by Ferenc Molnár in the National Library (closing time: 9 p.m.), if you can't find it in a bookshop.
The Municipal Circus: Dividing your attention between the show and the spectators.
Gay Cabaret in Angel Bar.
Evening Lecture in Collegium Budapest, on some scholarly subject (have a pre-lecture nap in the afternoon, it can be very heavy going and long).
Wichmann's: brooding over the meaning of life.
International Soccer Event in Kétballábas Pub, with Hungarian fans (definitely not for the faint-hearted).
Open-air Concert: Vajdahunyad or Martonvásár (the latter on the M1, devoted exclusively to Beethoven).
Watching the award-winning Hungarian film at the Filmszemle (Film Review) in early February (Corvin Budapest Film Palace).
Egghead party at an iconoclastic

poet/playwright/essayist's lavish home on the riverfront, overlooking both Inner City Parish Church and Erzsébet híd and Gellért-hegy. Practically every New Year's Eve.

TWELVE HUNGARIAN FILMS NOT TO MISS

During the summer months some cinemas and clubs show recent Hungarian films with English subtitles. (Most of them can also be rented from Mokép Videotéka.) The following are not to be missed:
Miklós Jancsó: *Confrontation* (*Fényes szelek*, 1969). A historical parable telling the story of some 'revolutionary guardists' in the late 1940's, who start to disrupt the ancien régime with gusto until they themselves are pushed off the scene. (The original title was *Shining Winds*.)
Péter Bacsó: *The Witness* (*A tanú*, 1969). A hilarious comedy about the Hungary of the early 1950's, when the authorities even experimented with growing cotton and lemons. Premièred only in 1979. ('A satirical comedy worthy to rank with Schweik' — *The Times*, London, February 1982.)
Zoltán Huszárik: *Szindbád* (1971). A sensuous, poetic film on the last days of an ageing hedonist, based on the writings of Gyula Krúdy, chronicler of small town fin de siècle. An exceptionally successful collaboration between director, cameraman, composer and actor. See also the introduction to 'Eating Well'. ('A striking tour de force of visual technique and metaphysical imagery' — *Films and Filming*. December 1981.)
Gyula Gazdag: *The Whistling Cobblestone* (*A sípoló macskakő*, 1972). A philosophical satire set in a summer student work camp — on the perspectives of the post-'68

generation. A feature film made using documentary techniques. Amateur cast, black and white. ('High-spirited and sly satire of government incompetence.' — *Village Voice*, October 1979.)

Pál Sándor: *Football of the Good Old Days* (*Régi idők focija*, 1973). A very funny and moderately sentimental film about an impoverished laundry owner, who persists in sponsoring a football team in the Budapest of the 1920's, during the first low ebb of Hungarian football, because 'The team must go on!'. Starring the great comedian Dezső Garas.

András Jeles: *Little Valentino* (*A kis Valentino*, 1979). A young man runs away with some ten thousand forints and loiters around some of the most depressing Budapest neighbourhoods. A malicious, black, but delightful film about human values in the late 1970's. Explains a lot about this city. (Filmed in black and white with an amateur cast.)

Gábor Bódy: *Psyché* (1980). A spectacular two-part epic; an intellectual, somewhat esoteric movie 'relating' the adventures of a fictitious poetess from the 1770's up to now. The greatest achievement of this avantgarde film-maker (1946-86), it gave a new twist to post-modernity. ('A chronicle of seduction and depravity in the experimental, avantgarde vein' — *Variety*, New York, May 1981.)

István Szabó: *Mephisto* (1981). A two-part, well-made, spectacular movie piece about the life of an actor in Germany during the first half of the 20th century, which explores the limits of cooperation between the gifted and the powerful. Starring Klaus Maria Brandauer. (An Oscar-winning film based on the novel by Klaus Mann.)

János Rózsa: *Kiss, Mummy* (*Csók, anyu*, 1986). Day to day life in an upper middle class family, described in the witty, somewhat sentimental vein of recent American cinema. Gives an insider's knowledge of present-day Hungary. In the role of the overworked, amoral father, the great all-rounder of Hungarian film and cinema, Róbert Koltai.

Bereményi Géza: *Eldorádó* (1988). A very funny and vivid story of a market vendor, his struggle to survive in the dark 1950's, and his love for his grandson. Excellent fun plus authentic acting, and even some startling music. The story ends in 1956. Starring Károly Eperjes, a marvellous actor — a kind of Dépardieu of the Hungarian cinema.

János Szász: *Woyzeck* (1992). A black-and-white rendering of the Büchner classic, transferred to an unspecified time in the 20th century. Excellent, breathtaking acting; dense, tense apocalyptic atmosphere all along. Also highly original photography. World famous.

Péter Gothár: *Vaska* (1996). 'A fairy tale from the Gulag.' A hilariously funny tragi-comedy, shot entirely in St. Petersburg, mostly, with Russian actors. With a lot of the Russian dialogue left untranslated in the Hungarian version — for Hungarian eggheads, who spent a decade at school struggling with Russian. A film with a beginning, a middle and an end. The English version is now available on video.

A NOTE ON THE DANCE-HOUSE MOVEMENT The end of the last century saw a large number of people moving to the capital; they cherished their folksongs here for a while but rarely passed them on the next generation. The middle class favoured (as they still do) a type of folk-music-like romantic songs, called 'Hungarian song'. (These are the equivalent of *Loch Lomond* in its connection to real Scottish folk-music.) Then around 1970, quite out of the blue, two young musicians, Ferenc Sebő and Béla Halmos, brought the real thing into fashion overnight. This music is still alive around the village of Szék in Transylvania, in a part of Romania which used to belong to Hungary. It was not only folk-music that became trendy at that time: traditional dancing also captured the imagination of the young. Many gathered in 'dance-houses' week after week to dance to live Transylvanian music, to learn new dances and to enjoy the melodies. Anyone could join at any time and newcomers were taught whatever steps had been mastered by earlier converts. Soon dance-houses for children also appeared. A one-day/one-night national dance-house festival takes place every year in the Budapest Sports Hall, as part of the Budapest Spring Festival, where folk musicians and dancers come together from all over the country and thousands of people dance together. These occasions are usually accompanied by a busy folk crafts market. Dance-houses have a unique atmosphere — the devotees regard each other as members of a large family. This rising interest in folk-music is reflected in a number of records.

It is a rewarding, quite unexpected experience to attend a dance-house session. Something you haven't heard about, and might fall in love with, there and then.

LIBRARIES *had a special significance in keeping free thought alive in Hungary. They were a link to the past, and also to the free world. Big libraries regularly ordered basic works of social sciences, and they were accessible to all university students. That was an intrinsic characteristic of the mild totalitarianism of the régime in Hungary: expertise was more or less allowed to develop — it just wasn't used; or very little of it.*

In Russia undesirable books had a special catalogue, accessible only to reliable comrades: in Hungary any system along those lines would have been unthinkable. There were two telltale letters stamped on the catalogue card of a couple of hundred openly anti-Communist books in English, or published by émigré Hungarian presses: Z.A.: 'restricted – literally, 'closed' – material'. But they were not as restricted as all that: any professor was willing to sign a request for a student: and with that the books became available.

I only once heard about a shameful trick that affected the given level of freedom of information: in the periodicals department of Gorkhy Library (see below) Time magazine and Newsweek were on the shelves — but certain issues somehow did not find their way there – the ones with politically sensitive features, of course. But by the beginning of the following year the issues were back where they belonged. In the bound volumes none of them is missing.

On the other hand, the library of the Academy was the cradle of the dissident movement. They helped everyone with inter-library loans: first they tried the Uppsala University Library, and if the book wasn't there, they were willing to contact a US library. As far as I was concerned, Uppsala had everything.

NATIONAL 'SZÉCHÉNYI' LIBRARY *(Royal Castle, Wing F, i.e. the huge part overlooking Buda. The easiest way in is by the special lift from Dózsa György tér. T: 175-7533. Open Monday 1 p.m.- 9 p.m., Tuesday to Saturday 9 a.m.- 9 p.m.)* In my student years the National Library – which bears the name of the father of the 'Greatest Hungarian', István Széchenyi, whom you can see on the 5000 forint bill – was housed in the National Museum building. (VIII. Múzeum körút 14-16.) One had to walk through long corridors with Roman tombstones on both sides. Inside there were high ceilings, creaky linoleum floors and elderly readers frowning at every whisper. I went there often, since they had everything. The National Library eventually moved to the Royal Castle. Huge and pompous, without being elegant; but the main reading room has natural, overhead light. Small electric trains come and go between the glass roof and the false ceiling — I always feel like a railwayman with defective hearing when I am there. Still, a singularly appropriate place to spend a whole day and sink into your work. There is a computerized catalogue which is very difficult to use — forget any computer routines you might have picked up in recent years.

LIBRARY OF THE ACADEMY OF SCIENCES AND LETTERS *(V. Arany János utca 1. T: 138-2344. Open Monday to Friday 9 a.m.- 8 p.m., Saturday 9 a.m.-5 p.m.)* Until the renovation, the library was housed on the ground floor of the famous, listed building (1862-65) to the left of the main entrance.

The Reading Room had not changed since the 1860's, with oil paintings of benefactors, famous scholars and writers on the walls. There were only 38 seats, of which four were reserved for academicians — who hardly ever came. It only slowly dawned on me that the library, where I went every day, almost religiously, was the hub of the dissident movement.

Since then the library has moved to the adjacent building. The reading room is on the first floor, and checking in is complicated. Sooner or later you find yourself standing in front of a lady in her seventies, who allots you a seat number, based on rank, or record of readership, or simply on how much she likes your smile. The quietest seats are near the smoking area. The lower the number, the better the seat. It's a modern library with hundreds of seats; the furniture is tailor-made and mildly posh. Now you don't have to wait two days for some of the books you want, the floor doesn't creak, there are computers, and yet... You know what I mean.

PARLIAMENT LIBRARY *(V. Kossuth tér 1-3. T: 268-4000. Open Monday to Thursday 9 a.m.-7.45 p.m., Friday 9 a.m.-2 p.m., Saturday 9 a.m.-6 p.m.)* Inside, the building (1887-1904) is a 'cross between a Gothic church and a Turkish bath', as a great 20th-century poet put it. As a student I sometimes went there. I found that the beautiful leather-bound volumes all around the gigantic Reading Room were the US Congress Papers. But when I wanted to use them they turned out to be entirely uncatalogued: I was given a ladder (sic!) to have a look. (But I did find what I needed.)

The Library is still beautiful (a visit here will save you the tourist trek round the rest of the building) but still makes one sleepy. There is still no catalogue of the US Congress Papers. But there are some new, computerized services. The other major change is in the surrounding building. It is being used for its original purpose again.

BUDAPEST PUBLIC LIBRARY, AKA. CENTRAL 'SZABÓ ERVIN' LIBRARY *(VIII. Szabó Ervin tér 1., off Kálvin tér. T: 138-4933. Complicated hours: Monday, Tuesday and Friday 9 a.m.-8 p.m., closed Wednesday, Saturday 9 a.m.-5 p.m., Sunday 9 a.m.-1 p.m.)* A lovely, traditional place, with a superb periodicals room with oak panelling up to the roof, plus incredible chandeliers. You should first visit the cloakroom in the basement. Apart from the usual Budapest notices (what to do and what not to do) there is a pleasing sentence from a great 19th-century poet, Arany: 'Oh, what a burdensome life/ Dressing and undressing every morning and night'. You should climb the great staircase to the first floor for the catalogue, the Main Reading Room, the Budapest Collection and the Periodicals Room. While waiting for the books I want to borrow, I love browsing through the new acquisitions. A great place to be at.

UNIVERSITY LIBRARY *(V. Ferenciek tere 6. T: 266-4634. Open: Monday 11-19, Tuesday to Friday 8 a.m.-8 p.m, Saturday 8 a.m.-6 p.m)* Originally established in 1561, transferred to Buda Castle in 1777, and here since this building was completed in 1876. It was seriously damaged when the underground was built under it in the 1970's, and has just been renovated. The Main Reading Room, on the first floor, traditionally the place where medical students spend all their lives, has an awesome, cathedral-like quality. That's where students feel they will never be able to remember all that stuff by exam day. Among the valuable treasures there are 171 codices, among them eleven of the famous 'Corvinas' from the legendary library of King Matthias Corvinus (reigned 1458-1490). They also have a Greek gospel of the 11th century. And subscribe to over 3000 foreign periodicals.

CENTRAL FOREIGN LANGUAGE LIBRARY or as it is still popularly called, 'The Gorky' *(V. Molnár utca 7. Open 9 a.m.-8 p.m; every other Saturday 9 a.m.-5 p.m; Monday 2-8 p.m.)* The building was a YMCA before the war but the only souvenir is a word under the front door mat: SALVE. After 'the changes' (the previous ones) it became a Russian language library, but from the early 1960's it began to collect literature in a dozen or so other languages. The Reading Room on the first floor has been redecorated three or four times in the last fifteen years, but except for the change of name and the disappearance of the statue of Gorky, hardly anything else is different. The typical noise is the not-so-easily-recognized sound of pigeons walking on the glass roof. The somewhat stocky, unshaven, curly-haired man of about forty, reading proofs or translating some Durrell or David Lodge book, is one of the funniest people in town and a very good friend of mine, and is often here on Wednesday afternoons. He loves to talk to foreign eggheads in his superior English.

SO MANY BOOKS! *Friends of mine from Western Europe remark with surprise on the number of books in peoples' homes here in Budapest. Because of a high level of state subsidy, books were very cheap compared to many other forms of entertainment in the 1970's and early 1980's. In 1989 the monopoly held by several state publishers disappeared and some 400 (!) small publishers sprang up. Anyone can publish a book in Hungary. Books are sold in all sorts of places, including the streets, pedestrian subways and supermarkets — which is quite a recent development, too.*

TWELVE GOOD BOOKS — NON-FICTION

Lukács, John: *Budapest 1900.* *(A Historical Portrait of a City and Its Culture.)* Weidenfeld and Nicolson, New York, 1988. An intimate and engaging look at an astonishing story. Budapest experienced a remarkable 'exfoliation' during the last third of the 19th century. It was one of the most vigorous metropolitan centres of Europe, both expansion-wise and exuberance-wise. This is a scholarly but very readable book, by a Budapest-born American historian. Not on sale in Budapest. (But try at the CEU–shop; see below.) *Budapest, anno...* Corvina, 1996.

This is a selection of the work of György Klösz, court photographer. A major photographer of the 19th century, his work gives us many scenes that have hardly changed, and many contemporary advertisements too. Klösz worked with glass plates, hence the fantastic detail. Some of his great pictures, covered with graffiti, are reproduced in the subway passage under Elizabeth Bridge.
Gundel's Hungarian Cookbook Corvina, 1997. The name Gundel is to Budapest as Sacher is to Vienna and Horcher to Madrid. Károly Gundel first published this book in 1934 and it has since gone through more than 30 editions. He is the great figure of Hungarian

cooking. Two (out of thirteen) children followed their father into the kitchen, and compiled this book.
István Örkény: *One Minute Stories* Corvina, 1997. Translated by Judith Sollosy. A selection from a cult book, by the master of Hungarian grotesque. The hilariously funny miniature stories give a deep insight into the Hungarian psyche, a funny and sorry picture, full of irony, cynicism and occasional self-hatred. A very good present to buy. Read by all Hungarian students.
Kosztolányi Dezső: *Darker Muses (Nero)* Corvina, 1990. A historical novel by the great master of twentieth-century Hungarian prose.
Ferenc Molnár: *The Paul Street Boys* Corvina, 1998. The children's classic: everyone in Italy and Poland (and other countries) knows it, but this the first English reprint since 1927. A funny, moving story, for kids and grown-ups alike.
Gerő, András: *Heroes' Square, Budapest: Hungary's History in Stone and Bronze*. Corvina, 1990. A fascinating story of a monument to Hungarian history, showing how it was designed and built, and how it was changed by successive régimes. Very well written, with superb colour and black-and-white pictures. Also available in German.
Csontváry album Corvina, 1994. The stunning great original of Hungarian art was like a gigantic comet. Sudden inspiration led him to take up art as an adult and the results, enormous bewitching canvases, are to be seen in the Nemzeti Galéria, and in the Csontváry Múzeum in the town of Pécs. See our First Walk. Better still, see the paintings.

TWELVE GOOD BOOKSHOPS

Bookshops are generally open between 10 a.m. and 6 p.m. on weekdays, 9 a.m. to 1 p.m on Saturdays. Times are only given in the following list when they differ from these. During the Book Week at the end of May/ beginning of June, the stalls that sprout up everywhere trade on Sundays too.
Bookshop at the Central European University (CEU) *V. Nádor utca 9, on the streetfront. T: 327-3096.* Open Monday-Friday 9 a.m. to 6 p.m., Saturday 2 p.m. to 5 p.m. A very serious academic bookshop without neglecting the good read, though the selection of Hungarian-related subjects, including literature, is limited. Operated, together with the nearby Bestsellers Bookshop, by Budapest legend Tony Lang, who returned to the land of his ancestors to start a bookshop. He had to learn the language, which he did brilliantly (see page 15). The bookshop carries the full range of Central European University Press books, of course.
Corvina *V. Kossuth Lajos utca 6.* Fair selection of Hungarian books in foreign languages to the left of the entrance, sheet music and records to the right. In an unbearably busy thoroughfare, where you can't park. You can also buy Corvina books, with a discount, in a more pleasant environment, in Vörösmarty tér, in the ugliest of the ugly office blocks, on the first floor. You'll see their ugly ad from the square.
Erkel *VII. Erzsébet körút 52.* Opposite the Royal Hotel. Three showrooms, with a large selection of sheet music, and records too. The latter are on the first floor and a stiff cardboard record sleeve is

cheerfully supplied on request to protect purchases. Catalogue.

Fókusz *VII. Rákóczi út 14.* Occupying two large floors, this is the biggest bookshop in the country. Maps, records and Hungarian books in translation all available. Remainder books on the first floor – if they haven't rearranged the stock, which they often do. Not as large and pleasant as any Barnes and Noble in the States, though, or Powell's.

Helikon *VI. Bajcsy-Zsilinszky Endre út, corner Hajós utca.* A large, lavishly decorated, recently opened, two-level bookshop, owned by the publishing house of the same name, itself owned by an investment fund. This investment is obviously a very long term one. The American-Hungarian CEO must have had Rizzoli of New York in mind. Experts say no business has ever flourished in this part of the town this century. We'll see. Large selection of Hungarian and foreign books, small café in the basement. Also CD-ROM's.

Kódex *V. Honvéd utca 5.* Not far from Parliament and on our Second Walk, this large, well-designed bookshop has two floors. The upper floor stocks books in many foreign languages.

Láng Téka *XIII. Pozsonyi út 9.* Also a video rental outlet, which is why it closes so late (11 p.m. every day). Also records and cassettes.

Le Pont *I. Fő utca 17,* in the Institut Français, and with hours of business adjusted to suit. Strangely enough, operated by the Pont Bookshop people. The word has a different meaning in French ('point' in Hungarian, 'bridge' in French). By far the largest selection of French books in Hungary, of course, and they order anything for you. Ground floor, to the left.

Litea *I. Hess Adndrás tér 4.* Opposite the Hilton — in the courtyard. The name is a portmanteau word made from Literature and Tea, and a really choice selection of each is available here. A singularly pleasant, recently built pavilion. A full range of Hungarian books in translation. Catalogues available. They also send books abroad, with postage free for purchases above 800 forints. Iced tea. Irish Coffee. Grog. Portuguese tea.

Osiris Könyvesház *V. Veres Pálné utca 4-6. Corner of Curia utca. T: 266-4999.* This is an unlikely place in such an expensive area. It's the eggheadiest of egghead bookshops. They operate a minority publications reading room, a small café, a book club, and a gallery space. A singularly pleasant place, not yet discovered by the expatriate community. Just go in, sit down, read anything. They should have the two English-speaking egghead quarterlies: *The Hungarian Quarterly,* and the *Budapest Review of Books.* On the inside and outside of the back page of the latter you will probably find my column on Budapest.

Pont *V. Mérleg utca 6.* This is clearly an egghead bookshop; the space is rented from the Alliance of Free Democrats, aka. the egghead party. (Their headquarters are upstairs.) All kinds of fiction and non-fiction. They operate a book-club, too. Now that the party is a member of the ruling coalition, there are fewer MP's browsing here. Still a pleasant, overcrowded place. Good advice is free and abundant here. There is a cheap and pleasant restaurant in the same building, called Mérleg ('Scales'), after the name of the street.

SECOND-HAND AND ANTIQUARIAN BOOKS *The distinction between these two categories has resurfaced fairly recently. For decades, the best shop had a characteristically socialist name: 'Központi Antikvárium' (Central Antiquarian Bookshop); and there the two activities grew so far apart that the shop was actually cut in two. (V. Múzeum körút 15. T: 117-3514.)*

OLD AND RARE BOOKS

Borda *(as already mentioned in your Crash Course: VII. Madách Imre tér 5. II. floor, only Tuesday and Thursday afternoon, otherwise by special appointment, T: 267-3723)* Fifty metres from Deák tér, where the three underground lines meet, in a red brick twin building originally designed in the 1920's to be the beginning of a new avenue leading from here to City Park.

Forgács *(V. Stollár Béla utca 8., T: 111-6874)* A pleasant, small shop in a silent sidestreet, near the Parliament. Open until 7 p.m., also Saturday afternoon, until 4 p.m. Strong on architecture and private press German and English editions, plus Hungarian fiction in German and English, especially the non-Hungarian editions. Also small works of art. Great service and paper bags.

Kárpáti és Szőnyi *(V. Szent István körút 3., T: 111-6431)* Small, crowded, well-stocked shop at the noisier end of Nagykörút, by the Pest end of Margaret bridge. Old books and prints at the back. They also give away a carefully compiled but poorly produced small list and map of all the second-hand bookshops in Budapest.

Kollin *(V. Bajcsy-Zsilinszky Endre út 34., upstairs, T: 111-9023., at Arany János utca underground)* Accessible through a second-hand bookshop called 'Nyugat'. Kollin opens at 2 p.m. and closes at 5.30 p.m. Specializes in old German travel books; there is an amazing collection of classic Baedekers,

including some volumes in English. Very elegant and well-informed.

Font *(VI. Andrássy út 56., T: 132-1646)* Near the Oktogon, this is a small shop with a Parisian Left Bank atmosphere, run by two bearded friends. Strong on old art books and eccentric postcards. Don't forget to go upstairs. The complete Köchel catalogue has been longing for a new owner there. Are you the one?

Philon *(VII. Dob utca 32.)* T: (0630) 346-985. Strong in Classical philology and Judaica. Open 12 a.m. to 7 p.m., 6 p.m. on Friday.

Honterus *(V. Múzeum körút 35.)* Strong on old maps and prints.

Horváth *(VI. Andrássy út 76.),* Takes pride in a large collection of classical authors (also scholarly and critical editions).

SOME MORE SHOPS, WITH A MISCELLANEOUS STOCK

Bibliotéka *VI. Andrássy út 2.* T: 131-5132.

Óbuda *III. Lajos utca 49/b.* T: 188-7332.

Ráth Mór *II. Margit körút 44.* T: 201-6793.

Uránia *VIII. Népszínház utca 23.* T: 114-2050.

Zenei Antikvárium — Second-hand Music Bookshop
V. Múzeum körút 17. Virtually opposite the Nemzeti Múzeum, with a huge selection of books on music and of sheet music. Occasionally amazing old East-European scores and records in good condition are to be found.

HOW DIFFICULT IT IS TO EXPLAIN IN PORTLAND, OREGON

Gentle Reader,

I know only too well that the word 'egghead' is an obsolete one, inherited from the years when Kennedy was running for the White House. It is a borrowing fuelled by an audacious, vain idea: if I use the word often enough, I will be able to bring it back from the dead. Moreover, though most of the time I omit the word 'Budapest', as a matter of fact I am always referring to certain 'Budapest eggheads'.

This section would like to provide some insight into a very special world in a very special town. To share the findings of my long and laborious explorations with you.

It is often asked what — if any — real benefits of the totalitarian regime went down the drain with the changes of Eastern Europe. Needless to say, there weren't many. The hugely excessive sums spent on high culture had an awful background of censorship. And in two ways: on the one hand, individual authors and publishers' lists were censored, and on the other, whole layers of consumer culture were kept from the people. They were more or less forced to read better quality things than they actually wanted. That explains how it could happen that Faulkner's *Absolom! Absolom!* printed – and sold – no fewer than 140,000 copies in Hungary (in a translation by the present President of the Republic), in the late 1970's. Who read all those copies, one might ask. Very few people, of course. Hungary has never been a country of eggheads. But books were cheap, i.e. subsidized by everyone, including the semi-literate miner, who never read anything, not even comics. (True, one of his kids might have been tempted to read books... an endless argument. Also, miners were much better paid than teachers and even doctors.)

In this slightly cruel, utterly frustrating but only mildly totalitarian society almost everything was hazy and dreamlike; not only books, but life in general was cheap. There the Budapest egghead as a species grew up, ambitionless, avidly letter-writing, gadget-happy, slightly privileged, with more and more contacts in the West, cosmopolitan, womanising, drinking semi-heavily, knowing that no real responsibilities would ever land on him.

Sub poena crescit palma — the palm-tree flourishes under the burden – is a Latin saying often cited in Budapest among intellectuals to explain the inexplicable: why, amidst frustration and general torpor the mildly totalitarian regime of the 1970's and 1980's was a sort of intellectual and literary Golden Age. Today, with the burden gone, Budapest is even more of an intellectually invigorating and colourful place, with beautiful, long-established libraries, rich classical music life and bustling student cafés. While the museum scene suffers from a scarcity of funds, the alternative and fringe art scene has grown enormously. The art cinema network almost equals that of Paris and New York.

For the foreign egghead there was always one insuperable obstacle: the Hungarian language, which isn't even Indo-European, but Central Asian in its ancestry. Now most students speak English, there are several English-language weeklies in the city, and information is no longer a problem here. All this amounts to something like paradise for any egghead.

A decade ago Budapest seemed to most visiting eggheads like a nice Roman province— some time after the Romans left. Now they return and rejoice: the Romans are back.

Sorry, they are not right. This piece would like to prove nothing less than that we were the Romans all along.

The Budapest egghead is an intellectual trained in a country where free thinking was confined to the egghead reservation, where political pressure forced eggheads to become members of a very closely-knit society, whose members were going to live a life without any real responsibilities outside the family or their own spiritual circle. A critical spirit became one of their fortes: an uncompromising, sweeping, easygoing critical spirit. Egghead society used to be much broader than any intellectual society in any given metropolis elsewhere in Europe. Students and young adults with all kinds of interests, stripped of normal career prospects, who would otherwise have browsed the stock exchange listings and looked for adventure there, or worked hard for an exotic holiday, or a sports car, or state-of-the-art hi-fi-equipment, were reading hard-to-read latest American fiction translated into Hungarian and discussing the findings of muck-raking Hungarian sociologists, who were given the money to do surveys that were then shelved in a room of the Communist Party headquarters. Budapest was a special place: the expertise was here, it was just that policy makers did not use it. Life was relatively cheap, everything was subsidized, even electricity and gas and rents. Oil was imported from the Soviet Union through some shady barter transactions. Food was cheap, books were cheap, an egghead could live on very little money. He could even buy some booze for the weekend party cum intellectual salon.

The typical egghead had some small job at a publisher or at a university or one or other think tank of the Academy of Sciences or a theatre, or a language school, but was also involved in some other odd job — like translating a long book of social science for a publisher (and many eggheads were involved in the underground press from the early 1980's on). There were the most improbable jobs — a key underground figure, now the Mayor of Budapest, worked in some Party-run institute where he commissioned translations of works of contemporary social sciences — for the use of comrades who wanted extra degrees, but who could not read the necessary English or German. So this egghead lived on that work, and could pay his egghead friends a lot of money. Another egghead, a writer, while writing his own books, among them the hilariously funny *1985*, a sequel to the Orwell classic, still not officially published, was translating Soviet war novels — into a tape recorder, without ever really looking at the typed version.

Eggheads worked a lot, but with varying intensity; work and leisure time made one continuum. Chance meetings in the street, in a library, at lunch could give the day a new direction. As in archaic society, news travelled by word of mouth. The national sport was to read between the lines. There were Them and Us, Them being the compromising intellectuals, with some power or other, the ones we looked down on. It was a highly interesting world full of information, misinformation, love, intrigue and pure scandal. The walls of possibilities were pushed forward and backwards an inch all the time. The system could not be more liberal than that. Nobody expected any real change in our lifetimes, especially not after 1981 in Poland.

The Budapest eggheads could not bring influence to bear on anything, so they developed a sense of universal interest. They could not change anything, so they wanted to change everything. They tended to become jacks of all trades and even masters of everything. Most of them developed eccentric traits. They grew interested in the minutiae of railway timetables, of sports records of long ago, of football team lists of particular matches and so on. One put together makeshift furniture for his very modest second home, the other wrote about hi-fi-equipment, the third collected antique typewriters, the fourth old stationery. But almost all of them were collecting the past. Some of them kept on returning to Transylvania, looking for Hungarian roots, ransacking lofts, taking home parts of looms and oxcart accessories. The better-informed also tended to enthuse about the contemporary avant-garde, more specifically about conceptual art with its habit of documenting the imagined artwork, so often substituting ideas for art proper.

Inside the typical egghead the citizen and the bohemian were wrestling all the time. A real bohemian and the shell of a citizen. The latter was a set of rules inherited and/or read in books. A citizen who had no other salary but what he earned. A citizen with no property, just pride and self-consciousness, what the Germans call 'sunken cultural goods' – 'gesunkenes kulturgut' – conjured into life. It's so interesting to see that some eggheads can fill that formerly empty shell. Maybe all of them could, but few have been given the chance...

Egghead society hinged very much on informal, clandestine information: everything that was 'not available in books'. It was important to know people in person — they were the source of knowledge, more than books, and much more than the media, which had no knowledge at all to give. Studying had some very archaic, even peripatetic characteristics. You followed Socrates into the cafeteria of the library of the Academy, and listened to his 20-minute lecture on some current issue, or on some eternal aspect of the arts. This egghead civilization tended to be based on verbal, face-to-face communication: it was archaic in this respect; and much less alienated.

Not only verbal communication, of course. After that 20-minute lecture one spent days in the same library, reading the books Socrates mentioned.

Archaic, human, verbal, metaphorical, funny, proud of itself, gossipy, idiosyncratic, experimental, self-destructive, enviably vigorous, friendly to talent. All that.

Of course, little of it is spotted now in Budapest — egghead society as it was.

But the scenery is still here. And most of the people are still here. Now middle-aged. Still unusually witty and original and creative with an unexpected twist here and there. Let's have a sample of Budapest egghead society right away.

RUNNING AMOK IN BUDAPEST EGGHEAD SOCIETY
An Imaginary Journey through the City Hour by Hour

But first, a couple of keynote remarks about

GLOOM AND CHANGES *No doubt, Budapest has become younger, more contemporary, more sophisticated, faster-paced, but also more segregated, in all the senses of the word, more scandal-ridden, more commercial and also more commonplace. There are bigger and bigger contrasts in wealth, in ambition, in the way people look at each other. Eggheads tend to find it more difficult to follow what has been happening all around them in ever-bigger concentric circles, as if they needed new lenses in their eyes: wide angle lenses. Eggheads were conditioned to live a different kind of life.*

Is Budapest still the intellectually invigorating and exuberant and turbulent place that it was in the last decade of the mildly totalitarian régime, which at the end even encouraged some optimism and hope for the future during the glorious years of transition? Most observers agree that it is and it isn't. Gloom is spreading and intruding into and protruding out of most minds; together with gloom's sister, disillusion.

Here is a worthy task for a factfinding tour: Have hearts and minds been damaged yet? If so, how much?

The generation of eggheads that so wanted change, seems a bit taken aback that change doesn't seem to stop. Things are not what they seemed at first. Liberty seemed at first to be destroying high culture, but later it turned out to be decentralizing and multiplying it. It has become less and less possible to have an overview of what is happening. That constant rearrangement of all the factors and layers of egghead lives makes many eggheads tired and worried. They had hoped to withdraw into their beloved ivory towers. After the thrill of '89 and '90 they hoped not to have to read the papers every day. They hoped Hungary would be an exception, and sulphurous notions be kept forever in a bottle.

7 A.M.: A SWIM IN GELLÉRT BATH If I were you, and had no friend to share his/her big apartment downtown with me, I wouldn't listen to siren voices and stay anywhere else but in Gellért Hotel. As an artist friend keeps telling me, it is a big, white, self-cleaning gem, a sort of Johnny come lately art-nouveau building, erected during World War I. There is direct access to the bath via an elevator. First, swim indoors in the small pool, and examine the stained glass windows. Then go outside: at this hour of the morning there is hardly anyone in the bath. I am sorry, but I don't think it will be possible to persuade anyone to go and swim and talk to you this early at the Gellért.

9 A.M.: CAFÉ GUSTO WITH LÁSZLÓ LUGOSI LUGO The first swallow, announcing a springtime for cafés: the first real new one in living memory. There is a pleasant street terrace: inside it is small, intimate, with brown furniture that does not look brand new. What really gives charm and flavour and personality to the place is the big oil painting of Augusto Piave. He is said to have been a café owner somewhere in Northern Italy, and the ancestor of one of the owners. A sort of patron saint of this place.

Lugo is a photographer, a chronicler of vanishing Budapest, a graduate of Hungarian and English studies; he has had an unusual, mixed career in Budapest demi-monde and intellectual salons. In his student days he looked like Apollo at his best: golden locks and ideal proportions — but he was not really successful with or interested in girls. He has never had a nine to five job, of course; instead he supported himself for ages by giving English classes, and spent his time going around town and having more or less private classes from some of the greatest figures of Hungarian photography.

Then in the early 1980's Lugo decided that Hungary was hopeless and frustrating and he moved to New York. Then back. Then he found his real subject: the old and the new in the city. He is a born perfectionist, and is constantly changing to bigger film formats.

Recently he discovered hundreds of hitherto unknown pictures by György Klösz, the classic photographer of the last century. He is currently working on a biography of Klösz. And for the first time in many years, he has a steady income (which comes in handy for the father of a baby daughter): he has become the staff photographer of a design journal.

Try to grill him about new, positive developments in Budapest, and whether 4 x 5 is big enough for him, and does he want, one day, to change to large glass plates. (II. Frankel Leó utca 24.)

11 A.M.: LUKÁCS BATH, WITH GERGELY BIKÁCSY This run-down, open air bath, amidst hundred-year-old trees hung with hundreds of small ex-votos, used to be the hotbed of free thought, a kind of witty intellectual salon, even in the Darkest Fifties. The last of the Mohicans, who could hardly see the highest days of the place, spends almost all his days here, from spring to autumn, eccentric film critic and short story and porn-epic writer, bald, white-bearded, muttering Gergely Bikácsy, aka. Tamás Glauziusz. He is a French egghead, theoretician of the French Nouvelle Vague, and lover of Paris, slipping between Paris and Budapest all his adult life. He feels that he always makes the wrong decision. He would like to be in both places, at the same time, all the time. It's no use asking him about gloom, since he is the gloomiest of all Budapest eggheads. 'Have you found a publisher for your porn-epic yet?' could be a good question to rattle his cage with. The epic follows the legend of the Holy Grail: the most indecent, most parodistic work of travesty since Apollinaire and Bataille. He is also famous for his novel *A Tomboy in the Shady Lane*, which is a cruelly sincere rendering of his own love story, with the characters taken from the national classic early 19th-century tragedy *Bánk bán* which made the piece hilariously funny. His pseudonym Tamás Glauziusz refers to a character in a play and the film based on it: Uncle Glauziusz was a good-hearted accountant of the good old days who didn't understand the intrigues of these cruel, new times, but served his new masters nevertheless. Typically Budapest egghead manners. (II. Frankel Leó utca 25-27.)

1. P.M. LUNCH WITH ÁDÁM NÁDASDY AT MERLIN The Merlin Theatre is five years old and housed in the City Hall complex, which was originally an old soldiers' home built in the mid 18th century. The theatre itself is in an independent building from early this century: it started as a drama school, and is now a host theatre for visiting productions, and also an English-speaking theatre in the summer.

The restaurant (which is a jazz club at night) was meant to be elegant, expensive and profitable, to sponsor the other activities. Instead, it became a sort of cross between an avant-garde café and a city hall canteen. The latter at noontime, the former especially in the afternoon. Ask Ádám to point

---

BUDAPEST BESTS : : BUDAPEST BESTS : : BUDAPEST BESTS

András Váradi, Biochemist, Collector of Watches, Fleamarket Freak

For over 12 years now I have been going to the Ecseri fleamarket, every Saturday morning. I get up brutally early — I prefer to get there before 7 o'clock. During the last four or five years my interest has focused more or less exclusively on old mechanical wristwatches. At roughly the same time I became a really advanced flea-market addict: I can be happy now even if I leave the market empty-handed.

'How much discount would you give off half your price?' is an age-old Ecseri fleamarket witticism, still often overheard. Here are some thumb rules, for your use:

Don't ask for a price unless you really want to buy the stuff. • *Always decide the maximum you are willing to pay.* • *Be a Man (even if you are a woman), and stick to this maximum.* • *Don't Let Yourself Be Tricked: if you are asked about the price, hand the object straight back. Or offer half of your maximum. Or try one third.* • *It is forbidden to interfere. If the piece is in somebody else's hand, wait until he/she puts it down.*

Practically *everybody is a character* in the fleamarket, except for the Noisy Tourists With Too Much Money. A man in his early fifties comes here every Saturday and sells old Hungarian 'peasant glasses' — wine and brandy-bottles from the 18th and 19th century. On weekdays he is a murder squad detective. And there is a remarkable high-school teacher of physics who sells old telephones and vintage radios.

The most prominent obsessed fleamarket-goer is certainly a somewhat small, bearded man in his late forties, with a small golden earring in his left ear and with ponytails, almost always in boots: Vladimir ('Jani') Péter, professor at the Academy of Arts and Crafts, silversmith, designer of the Wladis range of jewellery. He is a very attentive listener generally: but not here, where he hardly notices friends, he is so immersed in scanning 'the stuff'. (A mere pile of junk to the uninitiated.)

Eating at the Fleamarket is no gourmet occasion. In front of small buffets people are enjoying the traditional ultra high cholesterol 'diet': juicy sausages, grilled pork ribs, smoked knuckles with all the skin on, blood pudding or tripe stew. It is like a *real time* educational video on the theme 'Why Hungarians Die So Early.' I only eat sweets there.

A last piece of advice. Never go there with the idea of any definite article to buy. That very object won't pop up that day. Have fun and buy whatever you want, but if you happen to find a nice wristwatch, please, leave it for me. I am coming on Saturday to catch it.

out the hub and mastermind behind the 'venture', actor-director-manager Tamás Jordán. He runs the place now without his wife/co-visionary/actress (who was excellent here as Petra von Kant in the Fassbinder play here).

Ádám, the arch-egghead of Budapest, is a scholar, poet and wit, iconoclastic university lecturer in English linguistics, innovative university administrator, translator of *A Midsummer Night's Dream* and some other plays. He can be best enjoyed during one of his lectures, or on stage, or at home. To see his home is really a privilege, almost impossible, except if you are invited to one of his parties, which happen once practically every season.

BUDAPEST BESTS : : BUDAPEST BESTS : : BUDAPEST BESTS

Pál Schiffer, Trend-setting Documentary Film Director, Drop-out from a Dynasty of Politicians, One of the Most Intense Admirers of the Female Sex in Central Europe

I have many favourite cinemas in Budapest. Being a film director, it has been an intriguing task for me to decide whether I prefer making a movie or watching it. Nevertheless, I am risking the statement: my favourite cinema in Budapest is the Décsi (deh-tshi).

You might assume, that you are likely to find this name in one of the programme listings. Alas, you can't. No cinema bears this name today — just like street names, cinema names kept on changing in Budapest, especially during major political changes.

The Décsi is called Művész (l'Artiste) these days, though for a time it used to be called Új Tükör (New Mirror, after a weekly magazine). The original name goes back to a certain family name, that of the owner. The humble author of the present lines had the privilege to know old Mr Décsi in person, who, together with his entire family, happened to live in a flat just above the cinema, remaining true to an old tradition of crafts and business people, that of living above the business.

In the Décsi there used to be some balcony seats, and small loggias, and lavish gilded plaster decorations, as was the fashion of the early twenties. It was a typical 'cinema with bell sound', since five minutes before the end of every performance a bell was rung, as a signal: it was high time for couples to start to compose themselves. I clearly remember that a couple of years back I failed to lure my gentleman father to that cinema (then already called 'Művész') to watch a Nikita Mihalkov movie.

'Where is it on?' he asked.
'In the Művész' I replied, unsuspectingly.
'Which one is that?' he asked.

I came to my senses, remembering from my essential Péter Lengyel (p. 152 — *The Editor*) that a true Budapest gentleman remembers only one name per Budapest street, never mind how many times its name is changed... And it's valid for cinemas, too. So I added:

'Well, you know... the Décsi.'

His natural habitat is a mixture of high class art, thousands of books and low-tech, naff home electronics.

You should read his 'egghead manifesto', *The Name of the Captive*, (in the very first issue of BOOKS, Winter 1991), and ask what has happened since. Ask about the gloom in him, about how he tried to reform his university, about changes. You can talk to him in English, German, Italian or French. He is much less eloquent in Russian, Polish or Persian.

He's not tall, he has a round face, grey hair and beard, and he's generally speaking a bit stockier than he'd like to be. He uses Wordperfect (DOS-

---

He objected, angrily:

'One does not go there. That is a cinema with a bell!...' And he really did not come, though I insisted that they had stopped ringing the bell decades ago.

Changing movie names did make the life of the serious movie buff hell. The Atrium was built in the thirties, became the May 1 (guess when), and now it is the Atrium again. The Royal Apollo was the Red Star for a trifling forty years, then regained its original name (and now might be pulled down). The one-time Forum was rechristened the Pushkin — and it was still called the Pushkin when this book went to press. The City became the Toldi. (It remains a mystery how this cinema got its new name from a legendary hero of the Hungarian Middle Ages, who was best known for his bodily strength...) And so on.

These days Művész is the flagship of the Budapest art movie network. (Most of the network is maintained by the City of Budapest, but there are some that belong to the film studios, and one that is operated by the Film Archives.) There is hardly anything like that in Europe — it obviously rivals Paris and London in variety of titles so regularly on offer...

The gilded plaster ornaments, the plush and velvet are no more, but there is air-conditioning and Dolby, and twenty or twenty-five films are shown every week now, on five screens, called Chaplin, Bunuel, Tarkovsky, Huszárik and Bódy. (The last two names remind the Budapest moviegoers of two outstanding Hungarian moviemakers, both of whom died young — the last very young.) A couple of years back the director of the British Film Institute could hardly believe me when I mentioned to him that there is a cinema in Budapest where one can see no fewer than five Peter Greenaway films inside a week. I meant the Művész, needless to say.

So, Gentle Traveller, if you feel the urge to watch a film by Mihalkov, or Hartley, or Kusturica, or Jarmusch or Jarman, or Menzel, or Kieslowski, or Wang (or the like), it is Művész you should come to... Don't panic, unlike many cinemas in Budapest, there are no dubbed films shown here. Just subtitles. And a lovely café to sit in. Called Café Fellini.

(Művész cinema, VI. Teréz körút 30.)

version). He'd like to have a phonetic symbol set for this software. He hasn't been able to find it, even in England. Could you help him, do you think? (V. Gerlóczy utca 4.)

3 P.M. CAFÉ NEW YORK WITH THE EDITORS OF *2000* What was once one of the foremost literary cafés tends nowadays to be deserted: the building upstairs, formerly a sort of Fleet Street in itself, has been emptied: it's for sale. It's 99 years old and big — it has a past and a future. The editors of *2000* gather in the gallery, literally but not figuratively looking down at the ground floor, where tourists video each other, and over the luxury restaurant called Deep Water, where occasional, lost travellers and nouveau riche tycoons have lunch, mistaking it for a gourmet place.

By three all the editors are there, except for those who happen to be in London or Florence or Vilnius or St Petersburg or at the University Council in Budapest, and the one who is permanently stationed in Vienna. After 3 o' clock only promising, young, hitherto unpublished poets still have the courage to risk a visit. The editors, seven in number, form a brotherhood of love and hatred. They have loud quarrels over books, though not necessarily here, in front of the authors.

They are often deep in conversation with their overqualified secretary, a retired, Russian-born lady, who is a research fellow in literature. But if you come to leave a manuscript with them, don't expect a very quick answer. There is no editor in chief — a blessing and a curse. One of the curses: slow decisions. (VII. Erzsébet körút 9-11., only on Thursday, otherwise by special appointment.)

5 P.M. THE COURTYARD OF 'THE NEST' WITH MIKLÓS VAJDA

Miklós Vajda is the 'last literary gentleman', the editor of *The Hungarian Quarterly*, an English-speaking quality journal, indispensable for serious eggheads interested in Hungary anywhere in the world. He is the translator of maybe as many as a hundred plays from English. He looks and behaves like a gentleman, has read everything, old and new, and has lived a remarkably colourful life. Born into a wealthy upper-middle class family, he had his cake and ate it too in terms of mothers, since his father's first wife, the greatest actress on the Hungarian stage, lavished adoration on him. Later he went through awful experiences that he has yet to write about in his memoirs. He has singularly unbiased opinions about life and literature today. Of course, ask him about gloom, about Hungarian literature in English. Try to get out of him the name of one (just one) Hungarian novel in English that is a must for visiting eggheads.

The 'Nest' or Fészek is an artists' club established in 1903, one that has always retained some form or other of self-government, but that has become increasingly naff in the eyes of the younger generation, perhaps because of the leadership padded with 'favoured' artists. The restaurant, recently leased by the wife of a successful Budapest restaurateur, is different. It does not really belong to the club.

Miklós is the figure on the left in the legendary painting *Three Editors* from the fifties. (This is for the Advanced Egghead Tour, for next Summer.) (VII. Kertész utca 36.)

7 P.M. A BEER OR TWO (OR THREE) WITH FERENC TAKÁCS AT WINSTON'S, AN ENGLISH PUB Takács is perhaps the most curious fruit from the intellectual orchard that was Budapest over the last twenty years. Gargantuan, rebellious, scholarly, without ambition (though newly married in the 1990's), he is the storyteller champion and the Joyce-and-Eliot lecturer at Budapest University. His English is phenomenal, rich in idiom and meta-language features. He even translated *The Transporters* of Péter Esterházy, the paradigmatic contemporary writer, into English: short, but impossibly difficult and metaphoric. Cynical to the utmost, or so he pretends, he does his best to camouflage larger than life vanity by flaunting his ego. A brilliant mind and a fine stylist, he published an allusion-rich first chapter of a Gargantuan novel. He's just turned fifty, and seems to have begun to long for everything: power, fame in the eye of the man in the street. Be careful what you say: he will always contradict any statement you make. So just ask questions. 'Was life in the Kádár era really sweet?' could be a good start with him. He seems to pay attention only to himself; he is a very attentive listener indeed. Was recently promoted to be the Head of the English Department, Eötvös University. (VI. Jókai tér 4.)

9 P.M. SEMI-FORMAL DINNER WITH THE EDITORS OF *HUNGARIAN BUKSZ* MAGAZINE Ideally this should take place in the home of one of the editors, possibly in István Rév's flat, in a dreamy Buda villa, because then you can take a look round at middle-aged-egghead-style at its best. Second choice is Mr Klaniczay's home, the third is Gundel's, in the small private room upstairs.

Most of the editors have been friends since undergraduate years. This is a closely knit brotherhood with a shared vision of quality and right and wrong. They seem to believe in scholarly life and scholarship in general. They indulge themselves with independence and sarcasm; they are cruel and devastating if necessary. They are intelligent to the nth degree, workaholic and cantankerous, according to many. An independent power centre, but they also know how to enjoy life (yes, perhaps even all of them). You should test the gloom theory and their beliefs, you should ask if Hungary is big enough to provide an independent reviewer for every topic. And whether they have ever published a review that was unconditional praise. And whether any one of their readers ever realized that the design of their title page logo changes with the season (the way the sun shines from different directions). (XII. Virányos út 16., if the first choice.)

11 P.M. CAFÉ GARAGE WITH ANDRÁS BARABÁS He is one of the funniest and most entertaining, also most tiring and amazing and complex guys in the Budapest egghead scene as of today. Fun is his natural vernacular, no doubt. His favourite subject is himself, his awkward personality, his alleged physical clumsiness. He is the editor of a music monthly, an expert conjurer of English and Hungarian, a translator of Wodehouse and Lodge and Durrell and Carver. Mr Barabás (or, as commonly nicknamed, "Bari", which is partly an abbreviated form of his surname, partly an epithet, referring to his sheepish hair) the lengthy process of adaptation to grown-up life has not come to an end. His discourse is rich (almost overburdened, to put it so) with metaphors, allusions, references and camouflaged quotations. And he is above all interested in the opposite sex. Agreed with his wife to tell each other everything just after having turned 60. He could easily agree, he says, since he finds it fantastic to live up to that age.

You don't have to ask him about gloom. He emanates it without being asked.

The three-level theme place is a newcomer on the scene, and flaunts car and motorcycle memorabilia. A place designed with utmost care and a tongue-in-cheek.

AFTER MIDNIGHT, POSSIBLY ALONE ON LIBERTY BRIDGE I bet you will not ponder the answers to questions of a theoretical kind. The only exception might be: 'Hey, civic boosterism, so widespread in Budapest in the last couple of years, is scarcer nowadays. But it's not all gone. Not yet, anyway.'

The night lights of the city. Trying to gather up the stamina needed to crawl to your bed. Try harder, you'll get there. Some day.

MORE REMARKS ON THE ORIGINS OF EGGHEAD SOCIETY The

real egghead enjoyed the egghead way of life, reading a lot, discussing a lot, partying a lot, also working a lot, but rarely meeting a deadline, seeing the outcome of work rarely, late or never. Knowing everybody who counts, never hoping to hear the starter's pistol. He or she was an intellectual, eminent (or at least promising) in something, but his (her) intellect was more developed than his counterpart's in a free society. One had the feeling that the Budapest egghead used a higher proportion of his/her brain than the ones in the ideal position — over there. Also the Budapest egghead could and did make the most improbable connections between his/her pieces of information. To put it in short — he/she was an artist as well, apart from being a scholar (at least a budding one).

Also the Budapest egghead made an effort to explain everything. He did it with gusto. He either supposed that everybody was well aware of the basic principles of his field or carefully and evocatively explained them to the interested fellow eggheads — especially to younger egghead ladies.

Some egghead-inclined people some time or other grew tired of talking and playing and tried doing something instead: going to teach in a small village for a year or two, starting a club for gypsies somewhere in the outskirts of Budapest, or trying out some barely tolerated activity. There was a continuous spectrum of eggheads, former eggheads, eggheads with jobs, former eggheads-with-jobs now dropped out, artists, girls of the demimonde, even young, serious scholars, deprived of their due position, and of course banned or rarely published writers. It was a colourful society of about a thousand people, the hotbed of political, intellectual and artistic dissent. This transitional-seeming existence forced people to form their own opinion. It worked against stereotypes. You never knew who you might sit next to at a party: a great, trend-setting philosopher of international rank, a rich dentist, a pope of the avant-garde with his unlikely, fragile companion, or the beautiful, 'enfant terrible' youngest daughter of the greatest psychologist of the day, the hero of 1956.

PRIVILEGES Privileges were of many kinds: politicians, or retired politicians as parents, who could arrange a special bank loan to buy a small flat in a modern housing estate, relatives in Britain, where one could pass the summer, access to one of the private children's camps, especially the one in a village called Bánk, where a substantial part of the egghead society knew each other from.

Some of the privileges were natural, inherited ones, from middle-class parents, simple privileges like a big home library, a nice home in Buda, grandparents who spoke foreign languages. Among the fathers were a painter working as a journalist, a long-dead writer, an opera director and great educator, a leading historian who never misused his power. But the typical family enjoyed the slight privilege of a relatively affluent, unknown father. The general director of a food wholesale company, a head of a small film studio, even a small businessman. Then there were the kids of déclassé families, with very old aunts and nice vases and china sets in the cupboards. But now, remembering the good old days, I realize that at least half of them were of first generation intellectuals — in many cases with parents who had taken degrees at evening courses in the 1950's, or who had no degrees.

Many of these kids fulfilled the social ambitions of their families: but they were also somehow touched by the amazing aura of free thought. Most of them lost all intellectual contact with their parents, who desperately wanted to fit the cookie-cutter mould of the mildly totalitarian regime of the late 1960's and early 1970's. But once they were in egghead society, they became privileged overnight: they had access to the information one needed to outwit the Communist régime. In everyday matters, I mean. In housing regulations, in getting odd jobs, a council flat or a telephone line, or maybe just keeping hold of what they had got. The egghead has become a member of one huge credit card system of favours. Where you could have some help from some fellow-egghead. Information meant a lot in that archaic, mildly totalitarian society. But of course you couldn't overdraw on your credit — without becoming a pariah.

A GLASS HOUSE THREATENED Living in the egghead society, in this glass house of pseudo-existence was nice and frustrating, intellectually very invigorating. This human tapestry served as a highly scenic backdrop for that Golden Age in literature and film. Backdrop and Golden Age came to an end together, when the earth beneath them began to tremble: politics started to become more interesting. With the advent of liberty, normal opportunities emerged for the egghead: to start new careers, albeit somewhat late in life: to become multimillionaire businessmen, or nationally known politicians. The last happened en masse when something singular occurred in 1988-89: an egghead party was formed and it almost won the national elections. It has just undergone the painful process of getting rid of egghead characteristics.

Being an egghead now is totally anachronistic. Still, occasionally, it can be charming. Come and see and experience it.

THE INGREDIENTS

An Index to Budapest – a Good Read in Itself

BUDAPEST BESTS : : BUDAPEST BESTS : : BUDAPEST BESTS

György Tibor Szántó, Historian, Publisher, Translator, "Godfather"

When you are tired of the constant traffic noise and the window shopping inevitable on Erzsébet körút, you might want to find some peaceful island nearby with benches for long distance walkers. Rescue is at hand! Please turn to the right at either Barcsay or Wesselényi utca (with your back to Blaha Lujza tér) and go just one or two blocks. You cannot miss Almássy tér, a triangular square that serves as a playground for the young and the youthful, and also fulfils the strange notion of a green park for the elderly. They must all live in the surrounding picturesque late 19th, early 20th-century apartment blocks built in a great number of styles, ranging from mock-Gothic to Art Deco.

The man who gave his name to this surprisingly colourful and well-proportioned, small-town-like square, is Pál Almássy (1818-1882), a hero typical of the 19th-century landed gentry.

The statue in the middle of the square, however, is of another hero of the same ardent period: Antal Csengery (1822-80; by János Csiszér). He is regarded as the father of public schooling in Hungary, who brought education to the lower middle class, that is, the young people who had to start work at the age of 18.

Take your time looking around Almássy tér. Note the houses once designed for 'petty bourgeois' families in a definitely working-class neighbourhood. If you happen to find an open gateway, you will see the pretty, hundred-year-old staircases with wrought iron railings, amazingly shaped floortiles even on the circular foyers popularly referred to as 'gang'. Each house is subtly different from the others. The smell that comes from the kitchens, though, is identical throughout and must also be a hundred years old.

The southern part of the square is in fact a short pedestrian street (Almássy utca) with wooden benches and some (usually thirsty looking) greenery in graffiti-covered containers. The pavement here is for children to draw on.

The little public convenience on the northern side of the square is unfortunately closed for the better half of the year. You may find what you need at the opposite end of the square, in the old café called Bohém Presso.

Almássy tér may look shabby and battered and in bad need of refurbishment. This look, however, is probably as old as the square itself.

Dear Reader,

I am really interested in your opinion.
Both about the book itself, and also your
experiences on the spot.
So please detach this page and send it back to me.
You can also e-mail me: torok@datanet.hu.

Your Invisible Host: *András*

To: András Török

Budapest
Perczel Mór utca 4.
Hungary

H-1054

Dear András,

I found your book:

I missed the following:

I found the following things inaccurate:

I can add from my experience:

My name:

My Sex and Age:

My Address (Optional):

My E-Mail:

Date of My Visit:

Printed in Hungary, 1998